Early Modern English News Discourse

Pragmatics & Beyond New Series (P&BNS)

Pragmatics & Beyond New Series is a continuation of Pragmatics & Beyond and its Companion Series. The New Series offers a selection of high quality work covering the full richness of Pragmatics as an interdisciplinary field, within language sciences.

Volume 187

Early Modern English News Discourse. Newspapers, pamphlets
and scientific news discourse
Edited by Andreas H. Jucker

Early Modern English News Discourse

Newspapers, pamphlets and scientific news discourse

Edited by

Andreas H. Jucker
University of Zurich

John Benjamins Publishing Company
Amsterdam / Philadelphia

∞™ The paper used in this publication meets the minimum requirements of
American National Standard for Information Sciences – Permanence of
Paper for Printed Library Materials, ANSI z39.48-1984.

Library of Congress Cataloging-in-Publication Data

CHINED (Conference) (2nd : 2007 : Kartause Ittingen)
　Early modern English news discourse : newspapers, pamphlets and scientific news
　　　discourse / edited by Andreas H. Jucker.
　　　　p.　cm. (Pragmatics & Beyond New Series, ISSN 0922-842X ; v. 187)
　The papers in this volume were presented at the second Conference on Historical News
　　　Discourse (CHINED) held at the Kartause Ittingen (Switzerland), on August 31
　　　and September 1, 2007.
　Includes bibliographical references and index.
　1. Journalism--Great Britain--History--Congresses. 2. Journalism--Great Britain--
　　　Language--Congresses. I. Jucker, Andreas H. II. Title.
PN5115.C55　　2007
072--dc22　　　　　　　　　　　　　　　　　　　　　　　2009008214
ISBN 978 90 272 5432 0 (HB; alk. paper)
ISBN 978 90 272 8947 6 (EB)

John Benjamins Publishing Co. · P.O. Box 36224 · 1020 ME Amsterdam · The Netherlands
John Benjamins North America · P.O. Box 27519 · Philadelphia PA 19118-0519 · USA

Table of contents

Preface   VII

Newspapers, pamphlets and scientific news discourse
in Early Modern Britain   1
   Andreas H. Jucker

Newspapers

Crime and punishment   13
   Udo Fries

Reading late eighteenth-century want ads   31
   Laura Wright

"Always in te Orbe of honest Mirth, and next to Truth":
Proto-infotainment in *The Welch Mercury*   57
   Nicholas Brownlees

Religious language in early English newspapers?   73
   Thomas Kohnen

"As silly as an Irish Teague": Comparisons in early English
news discourse   91
   Claudia Claridge

"Place yer bets" and "Let us hope":
Imperatives and their pragmatic functions in news reports   115
   Birte Bös

Pamphlets

Comparing seventeenth-century news broadsides and occasional
news pamphlets: Interrelatedness in news reporting   137
    Elisabetta Cecconi

"From you, my Lord, professions are but words – they are so much bait
for fools to catch at": Impoliteness strategies in the 1797–1800 Act
of Union pamphlet debate   159
    Alessandra Levorato

Scientific news discourse

"Joyful News out of the Newfound World":
Medical and scientific news reports in Early Modern England   189
    Irma Taavitsainen

News filtering processes in the *Philosophical Transactions*   205
    Lilo Moessner

Index   223

Preface

The papers in this volume go back to the Conference on Historical News Discourse (CHINED) that took place at the Kartause Ittingen (Switzerland) on August 31 and September 1, 2007. It was the second conference on this topic after one held in Florence (Italy) on September 2 and 3, 2004. The papers of the first conference were edited by Nicholas Brownlees and published under the title *News Discourse in Early Modern Britain. Selected Papers of CHINED 2004* (Bern: Peter Lang).

My thanks go the contributors of this volume for their help and co-operation, to Danielle Hickey for her careful copy-editing and layouting work, and to two anonymous reviewers for the series for their pertinent and helpful comments and suggestions.

The date of the Ittingen conference was chosen to coincide with Udo Fries' retirement from his position as professor of English linguistics at the University of Zurich. Udo Fries has made a very significant contribution to the study of early English newspapers. He was the driving force behind the team who compiled the *Zurich English Newspaper Corpus* (ZEN), a corpus that was instrumental in many publications on early English newspapers, and indeed several papers in this volume are based on data from the ZEN. This volume, therefore, is dedicated to him.

Newspapers, pamphlets and scientific news discourse in Early Modern Britain

Andreas H. Jucker

The papers in this volume deal with news discourse in newspapers, pamphlets and in scientific writings in Early Modern Britain. This volume takes a broad and largely pragmatic view of what news is. The definition given by the *Oxford English Dictionary* may serve as a starting point:

> The report or account of recent (esp. important or interesting) events or occurrences, brought or coming to one as new information; new occurrences as a subject of report or talk; tidings. (OED "news" n. 2)

This definition is broad enough to encompass the contents of newspapers, of pamphlets and of scientific news discourse, but some qualifications are necessary. Generally speaking, newspapers report on recent events, and they make a claim that this news is interesting enough for the reader to warrant the purchase of a copy of the newspaper. The definition also applies to scientific news discourse, in which scientists share the results of their research with their colleagues. In this case, too, the news contains a "report or account of recent events or occurrences", where "events and occurrences" are understood in the sense of scientific findings. Newspapers and pamphlets are addressed to a wide audience; scientific news discourse, on the other hand, is addressed to a small and exclusive audience, but in both cases, the audience expects to receive reports and accounts of a largely factual nature on "recent events and occurrences". In fact, critical readers may often wonder about the factual status of the contents of newspapers, pamphlets or even scientific writing, but, by and large, authors of all three formats clearly expect their readers to accept their texts as factual.

For pamphlets, the situation is perhaps less clear-cut since many of the early pamphlets did not report events or occurrences but were largely argumentative. Newspapers, too, publish material that cannot be described as news in the narrow sense, for instance in the form of editorial comments or advertisements. For the purpose of this book, however, such content will be included, too. The papers of this volume are, therefore, concerned with early newspapers, pamphlets and scientific writings in general.

In a handbook article on mass media (Jucker 2005), I distinguished between a narrow definition and a broad definition of mass media. For today's world, the narrow definition comprises print media, such as newspapers and magazines, electronic media, such as radio and television, and online media on the Internet, while the wide definition of mass media also includes other printed materials including books, leaflets, billboards and manuals, and even non-verbal information channels, such as street signs or icons at airports or railway stations, and artistic forms of communication to mention just a few. In Early Modern Britain the range of mass media channels was obviously much smaller, but the three forms chosen for this volume can be seen as representative for early modern mass media news publications. Like their modern counterparts, what they have in common is that they constitute a form of one-way communication. An author communicates to a large and anonymous audience. For modern forms of mass media communication, several qualifications are needed for this. Mass media content is almost always produced not by a single author but by a large production team, which shares different responsibilities for the content, form and transmission of the news content. There are also many ways for the audience to talk back especially in the new online media, e.g. in letters to the editor, in comments sections or discussion forums. In weblog publishing, the traditional distinction between institutionalized senders of mass media messages and an audience of private individuals disappears altogether. In this form of mass media communication, the senders, too, are private individuals. The distinction between personal and mass media communication and, more generally, the distinction between private und public become increasingly blurred (cf. Dürscheid 2007).

In the early modern forms of mass media communication, the communication was more clearly asymmetric. The author communicated to a large audience which was not in a position to talk back. However, the typical authors or senders of the messages also differed somewhat from their modern counterparts. Present-day newspapers are clearly produced by large teams. It is generally difficult, if not impossible, to ascribe the exact wording in a newspaper article to a single individual because of the complex production process. The source of an individual article may be a text written by a news agency journalist. This text is then re-written by a newspaper journalist before it undergoes several rounds of revisions by news editors and subeditors (see Bell 1991: 36–44). Even scientific news publications are the result of editorial processes involving not only an author but also reviewers, desk editors and general editors.

In contrast, some of the early modern news publication formats were still dominated by single individuals. The first newspapers consisted of a sequence of letters from correspondents which were published without any further editorial intervention, except that they often had to be translated (cf. Brownlees 1999; Griffiths 2006). The translator and "editor" was also the publisher and printer of the newspaper. Pamphlets, too, were in an obvious way the result of individual authors rather than institutionalized publishing houses.

But even scientific news discourse was more personalized than it is today. In her contribution to this volume, for instance, Moessner shows how the early volumes of the *Philosophical Transactions,* published by the Royal Society, were initially dominated by their editor, Henry Oldenburg, who published his own version of the news that he received through his large network of correspondents. It was only in later years that the editorial voice became more and more backgrounded.

Early English news discourse has recently enjoyed a fair amount of scholarly attention. Raymond (1996), Sommerville (1996), Brownlees (1999), auf dem Keller (2004), Griffiths (2006) and Studer (2008) are all book-length studies of early English newspapers, while Raymond (2006) provides a collection of papers on early English newspapers. Grabes (1990) and Raymond (2003) are useful histories of pamphlets and pamphleteering in Early Modern Britain, and Hüllen (1989), Gotti (1996), Valle (1999), Taavitsainen and Pahta (2004) and Taavitsainen (2006) provide detailed information on the history of scientific news discourse in Early Modern Britain. A particularly noteworthy collection of articles is, of course, Brownlees (2006) because this volume, like the present one, includes papers on all three types of news discourse.

The papers in this volume, therefore, fall into one of these three large groups devoted to newspapers, pamphlets and scientific news discourse. The first group, with papers on early English newspapers from their beginnings in the seventeenth century up to the nineteenth century, covers a broad range of different text types that occurred in these papers, from advertisements and announcements to news reports and religious texts. Most papers in this section focus on a particular text type and provide detailed descriptions of typical structures and typical phrases. Text categories were fuzzy and they developed over time; the papers demonstrate how the recurring patterns came to be established and how these helped to identify the text categories.

The first two papers of this section deal with particular text types in early newspapers: the reporting of crime and punishment, and want ads. **Udo Fries** deals with early forms of soft news, i.e. reports on crime and punishment in the *Zurich English Newspaper Corpus.* He discusses the text classes in which information on crime and punishment appeared. The identification is not always straightforward because the newspapers were inconsistent in their designations and the classes were developing over the period under investigation. In fact, in the early newspapers of the period, reports on crimes may even have occurred in advertisements or announcements. Advertisers promised a reward for information or the retrieval of lost or stolen horses or runaway servants. Such advertisements were stereotypically introduced by *whereas* or by a past participle, such as *stolen* or *deserted*. The crime reports proper showed fairly conventionalized structures and stereotypical phrases, and Fries shows how these changed in the course of the eighteenth century. They tended to be matter-of-fact reports that might be classified as hard news, but, in the course of time, the reports became longer and included evaluative elements and superlative expressions ("a most bloody and cruel murder"), and journalists started to speculate on the social reasons of crime, as in this report on the execution of a culprit who had been transported but who returned to England before being allowed to: "His unhappy Exit seem'd to be owing to the Neglect of his Parents, who, giving him no sort of Education, nor bringing him up to any Employment, he begun, when very young, to pilfer and steal for his Livelyhood" (Fries, example (39)).

Laura Wright's paper deals with want ads that appeared in the London newspaper *The Morning Herald* in the 1780s. Employers used such ads to seek servants, and servants used them to seek employment. Wright discusses how the writers of these ads used the restricted space to give a clear picture of what they were looking for. Words were expensive and therefore the information had to be conveyed in as few words as possible while still making clear what kind of servant or what kind of employment was being sought. The paper discusses a range of conventionalized words and phrases that are not immediately transparent to the modern reader of these ads and explicates them on the basis of her data and of additional information from the *Oxford English Dictionary*, the *Zurich English Newspaper Corpus*, contemporary literature on the employment of servants, and contemporary fictional accounts of servants seeking adequate employment. Not all of the phrases can be assigned clear meanings, but together they create a fascinating picture of late eighteenth-century society with the precarious situations of servants and, in particular, women servants.

The third paper in the section on newspapers deals with one particular early newspaper, *The Welch Mercury*. It was not a particularly successful paper, but in some respects it already anticipated later developments. It appeared in only nine issues under two different names at the time of the English Civil War in the years 1643 and 1644. **Nicholas Brownlees** argues that the lack of success of this newspaper makes it particularly interesting for an analysis of early newspapers. Not only was it the first newspaper to employ early forms of infotainment but, in later issues, it tried to avert its fate by experimenting with new journalistic formats. The paper was written in mock Welsh English by a fictional Welsh author, who purportedly supported the King against the Parliamentarians. Thus, the paper satirizes itself both in form (mock Welsh English) and in content (anti-Parliamentarian). It was its editorial intention to both inform and to entertain, and it used stereotypes of a Welsh accent and what was supposed to be Welsh foolishness. In the later issues it was particularly news on Royal issues that was heavily marked by a Welsh accent, while Parliamentarian news was presented largely in Standard English. Brownlees' analysis also draws attention to such features as early forms of headlines whose purpose it probably was to highlight the news values of the articles. They were not to be perceived as anti-Welsh satirical pamphlets.

The remaining three papers in the section on newspapers focus on stylistic peculiarities of early newspapers. **Thomas Kohnen** compares the style of the early newspapers of the *Zurich English Newspaper Corpus* (1661–1791) with a corpus of prayers in order to find out more about the religious features contained in early newspapers. He focuses on the lexical aspects and provides a keyword analysis, that is to say, he picks out those words that show an unusually high frequency in one corpus in contrast to the other corpus. Words like "Oh", "Lord" and "God", for instance, occur very frequently in the prayer corpus but with limited or rare frequencies in the newspaper corpus. In his analysis, Kohnen looks in detail at how such words are used in late seventeenth- and in eighteenth-century newspapers. It turns out that they are either used in fixed formulae or routines, or in the few instances of religious texts that are explicitly framed as such in these newspapers. In an analysis of typical collocational patterns, Kohnen demonstrates that the identified keywords occur in the two corpora with very different patterns. Thus, the analysis provides interesting insights into the use of religious language in early newspapers but it also suggests that religious language was felt to be archaic in the eighteenth century. In the newspapers, it had the status of a clearly distinct special register.

Claudia Claridge analyses the use of comparisons in seventeenth- and eighteenth-century news discourse. She focuses on the two constructions using *like* and *as ... as* with one, two or three intervening items. Her analysis is also based on the *Zurich English Newspaper Corpus* and – for comparative purposes – the press genres of the *F-LOB Corpus*. She argues that comparisons are not, strictly speaking, necessary to convey new information. They are useful because of their elaborating functions. In particular, she distinguishes between four main functions, i.e. intensification/emphasis, evaluation, providing information and explanation/clarification. Her data reveals that many comparisons have a persuasive function in that they highlight or provide common ground between the writer and the reader. They are conscious stylistic choices on the part of the journalist. However, they turn out to be less frequent in early English news discourse than in Present-day English newspapers. Claridge surmises that the oral flavor of comparisons made them less obvious choices for seventeenth- and eighteenth-century journalists than for their modern counterparts.

Birte Bös, finally, deals with the pragmatic functions of imperatives in news reports. She uses the *Rostock Newspaper Corpus* as data, which comprises samples of news reports from English newspapers from 1700 to 2000, amounting to a total of about 600,000 words. Bös starts from the hypothesis that imperatives should be more frequent in more recent newspapers because of the personalization of mass media communication and the function of imperatives as a device to address the audience directly. However, she finds that the situation is more complex. Imperatives are not attested in the first half of the eighteenth century, but, from 1760 on, they occur regularly in her data with a steady increase until the mid-nineteenth century, and a surprisingly stable frequency in the twentieth century except for a peak in 1960. Imperatives can be directed from the journalist to the newspaper audience but in many cases the imperatives have different originators and different targets. They may, for instance, be directed from the author to the referents of news reports or they may occur in quotations with a direction from one referent to another. It is also necessary to look at the very frequent *let us* or *let's* construction separately and the different communicative situations need to be taken into consideration. The illocutionary force of this construction can vary from orders and commands to requests, recommendations and invitations depending on the force that is exerted on the addressee of the imperative to comply.

The second part of this volume contains two papers on pamphlets and other forerunners of newspapers. **Elisabetta Cecconi** deals with broadsides and pamphlets in the seventeenth century. News broadsides or broadside ballads were short verse narratives printed on one side of a single sheet of paper. They were popular from the mid sixteenth to the mid seventeenth century. Occasional news pamphlets, on the other hand, were short "books" which also were very popular from the middle of the sixteenth century. Broadside ballads were intended for oral performance, while pamphlets were intended to be read either privately or collectively. Thus, both formats mark a transition from oral to written news transmission.

In her analysis, Cecconi compares stories that were published both in the format of broadside ballads and of news pamphlets. She points out the dramatic quality of the broadsides which suited their oral performance and the more argumentative nature of pamphlets which were intended to be read either privately or collectively. In addition, there are interesting differences between broadsides and pamphlets, on the one hand, and early newspapers, on the other. The former display a mixture between factual reporting and religious preaching. Many elements, including typographical choices, pictures and lexical choices, are designed to catch the readers' interest. In contrast, early newspapers stick to more sober reporting of facts. At the same time, broadsides and pamphlets already anticipated developments that newspapers adopted only later on, such as interest-inducing headlines and a text structure that highlights the result of the reported events.

Alessandra Levorato focuses on a much later period in the development of pamphlets by analyzing those written at the end of the eighteenth century during the so-called "pamphlet war" that ensued around the prospective union between Ireland and Britain. She looks at a corpus of pamphlets that were published in Dublin during the years immediately preceding the union in 1801. The corpus separates those pamphlets that were in favor of a union and those that were against; both types used a range of persuasive strategies to argue their point. She looks, in particular, at the impoliteness strategies employed by the two different sides and distinguishes between on-record strategies and off-record strategies. On-record strategies can be further subdivided into negative and positive impoliteness strategies. The former include strategies such as challenging questions, condescension, scorn, ridicule or threats, while the latter include snubs, derogatory denominations, epithets and disagreements. Off-record strategies are less frequent. One example would be sarcasm. The analysis reveals that both proponents and opponents of a union between Ireland and Britain made use of impoliteness strategies, but these strategies were clearly more frequent and more eye-catching among the anti-unionist writers, who were calling their fellow countrymen to unite against the intrusion from outside.

The third and final part of this volume contains two papers on scientific news discourse. **Irma Taavitsainen** presents evidence for early forms of scientific news discourse in the sixteenth century. As a first step, she uses the corpus of *Early Modern English Medical Texts* to retrieve occurrences of the word *news* in these texts in order to find out how sixteenth-century authors of scientific texts used this term. As a second step, she studies several news reports in detail by contrasting them with the well-known features of modern news reports. The sixteenth century was particularly interesting in this respect because of the many reports from voyages to the new world of the American continents, with accounts of new plants and animals. Taavitsainen shows how the accounts from the new world changed over the course of the sixteenth century. The earliest ones, dating from around 1520, took the form of medieval travel literature depicting the new world as both marvelous and monstrous. New modes of reporting emerged only in the second half of the sixteenth century with additional emphasis on factual descriptions. The enthusiasm about the promising medicinal potential of the newly discovered plants replaced the earlier sense of marvel and excitement about the monstrosities and "savages" in the new territories.

Lilo Moessner's paper deals with important changes in the scientific news discourse of the seventeenth century. Early scientific news discourse relied to a large extent on letters exchanged within European networks of scholars (see e.g.

Valle 1999, 2003; Gotti 2006). Letters that described scientific experiments, new discoveries and other results of scholarly work were circulated in these networks. They were translated into other languages to reach a wider audience. In the seventeenth century, the Royal Society was founded, and in 1665 the *Philosophical Transactions* was set up as a new channel for the dissemination of scientific news. Henry Oldenburg was the first editor and he had a very considerable influence on the published material. At the beginning, he published his own version of the news that he had received through his own extend network of correspondents, but – as Moessner shows – in the first decade of publication, the editorial voice was backgrounded more and more, and the authorial voices gained in importance. A new medium of news publications established itself.

Thus, all the papers in this volume strive to situate their linguistic analyses not only in the larger context of the changing news discourse of the early modern period but also in the context of more specific text types. Language change is situated in a linguistic and cultural context. In order to understand the developments, it is necessary to look carefully at the details of how language is used in specific situations. News discourse is particularly interesting. In all the case studies assembled in this volume, an author communicates to a large and diverse audience, and generally can only make guesses about that audience. The audience itself is the justification for the production of these texts but it cannot talk back to the author in any direct way. The papers in this volume remain focused on the linguistic details under analysis and, at the same time, they try to provide a larger picture of the developments in the language of news discourse in Early Modern Britain.

References

auf dem Keller, Caren. 2004. *Textual Structures in Eighteenth-century Newspaper Advertising. A Corpus-based Study of Medical Advertisements and Book Advertisements*. Aachen: Shaker.
Bell, Allan. 1991. *The Language of News Media*. Oxford: Blackwell.
Brownlees, Nicholas. 1999. *Corantos and Newsbooks: Language and Discourse in the first English Newspapers (1620–1641)*. Pisa: Edizioni ETS.
Brownlees, Nicholas (ed.). 2006. *News Discourse in Early Modern Britain. Selected Papers of CHINED 2004*. Bern: Peter Lang.
Dürscheid, Christa. 2007. Private, nicht-öffentliche und öffentliche Kommunikation im Internet. *Neue Beiträge zur Germanistik* 6.4, 22–41.
Gotti, Maurizio. 1996. *Robert Boyle and the Language of Science*. Milano: guerini scientifica.
Gotti, Maurizio. 2006. Disseminating Early Modern science: Specialized news discourse in the *Philosophical Transactions*. In Nicholas Brownlees (ed.). *News Discourse in Early Modern Britain. Selected Papers of CHINED 2004*. Bern: Peter Lang, 41–70.
Grabes, Herbert. 1990. *Das englische Pamphlet I. Politische und religiöse Polemik am Beginn der Neuzeit (1521–1640)*. Tübingen: Niemeyer.

Griffiths, Dennis. 2006. *Fleet Street. Five Hundred Years of the Presss*. London: The British Library.

Hüllen, Werner. 1989. *"Their Manner of Discourse": Nachdenken über Sprache im Umkreis der Royal Society*. Tübingen: Gunter Narr.

Jucker, Andreas H. 2005. Mass media. In Jan-Ola Östman and Jef Verschueren in collaboration with Eline Versluys (eds.). *Handbook of Pragmatics* 2003–2005. Amsterdam and Philadelphia: John Benjamins, 1–18.

Raymond, Joad. 1996. *Invention of the Newspaper: English Newsbooks 1641–49*. Oxford: Clarendon Press.

Raymond, Joad. 2003. *Pamphlets and Pamphleteering in Early Modern Britain*. Cambridge: Cambridge University Press.

Raymond, Joad (ed.). 2006. *News Networks in Seventeenth Century Britain and Europe*. London: Routledge.

Sommerville, John. 1996. *The News Revolution in England. Cultural Dynamics of Daily Information*. New York and Oxford: Oxford University Press.

Studer, Patrick. 2008. *Historical Corpus Stylistics. Media, Technology and Change*. London: Continuum.

Taavitsainen, Irma, and Päivi Pahta (eds.). 2004. *Medical and Scientific Writing in Late Medieval English*. (Studies in English Language). Cambridge: Cambridge University Press.

Valle, Ellen. 1999. *A Collective Intelligence. The Life Sciences in the Royal Society as a Scientific Discourse Community, 1665–1965*. (Anglicana Turkuensia 17). Turku: University of Turku.

Valle, Ellen. 2003. "Let me not lose yr love & friendship": The negotiation of priority and the construction of a scientific identity in seventeenth-century natural history. In Risto Hiltunen and Janne Skaffari (eds.). *Discourse Perspectives on English. Medieval to Modern*. (Pragmatics & Beyond New Series 119). Amsterdam and Philadelphia: John Benjamins, 197–234.

Newspapers

Crime and punishment

Udo Fries

1. Introduction

This paper deals with the reporting of crimes perpetrated in the late seventeenth and in the eighteenth century as we find them recorded in the newspapers of the day. The texts discussed here are taken from the newspapers collected in ZEN, *The Zurich English Newspaper Corpus*, which covers the period from 1671 to 1791, in ten-year intervals.

In modern newspapers, a variety of text classes or genres have been identified. In the analysis of modern English newspapers the distinction between hard news and soft news has become generally accepted. This distinction refers to "a concept mostly applied to the content of the news" (Xekalakis 1999: 91). Hard news is, according to Bell (1991), concerned either with so-called "spot news" – accidents, disasters, crimes – or with important events in politics, economics, and diplomacy. Soft news, on the other hand, presents human interest stories – often in an "involved, personal and colloquial style". Hard news is said to be presented in a neutral, formal and distant style (Xekalakis 1999: 92).

Looking at earlier English newspapers, Schneider (2002) also distinguishes between hard and soft news, a distinction seen by her to parallel that between quality and popular papers. Hard news, according to Schneider, consists of foreign politics (e.g. reports on wars), home politics (e.g. parliamentary reports or local elections), appointments, commercial information and ship news, but also of short factual reports on marriages, deaths, festivities, and leisure activities. Soft news, on the other hand, consists of reports on ordinary people, e.g. births, marriages, diseases, deaths, crimes (e.g. stealing, robbery, murder), but also of fights, suicides, court trials, natural disasters, and tragic accidents.

Quality papers are said to consist mainly of hard news, whereas popular papers consist of soft news. Information correlates with the quality press and entertainment with the popular press. Reports of crimes, therefore, would belong to entertainment, or soft news, and therefore predominately to the popular press.

What I want to point out here is that reports on crime can belong to both sections: hard news, i.e. short factual reports designed to inform, and soft news, i.e. longer reports that may also entertain – or rather frighten or excite their readership.

Within the section of hard news the distinction between foreign news and home news is also relevant. The inclusion of home news in early English newspapers depended largely on the fluctuating political situation. Between 1620 and 1640, home news was not always allowed to be printed (for details cf. Brownlees 1999). In 1665, the main contents of the *Oxford Gazette* were foreign reports, shipping movements, the weekly bills of mortality, King and court, lists of circuit judges and sheriffs – and crime and punishment. Their occurrence in the *Oxford Gazette*, later *The London Gazette*, would be an indicator that these reports were regarded as hard news, printed for the sake of information.

2.   Identifying text classes

Foreign news in early newspapers is easy to spot: it usually comes at the front of the paper and has a dateline, which specifies place and date of the report. The only other news on the first page of *The London Gazette* would be ship news. Everything that was not foreign news would be home news: reports from within the shores of England – and Wales, Ireland or Scotland.

For the compilation of the corpus, home news in this wider sense would have yielded a very mixed bag of texts, which would make comparison through the centuries difficult. Therefore we established separate text classes for SHIP NEWS, BIRTHS, DEATHS, ACCIDENTS, CRIME and even a text class LOST-AND-FOUND (cf. Fries 2001). Theoretically at least, all these categories could also be part of foreign news. However, Continental run-away wives, servants or horses would not have been of interest in England and therefore not reported. It would have to be an especially wicked crime that took place somewhere on the continent to be reported in an English newspaper.

(1)   Ghent, Octob. 15
      One *Louis Pickar*, formerly a Captain of Dragoons in *Holland*, who is accused of having committed several Murthers, and other heynous crimes in the Province of *Utrecht*; having at the desire of the States-General been seized in this City, (whither he was fled) by order of the Prince of *Parma*, and committed prisoner to the *Castle*; and his Highness having Commanded, that he should be put into the hands of the *Fiscael* of *Utrecht*, pursuant to the Directions he had received from *Spain*, the same was executed yesterday;

but the said *Pickar* had not been long in the custody of the *Fiscael*, who was carrying him away in a Coach, when he was rescued by a number of Armed Men, and made his escape. (1681lgz01659)

For the following investigation, crimes committed abroad were not included.

Assigning a newspaper report to a text class is easiest when there are headlines such as *BIRTHS, BORN, DEATHS,* or *DIED.* For the text class SHIP NEWS, the headlines *SHIP NEWS* or *PORT NEWS* were commonly used from the middle of the eighteenth century onwards, with *HOME PORTS* used as an alternative in some papers for two decades in the eighteenth century. The problem encountered is that, during the whole period, there were similar texts without any headline at all – but with exactly the same contents: these texts we classified as SHIP NEWS as well. The criterion for inclusion was, therefore, only the contents of the article.

With the text class CRIME there are no headlines that could be of any help. We have, therefore, to define what we want to include in this text class solely on the basis of the contents of the texts, and, unfortunately, there will never be a solution that can encompass all cases. In the textclass CRIME we have not only included reports of crimes, but also reports of imprisonment and court hearings following a crime, as these closely belong to the crimes perpetrated. The assignation of text classes in the ZEN Corpus is, unfortunately, not absolutely consistent. Many of the crime reports discussed here are, in fact, classified in ZEN as belonging to the text class CRIME, but there are also items that may be hidden as HOME NEWS.

3.   Borderline cases

There are a number of borderline cases, which one might want to exclude from the study of crime reports proper.

3.1   Introductory *whereas*

There are instances of crime reporting that look like official, legal announcements or advertisements.

(2) WHereas on *Wednesday* last the 19th instant, between 5 and 7 in the Evening, there was taken away from a certain Gentleman in *Duke Street* in St. James's, One Olive-colour'd Cloth Coat, lined with a Shalloon of the same colour, Trim'd with Silver, and large Buttons, and Button-holes, very little wore, together with several other Goods of value. If any such Goods are offered either to be Pawn'd or Sold, you are desired to give Notice forthwith to Mr.

> *Robert Cleasby* at his House in Coal-Yard at the upper end Drury-Lane, and for Reward the Discoverer shall receive Four Guinea's, provided the Goods be recovered by the Discovery. (1701ept00057)

Texts of this type are characterised by an introductory *whereas* in the first sentence, followed by some advice of how to act (*If any such Goods are offered [...] you are desired to give Notice*), and concluded by a reference to the reward that will be given if the goods are recovered. All is expressed by a very formal use of language.

These texts are always bipartite in structure, basically consisting of a description of the crime and of the reward promised. The text type is also typical and commonly used for bankruptcy notices, which appeared almost exclusively in *The London Gazette*.

(3)   Whereas a Commission of Bankrupt hath been Awarded against George Fothergill, late of the City of York, Grocer, all Persons that owe him any Money, or that have any Goods or other Effects of his in their hands, are not to pay or deliver the same to any person, but to such only as shall be appointed by the Commissioners; but they are forthwith to give Notice of the said Bankrupts Goods and Effects to Mr. Daniel Oley, at his House in Bread-Street, London, or they will be sued. (1701fpt00884)

In the ZEN Corpus, there are 134 instances of these bankruptcy texts beginning with the phrase *Whereas a Commission of Bankrupt,* during the period from 1701 to 1791. They are certainly not texts written by the newspaper staff, but must have been sent to the paper by the Commissioners responsible for the matter. In the corpus, they were put into a text class ANNOUNCEMENTS. By the newspapers of the day they were also seen as advertisements.

During the first half of the eighteenth century such constructions are also used for reports of thefts or run-away servants, such as this one, in the advertisement section:

(4)   WHereas Henry Hibbert, a tall thin Man, with short black curled hair, aged about 34, Servant to Mr. Benj. Niccoll, Merchant in Watlin Street, London, has been absent from his service ever since Thursday last, and has carried with him a considerable summ of Money of the said Mr. Niccolls and other things. If he will return to his service, he shall be kindly received, or whosoever shall secure him, and give notice thereof to Mr. Mossey, Apothecary at the Rose and Crown in Watlin Street near Bread Street, shall have 5 Guineas reward. Benj. Niccoll. (1701pmn00946)

It is worth noting that until about 1730 these texts could also occur without the introductory *whereas*-formula, as in (5) and (6).

(5)　Charles Hoskins, about 17 or 18 years of age, ... went from his Masters House the 11th Instant, and carried with him a Desk, wherein were several Writings and Money, to a considerable value; Whoever gives notice of him to Dr. – in St. Martins-lane in Canon-street, or to Mr. John Pye at his Chamber in – shall have 5 l. reward. (1681lgz01615)

(6)　*A Male Child, about a Month old, in a* Flag Handbasket, was dropt in Twelve-Bell Court near Bow-Church Yard, on Tuesday the 29th of December last, about Eight of the Clock at Night. Whoever will discover the Parent or Person who dropt the said Child, shall receive Two GUINEAS Reward from the Churchwardens of the Parish of St. Mary le Bow.

　　Note, A Paper was pinn'd on the Child's Breast, in which was written these Words, PRAY CRISTN THIS CHILD. (1731djl03122)

In the corpus for 1741, there are exceptionally many of these short texts; on closer inspection, however, of the 16 instances found, 14 refer to the same person: there are five instances each in different issues of *The Daily Post* and of *The London Daily Post*, and four instances in different issues of *The London Gazette*. Due to the restrictions of the corpus, we can only say that, between May 30th, 1741 and October 3rd of the same year, John Waite, a cashier of the Bank of England, was desperately being sought. This is the story of John Waite:

(7)　Whereas John Waite, late one of the Cashiers of the Bank of England, about Forty Years of Age, and about five Feet eight Inches high, well set, round Visag'd, small grey Eyes, very light Eye-brows and Eye-lashes, and of a most remarkable fresh Complexion, absented himself yesterday from his Duty at the Bank, and is suppos'd to have secreted, or taken away with him from the Bank, East-India Bonds amounting to a considerable Value.

　　And whereas Warrants are issued for apprehending and taking the said John Waite, This is to give Notice, that whoever shall apprehend and secure the said John Waite, to be dealt with according to Law, shall receive of the said Governor and Company the Sum of Two Hundred Pounds as a Reward. DAVID LEGROS, Secretary. (1741dpt06780)

How often these texts were reprinted is difficult to say: it is not revealed by the corpus, but can only be found by going back to the newspapers themselves. There must have been influential people who made sure that the crime was not forgotten and the texts were reprinted over and over again.

3.2   Introductory past participle

A second group of examples which may be seen as borderline cases have the same bipartite structure but, instead of the introductory *whereas*, they begin with a past participle form. All are reports of theft or desertion. The following verbs occurred in the corpus:

Table 1. Past participle verb forms introducing reports of theft or desertion

Introductory verb	Number of instances in ZEN
Stolen, Stoln	38
Deserted	8
Taken	6
Escaped	4
Run away from	4
Rid away with	2
Absconded	1
Broken open	1
Robb'd	1
Stopped	1
Went away from	1

Once again, these texts tend to turn up in the advertisement sections of the newspapers. The most important type of crime we are dealing with here is theft of a horse (8) or, less frequently, of other goods like books, followed by the disappearance of persons together with goods (9).

(8)   SToln out of a Stable at Alresford in Hampshire a Black Gelding, about 14 hands high, full aged having all his paces, a white face, Wall Eyes, and 4 white Feet, goes near before, and has some Scars of cutting about his Fetlock, and one of his Knees being lately hurt the hair is not grown again. Whoever gives notice of him, so as he may be had again to Mr Udal, or his Ostler, at the Swan with two necks in Tuttle-street, Westminster, or at the George Inn in Alresford, shall have 40 s. Reward. (1701pmn00919)

(9)   RUN away from Neats Court in the Island of Sheppy Kent, about the 6th Instant, one Will. Greenfeild and his Wife, with a considerable Sum of Money; he is a Man of a Middle Stature, Aged about 40, Sandy Beard, longish Chin, wears a Wigg, and at present looks Meager and Sickly: Rode away on a truss dark brown Nag, about 13 hands high, without any mark, with new Bridle and Saddle: His Wife is middle Siz'd, black Ey'd, lost an upper Tooth before, and very big with Child. Whoever secures the said Will. Greenfeild, and gives Notice to Mr. John Edwin in Austin Friars, London, shall receive 10 l. Reward

and Reasonable Charges, for his Wife 5 l. and for the Horse one Guinea. (1701pby01068)

The London Gazette was famous for its inclusion of reports of stolen horses, but they were included in other papers as well, right up to the end of the eighteenth century, as *announcements*. From the 1770s onwards, the term *advertisement* tended to be restricted to its modern sense: consisting of texts that offered some goods or, for example, theatre tickets for sale. Stolen horses would no longer appear in this section of the papers. Another reason for regarding these instances as borderline cases is the fact that, while stealing a horse is certainly a crime, many horses simply disappeared without any evidence of a crime having been perpetrated. Therefore the most common introductory phrase is *Stolen or strayed*:

(10)   Stolen or strayed the 17th past, out of William Borehant's Grounds in Gosfield Parish near Brantre in Essex, a bright-bay Mare above 14 hands, 5 or 6 years old, a Star in her Forehead, her near hind Foot white, and W. B. branded upon the near Buttock, the W. a little blurr'd. Whoever secures her, and gives notice to the said William Boreham, shall have a Guinea Reward, and reasonable Charges. (1701lgz03746)

Of the 38 examples of *Stol(e)n*, 20 are *Stol(e)n or strayed*. These would be classified as instances of CRIME, whereas, were the phrase the other way around, one might well regard them as instances of the class LOST AND FOUND. Of the six instances of an initial *Strayed*, five, however, are *Strayed or Stolen*. Apparently one could never be too certain whether a missing horse had simply got loose and run away or was removed by stealth.

4.   Crime reports proper

When we turn now to straightforward crime and punishment reporting, the distinction between brief, factual reports on the one hand, and longer articles with many gruesome details on the other, should be one aspect worth looking into. But this is not necessarily a distinction of the eighteenth century, as there are many stages between short and long, depending also on how much is known about a particular crime. Reports on murders tend to be generally longer than those on robberies.

In the shortest, most matter-of-fact way, crime reports consist of: 1. a time adverbial; 2. a reference to the victim or the criminal; 3. a verb phrase expressing the criminal act; and, perhaps, 4. a place adverbial.

Here are some examples from 1751:

(11)   Last Friday Night Mr. Highmore going for his Lodgings at Newington, was robbed near the Green by two Fellows, of a Gold Ring, seven Shillings, and other Things. (1751gat05209)
On Tuesday Night, about Seven o'Clock, four Ladies were robbed, in Holloway-lane, going to Highgate in the Stage, of eight Pounds. (1751lda00156)
On Monday Night three Fellows, well armed, robb'd two Gentlemen in a Coach, at the Foot of London Bridge, next the Borough, of a Watch and Money. (1751lmp01416)

4.1   Time reference

What many of these reports have in common is that they begin with a time reference, which may be very general or surprisingly detailed. Such time references occur, of course, also in other text classes, from foreign news to home news, to notices of births and deaths, and are therefore not a distinguishing feature of the text class CRIME, but there are definitely more news reports on crime that have this as an initial element than those that do not.

During the seventeenth century it was only the weekday that was mentioned: *On Wednesday (last)* or *yesterday* were the standard forms. From the beginning of the eighteenth century more elaborate versions that give the reader not only the day but as exact a time reference as possible begin to appear:

(12)   Thursday last, about three in the Morning (1731cjl00242)
On Thursday Night, at Eleven o'Clock (1721apb01945)
On Tuesday Night last, between Nine and Ten o'Clock (1731rwj00328)

The numbers of these crime reports vary a great deal in the individual decades and they are also of varying lengths. For 1751, there are as many as 139 instances in the corpus; short ones are more frequent, but almost a quarter are rather long ones.

4.2   The grammatical subject: The victim and the criminal

The subject slot in this type of news is filled either by the victim or by the criminal. Below are the most frequent constructions, with the victim being more frequently in subject position (13) than the criminal (14).

(13)   On Wednesday morning, about eleven, Mr. Wimwick, of Newbury, Berks, was robbed by a single highwayman on Hounslow-Heath, who refused his watch, but took his money, to the amount of seven pounds. (1771lev06825)

(14)　On Saturday last, about 10 a Clock at Night, 7 or 8 Footpads attacked a Gentleman in his Coach, going to Old-Ford; and robbed him of 14 l. after which, they rifled a Cart coming from Row, with Goods that had been Dyed there and carried off to the Value of Two Hundred Pounds in Velvets. (1701lpt00270)

Depending on the crime, the victim is identified by name or, alternatively, with just a generic reference, e.g. *a gentleman, a young lad.*

Identification by name simply presupposes a well-known person and is relatively rare. Instead, we find profession and place of abode added:

(15)　Mr. Hart, a Taylor in Long-Lane (1731dat00130)
　　　Mr. John Saunders, a Butcher of Keinsham (1751gat05396)
　　　Mr. Smith, a Sail-maker in Shad-Thames (1751lda00184)
　　　Mr. Norton, a Dyer, in Brick Lane (1751lmp00406)

A victim's position in society would be another specification:

(16)　Mr. Penny, Treasurer and one of the Principals of Clement's-Inn (1741dpt06807)
　　　Mr Wilson, Farrier to his Royal Highness the Duke of Cumberland (1751lmp01416)

Many robberies seem to have happened on the victim's way home:

(17)　Mr. Cambell of Bloomsbury, on his return Home from Rathbone-Place (1751lmp00406)
　　　Mr. Jackson, of the Borough of Southwark, returning from Croydon (1771wlp01384)

Very rare is the construction with *one* + surname, as far as the victim of a crime is concerned (18), but it is normal with reference to the criminal when he is committed to prison (19).

(18)　one Mr. Smith, a Stationer, in Gutter-Lane (1721apb01945)
　　　one Bennet, a hatter (1771lev06825)

(19)　On the 21st Instant one Elizabeth Smith was committed to Newgate, upon the Oath of one John Keate, for picking his Pocket of three Guineas. (1721apb02095)
　　　One Mr. Purcell, who formerly kill'd Mr. Love in Leicester-Fields, was lately committed to Newgate, for wounding an Officer belonging to the High Bailiff of Westminster, and rescuing from him a Debtor who he had arrested for a considerable Sum. (1721wjb01805)

The many cases of a gentleman, falling prey to some crime, whose name is not known, remain *a gentleman*:

(20)   A Gentleman Riding to Hampstead (1721wjb01835)
a Gentleman coming to Sackville Street through Hanover Yard in a Chair (1751ole00308)

More information about the criminals, their names or occupations, is not part of these reports, but it may occur in the reports of court trials and punishments (see Section 5 below).

4.3   The crime itself

In reports about robbery the objects taken are of obvious interest. The bigger the booty, one would think, the more interesting the news. There are cases where the stolen items are not mentioned at all but, more often, it is simply a certain amount of money that is mentioned.

(21)   robbed / robb'd […] of
nine Shillings (1731rwj00307)
of 3l. 17s. in Money (1751lmp00810)

Articles that were often robbed were watches – and hats:

(22)   robbed / robb'd […] of
about 16 pounds in money, and a Gold Watch (1681din00002)
seventeen Shillings, a Silver Watch, and his Hat and Wig
(1731dat00130)

If we are looking for human interest stories among the objects of robbery, we will find only the occasional one:

(23)   robbed / robb'd […] of
500 Ducats, which he had tied up in his Girdle, being, it seems, the com-mon Method, which these People use to carry their Money. (1751lda00156)
of seven guineas in gold, and 14s. in silver, all the money he had gath-ered together by his hard labour for months past, also his watch and wearing apparel tied up in a bundle, in which was a blue waistcoat, two pair of stockings, a shirt, and a pair of linings. (1771wlp01384)

4.4   Information surrounding the crime

Whereas the reports about robberies are fairly straightforward, it is what happened before and after that may rouse the interest of the reader. Breaking open (a house) or stopping a carriage may precede the robbery and lead to a complex verb phrase. *Broke open and robbed* is certainly more dramatic or emphatic than simply *robbed*.

(24)   This morning early the house of Mr. Herron, was broke open and robbed of cash and valuable effects to the amount of three hundred pounds. (1771msj00292)
Early yesterday morning the house of Mr. Meriton, who keeps a coal shop in Staining Lane near Foster Lane, was broke open , and robbed of forty pounds in cash, and plate, watches and rings, to the value of one hundred pounds more. (1761lcr00667)

Or, on his way, someone is *stopped and robbed:*

(25)   Last Saturday Morning three Gentlemen and a Lady were stopped in a Landau and Four by two Highwaymen, genteelly mounted, one on a Grey the other on a Bay Gelding, between Kitt's Inn and Wimms Wash, and robbed of what Money they had about them. (1751oen00014)
Last night, about seven o'clock, Mr. Mills, of Parliament-Street, was stopped and robbed in St. Margaret's Church-yard, Westminster, by two fellows, of his hat and a gold headed cane. (1771lev06858)

More often the expression is *stopped ... who robbed:*

(26)   Monday evening, between seven and eight o'clock, as Mr. Chester, Jeweller, in St. Martin's lane, was returning home from Chelsea, he was stopped by three footpads, who robbed him of his watch and near twenty shillings. (1771msj00292)
Saturday night Mr. Jury, of Fulham, was stopped between Little Chelsea and Stanfors-bridge, by three footpads, who robbed him of a gold watch, seals, &c. (1791evm00380)

After a robbery, the robbers or highwaymen normally disappear:

(27)   and hasted with all speed towards London (1681din00001)
and then rode off through Kingston. (1751lmp00406)

In order to provide more information, a second sentence is needed. These make the reports more memorable.

(28)   On Sunday Night last, between 11 and 12 o'Clock, a Gentleman was stopped
by two Foot-pads, on the Pavement on the West Side of St. James's Square,
who compelled him to go with them to the South Side of the Square, where
they robbed him of a Silver Watch, three Guineas, and some Silver. They also
threatened him with Death if he moved from the Spot till they were out of
Sight. (1751lmp00810)
On Thursday Night Mr. Thomas, Cryer to Lord Chief Justice Lee, was robbed
in Carey street Chancery-lane, by some Foot-pads, of about six Guineas and a
Gold Watch.One of them was pursued down Chancery-lane and Fleet-street,
but by having his Pistol cocked, frightened the Pursuers so much that he got
off. (1751lmp02427)
Sunday morning the northern mail was robbed on Enfield highway. The vil-
lains tied the postboy to a tree, and then with pix-axes broke open the cart,
notwithstanding it was made on the new construction. (1771wlp01388)

This may occasionally result in a whole story:

(29)   On Wednesday about two o'clock in the afternoon, Mr. Arnold was robbed
by a single highwayman, at no great distance from his own house near Seven
Oaks, Kent. Immediately after the robbery had been committed, Mr. Arnold
gave a general alarm, and an immediate pursuit was made by Mr. Pitman,
master of the Harrow public house, at Malmscott-hill, and Mr. Hall, master
of the White Hart, at Riverhead, and several others. The highwayman was
first overtaken by Mr. Pitman near Seal, and a pistol heard to fire; and on
Mr. Hall's coming up, he found the robber on the ground, and Mr. Pitman
lying upon him quite dead. What is very extraordinary, after the nicest
examination, no mark of violence which could be supposed to contribute to
his death, was found on the person of Mr. Pitman, except a small spot under
his ear. The highwayman who had received a shot in the head, was carried to
Riverhead, where the ball was extracted, and where he now lies dangerously
ill. (1791pad17660:s:231.1)

Note the commentary in the middle of the text. Another possibility for extension
is the phrase: *in the following manner* (30).

(30)   On Sunday last the house of – – – – Hill, Esq; in Dartmouth-street,
Westminster, was robbed in the following manner: A man came and pretended that he had business with Mr. Hill, when he was shewed into the par-
lour, where he wrote a note concerning some wine he had to sell to Mr. Hill
(who is a very great merchant, and deals wholesale) he went away then, and
came the next day, when he knew Mr. Hill was upon 'Change, wrote another
note, and took that opportunity to steal plate and money to the value of 270 l.
(1771bug00068:s:216.1)

4.5   Newspaper commentaries

Newspaper commentaries are not very frequent. They especially occur in reports of murder. Introductory commentaries consist of the newspaper's description of the crime, especially when the source of the news cannot be mentioned (for this type of news see Jucker 2006).

(31)   We hear from Durham, that some time last Week a most bloody and cruel Murder was committed at a Country Farm House call'd Gallylaw, near Sedgfield, viz. (1741ldp02034)
We hear from Dotton, near Black Torrington in Devonshire, of a very inhuman Murder lately committed there; a Farmer going into an Alehouse Kitchen, without any Provocation, began to be very abusive to the Company who were drinking there; (1751ole00360)

They may appear as text beginnings:

(32)   On Sunday last the most barbarous murder that has been heard of for many years was committed between Hilperton and Trowbridge on the body of one Mary Allen, by several men, who are yet unknown. (1761lep00614)
A shocking murder was, a few days ago committed near Norwich; the particulars of which we have not been able to learn. (1791evm00380)

They may also appear as summaries at the end of a report:

(33)   …forgiven Part of his Punishment, he not being able to undergo it according to the Opinion of the Surgeons. Prodigious Clemency! (1751oen00014)
Three fellows were apprehended on Saturday night, at the Albion Mills, who were detected cutting the hose, or leather pipe, which conveys the water from the engine to the directing pipe. A crime like this ought surely to be severely punished. (1791pad17683)

5.   Punishment

5.1   Imprisonment

The text class CRIME in ZEN also includes reports about imprisonment, court hearings and penalties. When a criminal is caught, he may be taken to prison; in London this may have been Newgate, a prison which was built in 1188 and rebuilt in 1770; *committed to Newgate* is a standard phrase.

(34)   One Mr. Purcell, who formerly kill'd Mr. Love in Leicester-Fields, was lately
committed to Newgate, for wounding an Officer belonging to the High Bailiff
of Westminster, and rescuing from him a Debtor whom he had arrested for a
considerable Sum. (1721apb01945)
Yesterday Clans Schlutingt, was committed to Newgate by Christopher Scott,
Esq. for stealing twelve stone soup plates, six earthen dishes, seventeen stone
plates, and eight stone milk pots. (1761pul00334)

One can easily detect a pattern: the culprit is caught and committed to Newgate
and the crime is normally specified.

In 60 instances in ZEN, someone was committed to Newgate, but there were
other places of confinement, for instance, the Gatehouse (19 instances) near Westminster, various Bridewells, especially Tothill Fields Bridewell (20 instances).

Other places to be sent, conveyed or committed to were the compters, prisons
for debtors, but also for criminals "convicted of misdemeanours, including homo-
sexuality, prostitution and drunkenness" (Wikipedia subject: "poultry compter").
Especially the London Poultry Compter, but also the Wood Street Compter, occur
in the corpus.

(35)   Yesterday a man was sent to the Poultry compter, by the Lord-Mayor for further examination, being charged with stealing the furniture of some coffins
out of a vault, in Aldgate church: one coffin was found broken to pieces, the
furniture taken off and the body exposed to view. (1771gep05813)
Last Wednesday night a porter in Honey-lane-market and his wife having some words, blows ensued, when he struck her with such violence that
she died in a few minutes after: he was secured and carried to Woodstreet
compter till the Coroner's Inquest shall sit on the body. (171gep05813)

5.2   Sentence

From 1751, we find that one could be *capitally convicted*: the phrase occurs in 32
instances right through to 1791. In the *Oxford English Dictionary*, the first and
only instance is from 1742 from the *Gentleman's Magazine*.

(36)   Yesterday twenty Prisoners were tried at the Old Baily. One was capitally
convicted, viz. Edward Ward for breaking open the Dwelling-house of
Miles Childrey of Hackney, and stealing from thence nine Pewter Dishes
and a Man's Hat. Ten were cast for Transportation, and nine acquitted.
(1751lda00042)

At Monmouth Assizes, Benjamin Hoskins was capitally convicted of the murder of his own child. He was hanged on Thursday, and his body delivered for dissection. (1791evm00327)

Reports on execution, formulated as *executed at,* occur in the corpus throughout the eighteenth century. They are very straightforward sentences: the place of execution and – optionally – the reason for execution are mentioned.

(37) Yesterday 3 Criminals Convicted last Sessions were Executed at Tyburn. (1701pmn00856)
Last Wednesday were executed at Tyburn the following Malefactors, viz. William Bond for returning from his Transportation before the Time was expired. (1721wjb01835)
Last Tuesday John Murphy, Gent. was executed at Clonmell, for the Murder of one Roger Rumbold, a Constable in Tipperary, whom he shot, on Rumbold's attempting to execute a Warrant against him sometime ago. (1751gat05250)

More information may be added in subsequent sentences:

(38) Wednesday morning the convicts under sentence of death in Newgate, were executed at Tyburn, pursuant to their sentence. They all behaved with decency except Hogan, who struck the Executioner when he was put in the cart, and behaved very badly to the last. (1771wlp01388)

(39) On Saturday last William Dunkan was executed at Tyburn, for Horse-stealing. He had been formerly transported, and returning before the Expiration of his Sentence, took on his old Trade again. He was about 20 Years of Age, and born at Beverly. His unhappy Exit seem'd to be owing to the Neglect of his Parents, who, giving him no sort of Education, nor bringing him up to any Employment, he begun, when very young, to pilfer and steal for his Livelyhood. (1751gat05250)

Transportation was the next mildest form of punishment. One got *sentenced to, ordered, convicted,* or most frequently *cast for transportation.* Instances of *cast for transportation* are found between 1751 and 1771. The first and only quote of this phrase in the *Oxford English Dictionary* is, however, from 1772.

(40) Eight were cast for transportation, and four acquitted. (1751lmp02427)
Yesterday the Sessions ended at the Old Baily, when six prisoners were tried, four of whom were cast for transportation, and two acquitted. (1761lcr00667)
Six were cast for transportation , three convicted of petit larceny, and nine acquitted. (1771csw00657)

The place for transportation is never mentioned. Until 1776, convicts could be transported to the American colonies – for a maximum of 10 years. Botany Bay in Australia opened only in 1786/1787, and could therefore be referred to in our corpus at the earliest in 1791. There is, in fact, a reference to Botany Bay in an article about malt taxes and the deplorable manners in pubs:

> (41)   But there is great danger, from an increase of Public Houses (a certain conse-
> quence of suppressing the family brewery), of the morals and manners of the
> lower class of people becoming more vitiated, already too much disposed to
> bad habits, as the Country Assizes, the Old Bailey Sessions, and the transpor-
> tation to Botany Bay but too clearly prove. (1791mcr06730)

5.3   Trials

The phrase *tried at* yields 34 instances in the corpus, 13 of which are trials at the Old Bailey. These are really COURT REPORTS. Often, there were many cases tried one after the other, which yielded very long reports (42), or lists of names and crimes perpetrated (43).

> (42)   Yesterday nine prisoners were tried at the Old Bailey, two of whom were capi-
> tally convicted, viz. Theodore Gardelle, for the wilful murder of Anne King;
> and Thomas Davis, for publishing two forged orders as true, for the payment
> of a seaman's wages, with an intent to defraud. William Darwell [thief-taker]
> was tried for the murder of John Lee [shot behind a coach near Highgate]
> and William Pentilow for being present, aiding, and assisting in the same.
> Darwell was found guilty of manslaughter, and Pentilow acquitted. William
> Platten, for the murder of Richard Snow, by flinging a piece of wood at him,
> and knocking him into the river Thames (by which he was drowned) was
> acquitted. One was cast for transportation, and three acquitted.
> Gardelle received sentence immediately to be executed on Saturday next, in
> the Haymarket, near Penton-street, and to be afterwards dissected and anato-
> mized. (1761lcr00667)
>
> (43)   The following were convicted to be transported, viz. John Cain, alias
> Blackeney, for stealing a pair of breeches and a pair of silver buckles, the
> property of Mr. Charles Hobson. John Knott, for stealing a gold watch in a
> shagreen case, the property of William Savage. John Hughes, for stealing a
> quantity of silk, the property of Matthew Davis, his master. Thomas Dodd,
> for stealing a silver watch, the property of James Camm. William Alpland, for
> stealing near eighty gallons of porter, the property of Samuel Reid, Esq; out
> of his store cellar in Church-street, Mile End. Lazarus Solomon, for stealing a
> linen handkerchief, the property of William Holloway. Elizabeth Doncaster,

for stealing a coat, and a pair of breeches, the property of Joseph Clewley. Edward Hammack, and John Bowler, for stealing 200 pounds weight of sugar out of a lighter on the river Thames. (1771bug00068)

6.   Summary and outlook

Crime reports in early English newspapers are a fascinating text class and their development during the eighteenth century can be observed by using the ZEN Corpus. The majority of these reports are brief and straightforward texts which, according to the distinction proposed by Schneider (2002), would belong to the hard news reports of quality papers. Yet, by the addition of only a few details that go beyond the mere facts they develop into human interest stories or soft news.

Many of the crimes referred to in early newspapers take the form of official, legal announcements or even advertisements. These texts show a fixed structure and have a restricted vocabulary. A large proportion of them are reports of the theft of horses or other goods, or of run-away servants. They provide a good argument for the inclusion of the text classes ANNOUNCEMENT and ADVERTISEMENT in a corpus of newspaper texts.

Crime reports proper, i.e. news, in particular about robberies and murders, may be very matter-of-fact, providing only those details absolutely necessary. But it is these texts that also provide the reader with exciting details. In spite of the fact that they are normally very brief, consisting of one sentence only, they give at least some interesting information on the criminals, the victims, and the crimes reported. From the middle of the eighteenth century onwards these short texts are gradually extended to more than one sentence resulting in stories of more than 150 words. Newspaper commentaries use more exciting language, especially superlatives (*a most bloody and cruel murder*), expressions which were also observed by Schneider (2002) in the introductory sentences of news reports in the popular press.

Reports about punishment are also included in the text class CRIME in the ZEN Corpus. They are either brief notices about imprisonment and sentences, or longer ones about trials, often yielding lists of all the criminals tried in one session.

What this study has also shown and what one should always bear in mind is that a corpus can include only a small number of the texts available for any period. Thus, the ZEN Corpus, in spite of its size, includes only a very small portion of the newspaper texts published in the late seventeenth and eighteenth centuries. In order to fully assess the writings on crime and punishment during that period one would not only have to extend the corpus but also include many other publications, from pamphlets and magazines to fiction.

References

Bell, Allan. 1991. *The Language of News Media*. Oxford: Blackwell.

Brownlees, Nicholas. 1999. *Corantos and Newsbooks: Language and Discourse in the First English Newspapers (1620–1641)*. Pisa: Edizioni ETS.

Fries, Udo. 2001. Textclasses in early English newspapers. *European Journal of English Studies* 5.2, 167–180.

Jucker, Andreas H. 2006. "but 'tis believed that…": Speech and thought presentation in early English newspapers. In Nicholas Brownlees, (ed.). *News Discourse in Early Modern Britain. Selected Papers of CHINED 2004*. (Linguistic Insights 31). Bern: Peter Lang, 105–126.

The Oxford English Dictionary. 1989. 2nd ed. J. A. Simpson and C. S. Weiner. Oxford: Clarendon Press. Online version: http://www.oed.com.

Schneider, Kristina. 2002. *The Development of Popular Journalism in England from 1700 to the Present. Corpus Compilation and Selective Stylistic Analysis*. Dissertation Rostock.

Wikipedia: http://en.wikipedia.org/wiki/Poultry_Compter.

Xekalakis, Elefteria. 1999. *Newspapers Through the Times: Foreign Reports from the 18th to the 20th Centuries*. Dissertation Zurich.

ZEN, *Zurich English Newspaper Corpus*, Version 1.0. English Department of the University of Zurich. http://es-zen.unizh.ch.

Reading late eighteenth-century want ads

Laura Wright

1.　Introduction

The study of historical pragmatics gives consideration to textual and social contexts, and nowhere is this more apparent than when reading old want ads (see *OED* "want", n^2 9. comb., *want ad*, first attested 1897). This paper looks at want ads from servants seeking employment, and employers seeking servants, in editions of the London newspaper *The Morning Herald* of the 1780s, and notes some formulae peculiar to this text-type. My starting-point is a short article by C. T. Onions (1931), who demonstrated that the phrases "distance no object", "rent no object", etc., developed in the context of eighteenth-century want ads whereby the principal aim of the advertiser was to obtain an agreeable post rather than a high salary. Salary was at first stated to be "not an object", then "no object", and then the phrase was extended in scope to include other terms like "rent" or "distance". The constraint of expense meant that servants usually tried to confine their advertisements to as few words as possible, with many of them seeking the same thing: a job, in a congenial workplace, with sufficient emolument. Unlike the lonely hearts advertisers in today's *London Review of Books* they did not seek to craft original works of literary merit, but to locate an agreeable employer as quickly as possible, and so certain collocations came to be preferred. That such collocations were specific to the text-type can be illustrated by the mid-twentieth century want-ad term "Girl Friday" (*OED* "Girl Friday" 'a resourceful young woman assistant (to a man)', first attested 1940, and calqued on Defoe's Man Friday), which older readers may remember. This phrase used to be common in want ads but is rarely met with nowadays, the term "PA" (personal assistant) or simply "assistant" having largely replaced it. (It is hard to say when the term "PA" was first attested in the specific sense of 'a secretarial administrator who works in an office setting', as *OED* lists it without illustration or definition under "P"). The demise of "Girl Friday" is probably due to late-twentieth century disapproval of the term "girl" for women in the workplace. In fact, eighteenth-century advertisers also dispreferred the terms "girl" and "woman"; "person" or "young person" being the more usual expressions. The term "person" had come to acquire overtones of low social standing by the beginning of the century (*OED* "person", n. II. 2. d.), and by the middle of the century it had become the normal term in want ads to refer to servants, both male and female (*OED* "person", n. II. 2. e).

2.   The conventions of the "WANTS a Place" advertisement

The Morning Herald in the 1780s consisted of a broadsheet of two folios, with the want ads appearing in a column on the dorse of the second folio – the back page of the newspaper. Want ads could be as brief as forty words, but were usually a little longer. This article will attempt to tease out the meaning of some of these words.

The advertisement itself usually began with the formula "WANTS a place", with the word "WANTS" in capital letters. Next came a noun phrase indicating the human agent (man, young person, footman, etc.), postmodified, often in considerable detail, listing accomplishments, and stating the post they were seeking (maid, cook, valet, etc.). There usually followed a clause stating that a character reference was to be had, and possibly a statement that the advertiser had no objection to travel, or to living in the country, or wearing livery, etc., with subject omitted. Typically, want ads from this time contained few subjects, with one or more verb-initial sentences. The default tense was the present, and auxiliaries, especially modals, were frequent. The advertisement usually ended with the imperative "Direct for/to [initials], at [address]". The address was either that of the *Morning Herald*'s office at 18, Catharine Street, Strand, or it was a private address. The initials, I suspect, were often made up. This is hard to prove, but it is surely unlikely that Londoners predominantly had the initials A. B. in the early 1780s, not to mention A. A., Z. Z. and even Z. Z. Z. An example of a want ad is given in (1):

(1)   Saturday, December 1, 1781.
       Wants a Place, a middle-aged Man, as Valet and Butler; has been in the same capacity before, can dress hair or wigs, and shave, can speak different languages, and handy in the cookery way, in three different manners, English, French, and Italian, and makes all manner of ice creams, fruits and preserves. Has no objection to travel to any part, having been used to travelling, to serve a single Gentleman, or in a genteel family, and can have an undeniable character. Direct for A. M. at Mr. Macke's, at No. 176, Piccadilly.

In (1) the subject (*a middle-aged man*) is postposed after the verb (*wants*), and thereafter not indicated; i.e. *has been, can dress, can speak, makes, has*, and *can have* all have a zero subject. Both the subject and the verb "to be" are omitted in the phrase *and handy in the cookery way*; such subject and "be" elision is typical. The main outer clause (*a middle-aged man wants a place to serve a single gentleman*), has non-contiguous subject, verb and object (indeed this is defined in a separate sentence). Two lexical items warrant comment here: "genteel" (see 2.1), and "character" (see 2.2).

2.1   "Genteel"

Since the 1850s, the term "genteel" has almost always been used 'in an ironic sense as being characteristic of those who are possessed with a dread of being taken for "common people"' (see *OED* "genteel", *a.* and *n.*). In the 1780s, "genteel" covered the qualities that the phrases "well-to-do" and "well-bred" might encompass today when used in the context of people or families, which is how it was frequently used in want ads. Stokes (1991:83) remarks that "genteel" "denoted a social class, contradistinguishing members of that class from their servants and tradesmen". "Genteel" comes from a re-adoption at the end of the sixteenth century of the French word *gentil*, which had been previously borrowed in the thirteenth century, and had developed to "gentle". In its re-adopted sense "genteel" meant 'belonging to or included among the gentry' (first attestation *OED* 1628); and then came to mean 'stylish, fashionably elegant or sumptuous' (first attestation *OED* 1599). By the 1780s, it no longer exclusively signalled gentry. There are slightly different senses of "genteel" in our want ads: when referring to persons, the sense is 'well-brought-up', 'well-bred', as in (2). When referring to the neighbourhoods such people lived in, the sense is 'well-to-do', as in (3). When referring to taste in dress, as in (4), or décor, as in (5), the sense is 'fashionably stylish'. The genteel boarding-school in (6) is 'suited to the station of a gentleman or gentlewoman'. When referring to address (*OED* "address", *n.* 10. 'manner of speaking to another, bearing in conversation'), as in (7), the sense is 'characteristic of persons of quality' (all of these definitions are to be found under *OED* genteel, *a.*).

(2)   Wednesday, June 26, 1782.
       Wants a Place, a middle-aged Woman, to take care of a Child from the month, or from the nurse, or the care of a Nursery, where there are two or three children, in which capacity she has lived 12 years in a genteel family, and can have an undeniable character. Direct for B. D. at Mr. Greenly's, Cumberland-street, near the Middlesex Hospital.

(3)   Thursday, July 4, 1782.
       Board and Lodging, together or separate, proposed to any Gentleman and his Wife, or Sister, desirous of avoiding the trouble of house-keeping; or single Gentleman induced to limit his expences, and wishing the comforts of a

regular family, may be accommodated in such society as, it is presumed, will be found unexceptionable: Apartments consist of an elegant drawing-room, three bed-chambers, dressing-rooms, &c. situation in a genteel neighbour-hood, contiguous to all the Inns of Court. Enquire at No. 172, Fleet street.

(4)   Tuesday, December 11, 1781.
Wants a Place, to wait on one or two Ladies, a person well qualified in that capacity, has dressed ladies to court and public places this eight years, can paper, crimp, and twist hair, has a genteel taste in millinery, cleaning and getting up crape to look like new, understands house-keeping perfectly well, if required, can be well recommended, and her character will bear the strictest enquiry. Any Lady who please to direct a line to S. B. at Mr. Elliot's, Haberdasher, in Vere-street, shall immediately be waited on.

(5)   Thursday, March 28, 1782.
Lodgings. To be Lett, genteelly furnished, in an airy situation, near Dean-street, Soho, a first floor, containing three rooms, with the use of a good kitchen, and every necessary conveniency for a Single Gentleman and Servant, or a small family. Enquire at Mr. Walker's, No. 7, James-street, Covent Garden.

(6)   Tuesday, June 24, 1783.
A Young Person, of good Address, who has been educated at, and Assistant in a genteel Boarding-School, in the vicinity of London, wishes to re-engage in the above situation, or to instruct two or three young Ladies in a genteel fam-ily. She flatters herself her character and recommendation, will, on enquiry, be perfectly satisfactory. – Address to K. S. at Mr. Moor's, Haberdasher and Hosier, Lamb's Conduit Passage.

(7)   Wednesday, June 26, 1782.
Wants a Place, in a Shop, or any other way, whereby he might be useful to his employer; a young Man of genteel address, and unexceptionable character. Direct for R. F. at Mr. Pressey's, Oilman and Grocer, in Henrietta-street, Covent-garden.

The slightly different senses of "genteel" are expressed by their collocations. When "genteel" is used with families, "regular" often collocates, as in (8).

(8)   Friday, March 28, 1782.
Wants a Place, a steady sober active Man, about 40 years of age, and single, as Butler in a genteel regular family, or to wait on a single elderly Gentleman, can shave easy, dress hair or wigs extremely well, and have an unexceptionable character from his last place, understands family business perfectly well, table, sideboard, &c. can bear confinement, and has no objection to the country. Direct to A. B. at No. 6, Hemming's Row, St. Martin's Lane.

For the duties of a butler see Hecht (1956: 46–47). The main duties were serving meals, looking after the plate and glass, and responsibility for the pantry and wine.[1] The definition of "regular" in this family context is probably to be found under *OED* "regular", *a., adv.*, and *n.* 4.b. 'orderly, well-ordered, well-behaved, steady', and led to the verbal form, as in (9).

(9) Saturday, April 6, 1782.
Wants a Place, as Butler, or Butler and Valet, a steady, single Man, free from any incumbrance, well acquainted with regulating a family, having lived in that capacity several years, has no objection to town or country, can be well recommended for ability, and integrity by the family with whom he at present lives, and whose only motive for parting with him, is his master's going abroad. Please to direct to Mr. Atkinson, Linen-draper, Coventry-street, Haymarket; or to R. B. at Mr. Palmer's, Cutler, in St. James's-street.

For the duties of a valet, see Hecht (1956: 45–46). Essentially these were: caring for the master's dress and hair, acting as a kind of servile companion, and, if there was no house-steward, directing the household staff. See *OED* "regulate", *v.* 1.b. 'To bring or reduce (a person or body of persons) to order. *Obs.*' for the general meaning of "regulate". However, the *OED* has no attestations of regulating a family, so I cannot be certain whether the noun or the verb came first in this context. Clearly both were well understood in the late eighteenth century.

We can thus paraphrase that the kind of situation so keenly sought was employment amongst a financially well-off, well-behaved group of people. The term "genteel" was, however, soon to lose its positive connotation. By the middle of the following century it was firmly associated with the servant class, as demonstrated by the following jest:

Cockney Domestic. – Servant girl.
"Well, mam – Heverythink considered, I'm afraid you von't suit me. I've always bin brought up genteel; and I couldn't go nowhere where there ain't no footman kep".[2]

This is taken from the 1858 edition of *Enquire Within Upon Everything*, which was a Victorian household compendium that sold in huge numbers – the ninth

---

1. "Insobriety is a very common failing amongst butlers" (A Member of the Aristocracy 1894: 53).

2. See discussion of "followers" in Section 2.8. This joke has a double meaning perhaps no longer immediately apparent: the servant girl pretends that she can't accept the job on offer as the household is insufficiently genteel, whereas contemporary readers would have understood that a footman in the household makes a prospective marriage partner.

edition boasts a printing of ninety-three thousand copies. The reader is being advised on how to avoid sounding like a Cockney. The stigmatised features are "h-insertion" and use of the voiceless velar stop instead of the velar nasal (*heverythink*), v~w interchange (*von't*), multiple negation (*couldn't go nowhere*), use of *ain't*, consonant cluster simplification (*kep'*), and use of *genteel* (without adverbial suffix). But in our want ads of the early 1780s, this pejoration had not yet set in, and "genteel" was an essential component as both servants and masters sought to ensure that their colleagues and surroundings would be civilised, stable and financially solvent. It is probably the frequency of this very usage (that is, by servants seeking a place) that caused its pejoration.

2.2   "Character"

In Present-day English the word "character", meaning 'a good character reference', does not stand unpostmodified. In late eighteenth-century want ads it could, as in example (10).

> (10)   Tuesday, April 2, 1782.
> Wanted, in a small, genteel family, a clever Footman, that understands his business well. He must be very neat and clean, have a good character from his last place, and know something of hair-dressing, as good encouragement will be given. Apply at No 22, Surry-street, Strand, any morning before Eleven o'clock.

For the duties of a footman see Hecht (1956: 51–52). Amongst other duties footmen were high-visibility servants, advertising their employers' wealth by means of their livery as they escorted them and ran errands outside the house.[3] *Character* alone is not a shortened form but a usage to be found under *OED* "character", *n.* 14.c. 'A formal testimony given by an employer as to the qualities and habits of one that has been in his employ', first attested 1693. It is frequently premodified by *undeniable* as in (11), or *unexceptionable* as in example (12), and is often to be found embedded in the string "can have a good/undeniable/unexceptionable character from his last place". *The Duties of Servants*, written by A Member of the Aristocracy (1894: 8–9) makes it clear that a "personal character" was transmitted by means of spoken interview between former and potential employer, in contradistinction to a "written character", which was considered less useful.

---

3. "In households where two or three footmen are kept, heads of families make a point of keeping tall footmen, and having men of equal height to avoid the incongruity of appearance that men-servants of unequal height would present. Where only one footman is kept, his height is immaterial" (A Member of the Aristocracy 1894: 59).

(11)   Thursday, April 11, 1782.
       Wants a Place, a middle aged Person, as Cook, that can dress plain victuals
       well, make made dishes, and perfectly understands pickling and preserving,
       to serve in a small genteel family, or to undertake the management of a house
       for a single Lady or Gentleman, in town or country. She can have an undeni-
       able character from her last place, where she lived a year and a half. Direct for
       A. B. No. 21, Devonshire-street, Queen-square.

A *made dish* was 'a fancy dish of various ingredients, depending for its success
on the cook's skill' (*OED* "dish", *n.* 2.b., first attested 1621). The reference to *plain*
victuals (like the reference to the man-servant in example (40) "who can dress
hair or wigs in a plain way") encodes something about salary. A Member of the
Aristocracy (1894: 81) explains that a *plain* cook is in contradistinction to a *professed* cook who commanded a far higher salary (see Section 2.5), and a plain
cook's duties included work outside the kitchen, such as cleaning other rooms.
The narrower the specialisation, the greater the wages.

(12)   Monday, July 1, 1782.
       A Footman wanted in a regular Family, who is master of his business, must
       understand hair-dressing, the Advertiser's place may be made very acceptable
       to any well disposed person; and it is requested that none do apply but those
       who can have an unexceptionable character for their sobriety, honesty, and
       attention. Further particulars may be had at Mr. Miller's, baker, Charlotte-
       street, the corner of Weymouth-street, Portland place.

(13)   Saturday, July 6, 1782.
       Board and Lodging offered in a small genteel Family, to any marieed couple of
       a cheerful disposition, or any single Gentleman desirous of society; situation
       retired, pleasant, and airy, within five minutes walk of the Park, and shilling
       fare of the theatres; apartments neat and modern, and family, presumed,
       unexceptionable. Direct to I. B. Parliament-street Coffee-house.

Unexceptionable as in (12) and (13) had a rather more positive sense, meaning
'perfectly satisfactory' (see *OED* "unexceptionable", *a.* 1.), than the current, more
pejorative sense of 'unremarkable, mediocre', which isn't listed in the *OED*. Note
how employers advertised themselves as being *presumed* unexceptionable, as already seen in (3). Similarly, the adjective *tolerable* had nuances no longer found
today, as in (14) and (15).

(14)   Friday, June 28, 1782.
       Wanted, a stout, active Lad, to carry out parcels, and open and shut shop. He
       must write a tolerable hand, and have an undeniable character for honesty and
       sobriety. Apply at No. 144, Fleet-street.

(15) Tuesday, April 9, 1782.
      Wants a Place, a young Man, of 31 years of a very good character for his hon-
      esty, sobriety and good behaviour, as Butler, in a reputable and genteel family;
      he can dress Ladies and Gentlemens hair tolerably well, tune harpsichords
      well enough to keep them in order, and has no objection to town or country.
      Direct to A. B. at Mr. Garrett's, Bookseller and Stationer, No. 24, Panton-
      street, Hay-market.

This usage is to be found under *OED* "tolerable", *a.* (*adv.*) 4. 'Moderate in degree,
quality, or character; of middling quality, mediocre, passable; now *esp.* moderately good, fairly good or agreeable, not bad', with attestations from 1548 to 1866.
However, the attestations listed are really fairly pejorative, meaning something
like 'bearable, put-up-able with', until the attestation of 1866, where *tolerable* is
qualified by *very*, which gives quite a different meaning.

> *OED* attestations of "tolerable", *a.* (*adv.*) 4.:
> 1548 UDALL, etc. *Erasm. Par. Matt.* v. 38 To the intent ye shoulde be of the
> meane and tollerable sorte.
> 1658 EVELYN *Diary* 9 June, The new front towards ye gardens is tollerable,
> were it not drown'd by a too massie and clomsie pair of stayres of stone.
> 1693 DRYDEN *Disc. Orig. & Progr. Satire* Ess. (Ker) II. 110 We have yet no
> English *prosodia*, not so much as a tolerable dictionary, or a grammar.
> 1706 PHILLIPS (ed. Kersey), *Tolerable*,... also indifferent, passable.
> 1835 SIR J. ROSS *Narr. 2nd Voy.* xl. 538 Found a tolerable road.
> 1866 MRS. GASKELL *Wives & Dau.* xv, He had eaten a very tolerable lunch.

By contrast our *tolerable* and *tolerably* in examples (14) and (15) surely mean that
the handwriting had to be legible, that is, where "tolerable" was synonymous with
"fair", and the hair was to be well-dressed, that is, synonymous with "quite" – it
would be perverse to interpret the young man's composition as advertising his
lack of skill. I suggest that the meaning given by *OED* of 'moderately good, not
bad', can be dated back at least as far as 1782.

   In (16) the word *character* is used slightly differently, as is found under *OED*
"character", *n.* 12. a. 'moral qualities strongly developed or strikingly displayed'
(first attestation 1735: Alexander Pope, "Most Women have no Characters at all").

(16) Tuesday, April 9, 1782.
      Wants a Place, as Lady's Maid, or Lady's Maid and Housekeeper, a Person that
      can dress hair, get up small linen very well, knows something of mantua-mak-
      ing and millinery, can have a good recommendation from the Lady she is now
      going to leave, and flatters herself of being capable to give satisfaction to any

Lady. Direct for A. A. at No. 19, Davis-street, Berkley square. It is to be hoped none will apply but people of character.

To *get up* small linen can be found under *OED* "get", *v.* l. "get up": 'to dress (linen), make ready for wearing'. The phrase *small linen* doesn't have an *OED* entry, it probably means underclothes, so to get them up probably meant to wash and press them, rather than to make them. (*OED* headwords "small-clothes" (first attestation 1796, "breeches") and "small", a. and n.[2] B. 9. *pl.* a. (first attestation 1837, "breeches") do not attest the sense 'underwear' until 1943.) Ladies' maids were often apprenticed when young to mantua-makers (see Hecht 1956:61).

The present-day sense of "character" was also used, where "character" meant 'the sum of the moral and mental qualities which distinguish an individual', as listed under *OED* "character", *n.* 11., first attestation 1647, and illustrated by examples (17)–(20). When used in this sense the word "character" is often embedded in the string "his/her character will bear the strictest enquiry/scrutiny" or something similar.

(17)   Thursday, June 27, 1782.
       To the Clergy. A Curacy wanted by a Clergyman in Priest's Orders, and a Graduate of a College. The Advertiser's character will bear the nicest scrutiny. A line addressed to Z. Z. Z. at Peele's Coffee-House, Temple Bar, Fleet-street, will be duly attended to.

The placer of the advertisement in (17) must have required anonymity as by using the initials Z. Z. Z. (actually, the initials A. B. are by far the most frequent in want ads of this era) and by receiving his mail at a coffee-house, he has successfully concealed his identity. *Nicest* is to be found under *OED* "nice", *adj.* and *adv.* 3.a. 'Precise or particular in matters of reputation or conduct; scrupulous, punctilious. Now *rare*' – although it should be said that this sense is now pretty much obsolete rather than rare. In fact, both the twentieth-century attestations are from the stories of P. G. Wodehouse, which gain their humour at this juncture from their old-fashioned language (*OED* "nice", *adj.* and *adv.* 3.a. 1938 P. G. WODEHOUSE *Code of Woosters* xii. 261 Bertram Wooster in his dealings with the opposite sex invariably shows himself a man of the nicest chivalry. 1948 P. G. WODEHOUSE *Spring Fever* xiii. 127 Up against this dark and subtle butler, we cannot afford to be too nice in our methods).

(18)   Tuesday, April 9, 1782.
       Wanted, by a Person of good Education and genteel address, a Place, to have the care of one or more young Ladies, where French is not required, and very fond of children; or would be glad to serve any Lady as her Maid and Housekeeper, as she dresses hair, and is every way qualified for such a place,

having lived in that capacity. No objection to a single Gentleman's place, if a regular, sober family, and her character will bear the strictest scrutiny. Direct for T. A. at Mr. Smith's, Milliner and Haberdasher, No. 59, Graet Marybone-street, Cavendish-square.

In (18) the sense of *strictest* here is to be found under *OED* "strict", *a.* 8.a. 'Accurately determined or defined; exact, precise, not vague or loose. Of particulars: Enumerated or described in exact detail'. As mentioned earlier, references for eighteenth-century servants were just as likely to consist of an oral question-and-answer dialogue as of a written testimonial. The difference lay in the wide range of questions that could be quickly posed face-to-face as opposed to the more limited range of topics likely to be covered by a writer.

(19)   Saturday, April 6, 1782.
Wants Employment, a sober, steady Man, as Butler, or Groom of the Chambers in a Noble-man's, or genteel family; or as Butler and Valet in a small, regular family, that are not used to change often. His character will bear the strictest enquiry, is well acquainted with the oeconomy of a table and sideboard, the care and management of a cellar, and can brew well, if required. Direct to A. A. at Mr. Scot's, Gentleman's Hotel, Pall Mall.

In royal and noble households certain prepositional phrases lingered, as in the context of (19). *OED* "groom", *n.*[1] 4. lists 'groom of his Majesty's removing wardrobe' (1731), 'groom of the stole to his Majesty' (1818), 'groom of the chambers' (1844), and 'groom-in-waiting to her Majesty' (1868).

(20)   Saturday, April 6, 1782.
Wants a Place, a young Man, out of Livery, who can dress both Ladies and Gentlemens hair, writes a good hand, and keeps accounts, to serve a single Gentlemen, or as Butler and Own Man in a genteel family, and whose character will bear the strictest enquiry from his last master. Direct to A. B. at Mr. Robinson's, No. 34, Duke-street, St. James's.

The word *man* meaning 'a male personal attendant; a manservant, a valet' is to be found under *OED* "man", *n.*[1] 7.a. However, I cannot find any entry for the phrase *own man* in the *OED*, nor can I find it in ZEN, although it clearly served as a meaningful job description in (20). *Old Bailey Online* has several ambiguous attestations of the phrase *own man*, where it is not entirely clear whether *own man* meant 'personal servant' or simply 'employee'. However, in (21) it seems likely that *my own man* was synonymous with *my man* and *my servant*, and had a meaning of 'personal manservant to a male employer':

(21)   "I had employed the prisoner occasionally as a driver of the cart, and so has *my servant*; but *my servant* is not in Court – I did not hear from him that the prisoner had my cart for the purpose of doing this job – he has been autho-rized to employ the prisoner to drive the van – on the 27th of September the prisoner came to me, between seven and eight o'clock in the evening, after *my man* had booked the work he had done in the day – the prisoner said he had taken my van for the purpose of taking a chest of indigo – he said he had received 3s. for it, which he gave me, and I gave him 1s.
COURT. Q. Did he tell you where it was taken? A. He said from Cutler-street to Whitechapel; but he did not say who had employed him – I should not have known my van had gone for indigo unless he had told me – I heard from *my own man* that the van had been used while he was away for five minutes; but he did not know by whom".
(*Old Bailey Online* Ref t18341016-99, 16th October 1834. Italics mine)

In perusing the want ads given under examples (1) to (21), the reader will have encountered some formulae that merit further explanation. These will now be discussed in the following sections.

2.3   "From the month"

Example (2), which was an advertisement seeking employment as a nursery nurse, contained the phrase *from the month*. This is further illustrated in (22) and (23).

(22)   Thursday, April 11, 1782.
Wants a Place, as Dry Nurse, a Widow Woman, 27 years of age, free from any incumbrance, who is capable of taking a Child from the month, as she has lived some years in that capacity, can have a good character from her last place, and has no objection to the country. Direct to M. J. No. 3, Welbeck-street, Cavendish-square.

(23)   Tuesday, July 9, 1782.
Wants a Place, as Dry Nurse, in a Gentleman's family, a sober, steady Person, about 39 years of age, to take a child from the month. She understands frock-making ' jams, &c, [probably the apostrophe before *jams* is a misplaced comma – LCW] and can be well recommended from her last place, where she lived upwards of three years, in that capacity. Direct to A. B. at Mr. Findlay's, Perfumer, No. 191, Piccadilly. None but people of credit need apply.

The locution "from the month" can be found under *OED* "month", *n.*[1.] 8.e., al-though the meaning is best found under 4.b. 'The month after childbirth, during which time a woman was formerly expected to be confined; in early use *esp.* the period before "churching"', first attested 1631. The definition under sense 8.e. reads 'from the time when a woman confined after childbirth is no longer attended by a monthly nurse', and the first attestation is 1808. I am not confident that the phrase "from the month" as used by our advertisers was exclusively directed at those who were attended by monthly nurses; presumably it could also have been directed at those with newborn babies who had just emerged from the month of confinement. The *dry nurse* is in contradistinction to the *wet nurse* of example (24).

(24) Thursday, April 4, 1782.
      Wants a Place, as Wet Nurse, a young Woman, with a good Breast of Milk, and no encumbrance, whose husband is gone abroad, and can be well recommended, to serve in a Gentleman or Tradesman's family. Direct to J. C. at Mr. Perry's, Glover, in Great Turnstile, Holborn.

The *wet nurse* was able to breastfeed an infant herself as she had also recently given birth (see *OED* "dry-nurse", *n.* (first attestation 1589) and "wet nurse", *n.* (1620)). The term "encumbrance" is still pretty well understood today in this context as a euphemism meaning 'without children', the likelihood being in example (24) that the woman's newborn has died (*OED* "encumbrance", 3. 'A person dependent on another for support; *esp.* in phrase *without encumbrance* = "having no children"', first attestation 1742).

2.4   "Understands business"

A verb frequently used to express mastery of a skill was *understands*, as in (25)–(27).

(25) Thursday, April 11, 1782.
      Wants a Cook's Place, in a Nobleman or Gentleman's family, a middle-aged Woman, who understands all manner of soups, made-dishes and pastery, can pickle and preserve, is very capable of her business, and has no objection to the country. If a kitchen Maid is kept, the more agreeable, as she has always been used to one. Direct to A. W. at Mr. Hippeth's, Gate-street, Lincoln's Inn Fields.

(26) Thursday, March 28, 1782.
      Wants a Place, a middle-aged Woman, as Housekeeper to a single Gentleman, or as Upper Maid in a small genteel family, who can work well at her needle, get up small linen, pickle and preserve, and understands the management of a kitchen. Direct for A. A. at No. 125, Wardour-street, Soho.

(27) Monday, July 1, 1782.
      Wanted, an active Lad, who understands the care of Horses, can comb a wig,
      and be well recommended from his place. Enquire at Hoyland's Coffee-house,
      near Somerset-house, Strand.

The phrase *understands sideboard* in example (8) would have indicated that the
advertiser was experienced in the profession of being a butler (*OED* "understand",
v. 1.b. 'To be thoroughly acquainted or familiar with (an art, profession, etc.); to
be able to practise or deal with properly', first attested 1533).

2.5 "Professed"

I provide five examples of "professed" (examples (28)–(32)) as this is now an unfamiliar usage, although common in the early 1780s. It meant 'professional' (see
OED "professed", *adj.* and *n.*).

(28) Tuesday, April 9, 1782.
      Wants a Place, in a Nobleman or Gentleman's family, as profest Housekeeper,
      a Person turned of 40 years of age, who perfectly knows her business, and can
      be well recommended from her last place. Enquire at Mr. Billing's, Turner,
      No. 10, Great Windmill-street, near the Hay-market.

(29) Friday, July 5, 1782.
      Wanted, a very good Woman Cook, whose abilities can be better proved than
      by her own opinion; for professing herself a Cook is not a professed Cook.
      She must understand how to spit meat as well as roast it, and to salt as well
      as boil; she must be cleanly, and rise early, and if she understands dressing
      fish, roasting fowl, and making hashes, in all other things she will be assisted
      by a Housekeeper; a Kitchen Maid, allowed no fees or perquisites; her wages
      shall be equal to her abilities, if her accomplishments are made known, but
      a trial must be had, as changing is intolerable. Any person reading this, and
      knowing their abilities and character will answer, may enquire for A. B. at the
      Parliament Coffee-house, Parliament-street.

The tone of this want ad is unusual, and A. B. has written a rather costly advertisement. The pragmatics of politeness were such that only employers could afford
to be quite so explicit in their requirements. I have yet to come across a want ad
placed by a servant stipulating that changing is intolerable and that the employer
must come up to standard.

(30) Wednesday, July 10, 1782.
      Wants a Place, a professed Cook, in a genteel family, that understands making
      all kinds of made-dishes, soups, pastry, jellies, blamanges, pickling, preserv-
      ing, and every other requisite for a compleat Cook, in which capacity she has
      lived several years, and can have an unexceptional character from her last
      place. Direct for A. B. at Mr. Pultney's, Fishmonger, Market-street, St. James's-
      market.

Complete is here used in its eighteenth-century sense, see OED "complete", a. 5.
'Of persons: Fully equipped or endowed; perfect, accomplished, consummate; esp.
in reference to a particular art or pursuit, as a complete actor, horseman, merchant.
Now arch.'. The blancmange mentioned in (30) is likely to have been the modern
pudding (see OED "blancmange", b. 'A sweetmeat made of dissolved isinglass or
gelatine boiled with milk, etc., and forming an opaque white jelly') rather than
the pre-eighteenth-century savoury dish of the same name, made of white ingredients such as fowl with almonds or rice.

(31) Wednesday, July 10, 1782.
      Wants a Place, as Professed Cook, or Cook and Housekeeper in a small family,
      a Person who has no objection to live with a single Gentleman, and can have a
      good character from her last place. Direct for M. L. at Mr. Grey's, Hays-court,
      Newport-market.

(32) Monday, April 21, 1783.
      Wants a Place, a young Man twenty-eight years of age, as Butler, in or out of
      livery, in a small regular family; has no objection to a single Gentleman where
      professed hair-dressing is not required. – Direct to B. H. at Mr. Billet's, taylor,
      Bolsover-street, Oxford-street.

Thus "professed" was a conveniently brief way of indicating that advertisers wanted only the skills advertised (the housekeeper in example (28), and the cooks in
(29)–(31)), or that they wanted multiple skills (not "professed"). The professed
servant required higher wages than the more general servant.[4]

---

4. "In the case of a professed cook, the elementary portion of the cooking, the plain cooking,
and all that relates to cleaning and scouring in kitchen, scullery, larder, and passages, and all
cooking utensils, is done by the kitchen and scullery maids, and only the cooking proper is the
duty of this class of cook" (A Member of the Aristocracy 1894: 74).

2.6   "In or out of livery"

Whether a manservant wore livery or not had cost implications for the employer, and status implications for the employee.

(33)   Wednesday, July 10, 1782.
Wants a place, a middle-aged Man, to live in the country, and has no objection how far, as Butler in or out of livery, or to live where only one man is kept, in a regular family, who can shave, dress wigs, or comb hair, and have an undeniable character from his last place. Direct for T. W. at Mr. Clark's, No. 41, Bell yard, Temple-bar. Letters, post paid, immediately answered.

(34)   Saturday, July 6, 1782.
Wanted, for a single Gentleman, a Servant in Livery, who can dress hair well. He must have a good recommendation from his last place. A Foreigner will be preferred. Enquire at Mr. Sweet's, Grocer, South Audley street.

(35)   Monday, April 21, 1783.
A Butler in Livery is wanted to live in a Gentleman's family; he must shave perfectly well, must clean plate in the best manner, understand setting out a side-board; laying a cloth, and every part of his duty; he must have lived some years in this station in London. As it is in all respects a very good place, it is desired that none will apply but those with the most undoubted good character. Mr. Gibson, Taylor, White-Lion Court, Cornhill, will give a direction to the place.

Providing livery (a uniform) was costly for the employer, as the magnificence of the livery reflected upon the status of the employer. However, the highest-ranking servants did not wear livery (*OED* "livery", *n.* 2.a. *in livery* and *out of livery*; Buck 1979:108; Meldrum 2000:200). Hence the men in examples (32) and (33) were indicating that they would accept posts as lower-ranking servants, whereas the men in examples (20), (41), (45) and (47) were indicating that they sought high-status posts with commensurate wages, tips and perquisites. The employers in (34) and (35) specified a liveried servant, as however costly the livery, it was cheaper than employing a non-liveried servant.

2.7   "No office-keepers" and "principals only"

(36)   Wednesday, July 10, 1782.
Wants a Place, a middle-aged Person, as Housekeeper in a genteel family, who has superintended a large family in the country for many years, and thoroughly understands her business, viz. marketing, cooking, pickling,

preserving, pastry, jellies, and syrups of all kinds. Whoever this may suit, please to direct for A. B. at No. [blotted – LCW], St. Margaret's-street, near Westminster-Bridge, and they shall be immediately waited on. N.B. No attention will be paid to any Office-keeper.

I cannot find mention in *OED*, ZEN or *Old Bailey Online* of "office-keeper" in the sense of 'agent' or 'employee of a domestic agency', only that of 'keeper of an office'. I surmise that *office-keeper* in (36) is in contradistinction to the *principals* of (37) and (38).

(37) Tuesday, December 11, 1781.
Any Gentleman or Lady having it in their power to procure a place under Government for a young man of genteel address, aged about 23 years; a premium will be given adequate to the salary, none but principals will be treated with. A line addressed to T. M. at the Morning Herald Office, Catherine-street.

(38) Saturday, April 6, 1782.
Matrimony: addressed to the Serious and Candid. A Widower, between Thirty and Forty, of good address and connexions in a lucrative line of business, which has been established at a great expence for some years, would be happy to meet with a Widow, or Maiden Lady of the above description, with a knowledge of the world; the loss of a valuable wife, and a close attention to business, is the real cause of this mode of application, in hopes that some prudent discreet Lady may see it. – A line directed to M. L. O. at Old Slaughter's Coffee House, St. Martin's-Lane, will meet with the strictest honor, secrecy, and attention, to principals only.

A *knowledge of the world* presumably meant something like 'conversant with the value of money'. I deduce this from the collocations of *lucrative, business, great expence,* and *valuable.* ZEN has four similar tokens in advertisement usage from 1741, 1781 and 1791.[5] Note how the widow in (39) wishes to deal only with respondents replying under their own names (although she does not give her own), indicating that there was a flourishing trade in estate-agents and employment-agents.

(39) Monday, December 10, 1781.
A Widow Lady, who has a small neat House in a pleasant situation, within a shilling fare of the Opera and Play-houses; would be glad of a single Gentleman, to lodge or Lodge and board, where he may have an opportunity of sometimes joining in agreeable family party; there are no other lodgers or

---

5. ZEN 1741, ldp02034:s:40.3:1741, ldp02073:s:54.1; 1781, mhd00148:s:365.2; 1791, mop05600:s:74.1.

children. The Lady requests no one will answer this out of an idle curiosity, as none but those who sign their real names, will be taken notice of. Letters directed to A. B. to be left with the printer, will be answered immediately. It will suit any one who is fond of reading, it being retired though centrical.

Retired meant 'secluded, sequestered; removed from places frequented by people' (*OED* "retired", *ppl. a.*); *centrical* was in use from the 1740s to the 1860s (*OED* "centrical", *a.*).

2.8   "Can bear confinement" and "followers"

Employers would often mention bearing confinement as a condition of employment, and servants would mention bearing confinement as being something they could endure (examples (40) and (41)).

(40)   Monday, June 30, 1783.
Wants a Place, a sober, single, diligent Man, aged 32, who can dress hair or wigs in a plain way, understands the side-board, cleaning plate, brewing, is a thorough family-servant, and used to confinement; he writes a plain hand, and salary is not an object; he lived six years in his last place, which he has just left; no objection to a place in the country for all the year, or to a place for the remainder of the summer. Direct to E. B. at Mr. Bristow's, Hair-dresser and Perfumer, Davis-street, Berkley-square.

(41)   Tuesday, April 15, 1783.
Wants a Place, a steady, sober Man, about 40, to wait on an elderly Lady or Gentleman, or in a small regular family, to be out of livery, or to be Porter to a merchant or banking-house; he can bear confinement, any security will be given, and wages no object, as he has a small income. Direct for J. C. at No. 100, Cheapside.

ZEN has the following two tokens:

(42)   Wanted an Upper Nursery Maid, to dress and attend on three young Ladies, from two to five years old: she must be from thirty to forty years of age; and of unquestionable good character, bear confinement, and have no followers; the Widow of a reputable Tradesman is the most likely. (ZEN 1781, mhd00132: s:343.1)

(43)   Wanted, as Under Nursery Maid, a sedate Person about 30 years of age, who can bear confinement, and of undoubted character; also a Housemaid of the same description, and age; they must not drink tea, and reasonable but no extravagant wages may be expected. (ZEN 1781, mhd00148:s:323.1)

The *OED* makes no mention of this usage under "confinement". I surmise that the phrase *bear confinement* meant that the servant was kept indoors for most of the day (I originally thought it meant that they were to be the sole servant in the establishment, but example (43) indicates otherwise). Serendipitously, the *OED* mentions *followers* as in example (42) in the context of servants, because Dickens included a want ad in *Nicholas Nickleby* (*OED* "follower" c. *colloq.* 'A man who courts a maidservant; *esp.* one who calls at the house to see her'). In Chapter 16, Tom is a domestic-employment agent in the General Agency Office:

> "Cook," said Tom, turning over some leaves of the ledger. "Well!"
>
> "Read out an easy place or two," said the fat lady.
>
> "Pick out very light ones, if you please, young man," interposed a genteel female, in shepherd's-plaid boots, who appeared to be the client.
>
> "'Mrs Marker,'" said Tom, reading, "'Russell Place, Russell Square; offers eighteen guineas; tea and sugar found. Two in family, and see very little company. Five servants kept. No man. No followers.'"
>
> "Oh Lor!" tittered the client. "THAT won't do. Read another, young man, will you?"
>
> "'Mrs Wrymug,'" said Tom, "'Pleasant Place, Finsbury. Wages, twelve guineas. No tea, no sugar. Serious family –'"
>
> "Ah! you needn't mind reading that," interrupted the client.
>
> "'Three serious footmen,'" said Tom, impressively.
>
> "Three? did you say?" asked the client in an altered tone.
>
> "Three serious footmen," replied Tom. "'Cook, housemaid, and nursemaid; each female servant required to join the Little Bethel Congregation three times every Sunday – with a serious footman. If the cook is more serious than the footman, she will be expected to improve the footman; if the footman is more serious than the cook, he will be expected to improve the cook.'"
>
> "I'll take the address of that place," said the client; "I don't know but what it mightn't suit me pretty well."
>
> "Here's another," remarked Tom, turning over the leaves. "'Family of Mr Gallanbile, MP. Fifteen guineas, tea and sugar, and servants allowed to see male cousins, if godly. Note. Cold dinner in the kitchen on the Sabbath, Mr Gallanbile being devoted to the Observance question. No victuals whatever cooked on the Lord's Day, with the exception of dinner for Mr and Mrs Gallanbile, which, being a work of piety and necessity, is exempted. Mr Gallanbile dines late on the day of rest, in order to prevent the sinfulness of the cook's dressing herself.'"
>
> "I don't think that'll answer as well as the other," said the client, after a little whispering with her friend. "I'll take the other direction, if you please, young man. I can but come back again, if it don't do."
>
> Tom made out the address, as requested, and the genteel client, having satisfied the fat lady with a small fee, meanwhile, went away accompanied by her friend.
>
> Dickens (1839: Chapter 16)

The references to tea-drinking both in real want ads (example (43)) and in Dickens' parody of want ads above were due to a considerable tax on tea in the eighteenth century. For example, Richard Hoare Esq. of Hoare's Bank in Fleet Street bought one pound of best green tea from Twining and Carter in Devereux Court in 1761, costing him sixteen shillings, according to a receipt still kept in Hoare's Bank archive. Sixteen shillings in 1761 was worth £60 of today's money, that is, the equivalent of £60 bought one pound of (admittedly best) green tea.[6] Dickens used the older term *direction* to mean 'address'. The *OED*'s first attestation under "address", *n.* 7.a. 'the direction or superscription of a letter, etc.; the name of the person and place to which it is addressed or directed; the name of the place to which any one's letters are directed' is dated 1712, so Dickens could have used the newer word *address* but chose not to. Possibly the older term was out of fashion, and Dickens was making a class distinction here, with the lower classes still preferring the traditional form. Notice how wages are not an object: Mrs Marker is willing to pay eighteen guineas, tea and sugar found; while Mrs Wrymug only offers twelve guineas, no tea, no sugar, and lives in Finsbury (trade) as opposed to Russell Square (gentry). Nonetheless the client preferred Mrs Wrymug's offer, despite the salary being a third less with no perquisites and being further down the social ladder. The implication is that Mrs Marker's five servants were female, with no male presence. The client would be unable to meet a suitable manservant as a future husband within the household, and followers were forbidden. At Mrs Wrymug's she would not only live under the same roof as the three footmen, she positively had to spend Sundays with them. The extract is amusing, but Dickens is making an observation on the social conditions of working-class women of the time, whose options for social and economic betterment were severely limited. The anonymous Member of the Aristocracy who wrote *The Duties of Servants* said of followers:

> The rule as to whether servants may receive visits from male acquaintances is a very important one, and the prohibition of such should be clearly expressed. In well-ordered households the visits of male acquaintants, commonly called "followers", are strictly forbidden; and all mistresses desirous of maintaining anything like order in their households, rigidly enforce the observance of this regulation.
>
> (A Member of the Aristocracy 1894: 11)

---

6.   Both Hoare's and Twining's still do business from their original Fleet Street sites. Hecht (1956: 156–157) discusses amounts of tea allowed to servants, or the allocation of tea-money in lieu; it is also discussed by Hill (1996: 70). For money equivalents see Currency Converter Old Money to New http://www.nationalarchives.gov.uk/ currency/default0.asp#mid.

Hill (1996: 54) comments that this rule was not just to avoid the inconvenience of strange men disturbing the household (possibly resulting in illegitimate off-spring) but also to avoid loss of servants due to marriage.

2.9 "Of light weight" and "either way"

These two phrases appear in advertisements by or for male servants who could drive coaches, such as in examples (44)–(46).

(44) Wednesday, April 23, 1783.
Wants a Place, as Groom, a young Man of light weight, who has no objection to waiting at table occasionally, and can bring an undeniable character from his last place, where he lived three years and a half. Direct to W. G. at Mrs. Fossey's, Poulterer, Leicester-street, Leicester-fields.

(45) Tuesday, April 15, 1783.
Wants a Place, a young Man, 28 Years of age, to live with a single Gentleman, or as Butler in a regular family, out of livery, who can shave and dress in the present taste, has been used to travelling, is of light weight, and can have an undeniable character from his last place. Direct for E. M. at Mr. Robbins's, Perfumer, No. 138, Oxford-street, near Bond-street.

(46) Wednesday, June 25, 1783.
Wants a Place, as Coachman, a Person about 26 years of age, of light weight, and thoroughly acquainted with either way of driving; he can be very well recommended from his last place, the occasion of leaving which, was the loss of his master. Should prefer a family that resides mostly in the country. Direct to W. H. at Mr. Barnes's, Stationer, near Temple Bar.

I surmise that the young men's light weight was an advantage as it would not wear out the horses. The ability to drive *either way* might mean from the horse, or from the coach. With some coaches, such as a barouche, the coachman sat on the box at the front of the coach; whereas with a post-chaise, the coachman rode on horseback. Post-chaises were in fashion in the 1780s, barouches a little later. The post of coachman was the highest-ranking of the lower (i.e. livery-wearing) servants (Hecht 1956: 51).

2.10 "Go a job" and "go the circuit"

(47) Tuesday, July 9, 1782.
Wants a Place, a young Man, 28 Years of age, to live with a single Gentleman, or as Butler in a regular family, out of livery, who can shave and dress hair or

wigs in the present taste, has no objection to go a job for the summer with any Gentleman or Lady, and his character will bear the strictest enquiry from his last place. Direct for Z. M. at Mr. Stockdale's, Bookseller, opposite Burlington-house, Piccadilly.

I have been unable to locate the phrase from example (47) *go a job* in the *OED*, ZEN or *Old Bailey Online*. I surmise that it meant to take a temporary job, probably for the duration of the London season (compare *OED* "jobber", n² 3. 'a person hired to do a particular job or employed by the job'). This was when wealthy people came up to London from the country, a custom influenced by parliamentary sittings. Parliament would adjourn for Easter, when the royal court would go out of London, and then return after Easter when the summer season would begin. The houses in Mayfair, St James's, Marylebone and Belgravia would fill up, as would the hotels and lodging-houses, and servants would be hired until the exodus to the country and the practice of country-house visiting began in the latter half of the summer.

(48)   Monday, June 30, 1783.
        Wants a Place, a single Man, 36 years of age, who can shave and dress hair, understands family-business well, can act as Butler or Game-keeper, brew, if required, and has no objection to live with a single Gentleman, or to go the circuit. Direct to G. h. at Mr. Pott's, Fruiterer, near the Image Yard, Piccadilly.

By contrast, the phrase *go the circuit* (in example (48)) is in evidence in our reference works and sources, but only in the context of the barristers' circuit (see *OED* "circuit", *n.*) which, for want of further evidence, this is assumed to refer to.

2.11 "Flatters him/herself"

(49)   Tuesday, June 24, 1783.
        Wants a Place, as Upper Maid, where hair-dressing is not required, a young Woman, who flatters herself to be every way qualified for such a situation, having in that capacity given satisfaction in her Last place, from whence she can have a good character. Has no objection to superintend a kitchen. Direct to A. O. at No. 5, King street, Cheapside.

(50)   Tuesday, June 24, 1783.
        A Young Person, of good Address, who has been educated at, and Assistant in a genteel Boarding-School, in the vicinity of London, wishes to re-engage in the above situation, or to instruct two or three young Ladies in a genteel family. She flatters herself her character and recommendation, will, on enquiry,

be perfectly satisfactory. – Address to K. S. at Mr. Moor's, Haberdasher and Hosier, Lamb's Conduit Passage.

(51)   Friday, July 5, 1782.
Wants a Place, to serve a single Gentleman, or as Butler in a family, where more servants are kept, or to live in a small genteel regular family where only one servant is kept, a person who flatters himself that his attention and sobriety will give satisfaction to his employer. He knows his business well in every respect, can dress Gentlemens hair in any desirable taste, and be well recommended. Direct to F. F. at Mr. Taylor's, Grocer, No. 42, Pall Mall.

Euphemisms were much in use: we've already seen "encumbrances" for children and "followers" for boyfriends. In (49)–(51) we see that the pragmatics of appearing to boast were too great for a simple copula (i.e. 'she is perfectly satisfactory'), despite the expense of extra wording (OED "flatter", v.[1] 7.b. 'To please with the belief, idea, or suggestion that. Now chiefly refl.').

2.12   "Both capacities"

I am not entirely certain that "both capacities" constituted a conventionalised phrase, but it would seem so from examples (52)–(54). In (52), the two capacities are those of footman and coachman, and in (53) they are those of butler and valet. However, in (54) matters are less clear:

(52)   Wednesday, June 25, 1783.
Wants a Place, a sober, steady young Man, as Footman in a genteel family, who understands his business well; has no objection to have the care of a pair of saddle-horses, as he has lived in both capacities, and can have a good character from his last place. Salary not an object. Direct to T. L. at Mr. Munday's, Green Grocer, Howard-street, Norfolk-street, Strand.

(53)   Wednesday, June 25, 1783.
Wants a Place, a steady, active Man, as Butler, or Butler and Valet, who has been in both capacities for many years, and flatters himself has given the utmost satisfaction in very genteel families. He can shave and dress, writes a good hand, and understands accounts; is still in his place, where he has lived several years. Has no objection to an employ by the month or week, and it will be his wish to make himself as useful as possible; has a perfect knowledge of the side-board table and cellar, and his abilities will be found equal to his pretensions. Direct to J. T. at Mr. Timberlake's, Wax-Chandler, Oxford-street, near Bond-street.

(54) Wednesday, June 25, 1783.
Wants a Place, a steady, sedate Man, aged about 30, to serve a single Gentleman, or a family where another is kept; can shave and dress hair well, having been in both capacities, and can have a good character from the family he has just left, where he lived upwards of three years. Direct to A. B. at No. 12, Great Windmill-street, the top of the Haymarket.

In (54), on the one hand, personal menservants were often required to shave and dress hair; on the other, the very fact that these skills were frequently specified perhaps meant that they should not be taken for granted, and so the barbering capacity might be the other capacity alluded to. Hecht (1956:48) notes that the dual post of butler/valet was quite common in eighteenth-century households.

3.   Summary

This paper has dealt with some of the conventionalised words and phrases to be found in London newspaper want ads of the early 1780s. Not all are entirely clear in meaning; in particular, "bear confinement", "either way", "go a job" and "both capacities" need further contextualisation in order to determine whether my surmises presented here are correct. Hecht (1956), Hill (1996) and Meldrum (2000) make it clear that each household had its own customs and that servants' job descriptions varied enormously from household to household, where the duties of a footman in one household could be quite unlike those in another. The precariousness of women-servants' livelihood is evident: single women angled to be employed alongside eligible males; being the sole woman servant in a household headed by a single male employer could be fraught (and is thus worthy of mention as in examples (18) and (31)); additionally, clarity of social status, so essential in eighteenth-century society, could be ambiguous – consider example (55):

(55) Tuesday, July 23, 1782.
A Young Person, of genteel Education, would be glad to be Companion to a Lady, or to be English Governess to three or four young Ladies; she can read well, and understands most fancy-works; she would have no objection to superintend the domestic concerns of a family, or to do any thing to render herself useful, provided she was not treated as a common servant: she can be well recommended. A line directed for A. B. at Mr. Richardson's, Stationer, the corner of King-street, Bloomsbury-square, will be punctually attended to.

Widows were often specified in want ads, there being less likelihood of potential difficulties that came along with young, unattached women. This ambiguous social status of course provided material for the literature of the day.

The taboo subjects necessitating periphrastic euphemisms in our want ads are death, the processes of finding a marriage partner, and appearing to boast about one's attributes. The conundrum of jockeying for position whilst not seeming arrogant or boastful was a problem for both those seeking servants and for servants seeking work. Face-work had to be done on both sides, leading to formulae such as *presumed unobjectionable* (3), (13) (written by employers, about themselves and their families) and *flatters him/herself* (49), (50) (written by servants, premodifying their abilities), despite the fact that such 'superfluous' wording caused extra expense.

In sum, want ads are of interest from a historical pragmatic point of view in that they were both placed and read by people from a wide social spectrum, indeed, they provided a means of communication across that spectrum. And, as always when dealing with historical data, there is far more extant material from the literate classes than from the uneducated. Want ads, then, for all their formulaic wording, provide us with evidence, albeit limited, of the language used and understood by servants in one text-type in eighteenth century London.

Sources

Currency Converter Old Money to New http://www.nationalarchives.gov.uk/currency/default0.asp#mid.

OED, Oxford English Dictionary online version: http://www.oed.com.

Old Bailey Online: http://www.oldbaileyonline.org.

The Morning Herald, and Daily Advertiser. London: Printed by J. S. Barr, No. 18, Catharine-street, in the Strand.

ZEN, *Zurich English Newspaper Corpus*: http://es-zen.unizh.ch.

References

A Member of the Aristocracy. 1894. *The Duties of Servants. A Practical Guide to the Routine of Domestic Service*. London: Frederick Warne & Co.

Anon. 1858. *Enquire Within Upon Everything*. London: Houlston and Wright.

Buck, Anne. 1979. *Dress in Eighteenth-Century England*. London: B. T. Batsford.

Dickens, Charles. 1839. *The Life and Adventures of Nicholas Nickleby*. London: Chapman and Hall.

Hecht, Jean J. 1956. *The Domestic Servant Class in Eighteenth-Century England*. London: Routledge and Kegan Paul.

Hill, Bridget. 1996. *Servants: English Domestics in the Eighteenth Century.* Oxford: Clarendon.

Meldrum, Tim. 2000. *Domestic Service and Gender, 1660–1750: Life and Work in the London Household.* Harlow: Longman.

Onions, C. T. 1931. Distance no object. *Society for Pure English.* Tract 36, 531–534.

Stokes, Myra. 1991. *The Language of Jane Austen. A Study of Some Aspects of her Vocabulary.* Basingstoke: Macmillan.

"Alwayes in te Orbe of honest Mirth, and next to Truth"

Proto-infotainment in *The Welch Mercury*

Nicholas Brownlees

1.   Introduction

In his authoritative account of the beginnings of the English newspaper, Raymond (1996) analyses the contents, style and socio-historical context of the periodical newsbooks and occasional pamphlets of the 1640s. According to the historian, this is the decade when periodical print news, in the form of weekly news pamphlets, assumed many if not all of the general characteristics commonly associated with newspapers.[1] The origins and evolution of journalistic rhetoric are exemplified by extensive reference to numerous publications of the period and, in particular, as is to be expected, to those which were most successful. Such newsbooks often ran for several hundred numbers.[2] However, apart from these well-established titles, there were many short-lived publications that came out once, twice, or just for a few numbers and then were heard of no more. One such publication, which ran for just nine numbers, was *The Welch Mercury*, or, at least, that was its title for the first three issues, after which it changed its name to *Mercurius Cambro-Britannus, the British Mercury, or the Welch Diurnall*. This new name was maintained for the

---

1.   The term 'news pamphlets' is used to refer to weekly news publications generally consisting of 8 to 16 quarto-sized pages. These pamphlets generally provided a wide variety of factual news and can be contrasted with many other pamphlets of the day which treated monothematically topical controversies relating to such matters as politics and religion. The term "newspaper" came into general use in the second half of the seventeenth century when print news appeared in single folio sheets.

2.   For example, *A Perfect Diurnall of Some Passages in Parliament* first came out in July 1643 and continued until November 1649.

rest of the newsbook's life, but despite the title's greater inclusiveness there is little to suggest it attracted a wider audience. It was not published on a regular weekly basis, did not come out at all between 5 December 1643 and 6 January 1644, and folded up definitively at the end of January 1644. In short it was not successful – but, nevertheless, it does reward examination. First, because it was the first periodical news pamphlet to introduce a form of news presentation which in the parlance of present-day media discourse could be considered proto-infotainment. Secondly, its very lack of success in attracting a steady readership around this editorial project meant that in later numbers it began experimenting with different forms of news presentation strategies so as to bolster what must have been declining sales. An analysis of these different forms of news presentation provides the news analyst with a profitable insight into how a mid-seventeenth-century news writer interpreted the textual and rhetorical possibilities of news transmission in the early years of the English press.

2.   The Welch Mercury

The Welch Mercury presents itself as a weekly newsbook written in Wales in Welsh English, or Welch as it was often disparagingly called at that time, and then sent up to London.[3] In this respect it sets out to be different from all the other London news pamphlets filling up the stationers' shelves in and around the St. Paul's area.[4] The editorial intention to provide an easily identifiable newsbook is underlined in the third number. In its mock Welsh English, which will be analysed below, the editor of *The Welch Mercury* writes:

> (1)   With bold confidence her will expose her selfe to the publicke view of te Reader; for tere be a great company of Mercuries that with pen feathers venter forth into the ayre of opinion; some fly abroad with long and slow wing, as te Diurnall; some on short wing, as *Mercurius Cilicus*, and te Informator; some on nimble flying wing, as *Brittanicus*, and out of tem sometime doe fly away on te lying wing, but te Welch Mercury carryed on te wings of wit and truth, will freely discover out new Inteligencers, free from passion or affections; but he will with moderate discretions and in an ingenuous

---

3.   Despite its later change of title, for the purposes of this paper I shall refer to the newsbook by its first name.

4.   See Raymond (2003: 53–97) for a description of printing practices in early modern England.

cleere way satisfie her understanding Reader of desired true Information.[5]
(3 November–11 November 1643)

In this self-presentation the key words are "wit and truth". While "truth" was what all news publications purported to provide, "wit", in the sense it is used here in *The Welch Mercury*, offered a novel feature in news presentation. In this specific case "wit" does not just incorporate the contemporary meaning of 'sharpness of mind' but also the other contemporary sense of 'bright, amusing thought'.[6] It is by means of these two characteristics, "wit and truth", that the *The Welch Mercury* aimed to distinguish itself from other parliamentarian news pamphlets selling in London in late 1643. *The Welch Mercury*'s twin objectives are, however, not only referred to in the newsbook's third number. They are likewise underlined in the fourth number of the publication where the pamphleteer says that while the newsbook lies "always in te Orbe of honest Mirth", it is also "next to Truth, for though her seem sometimes merry, yet her may be true and serious in her Resolutions" (11 November–20 November 1643). Therefore, unlike the factual, impersonal news style found in *A Perfect Diurnall of Some Passages in Parliament* and *The True Informer*, or the exclusively comic portrayal of Welshness in the occasional pamphlet *The Welch-Mans Complements* (1643), *The Welch Mercury* attempted to provide both elements in the same publication. In the rest of this paper I shall analyse, first, how *The Welch Mercury* initially set about achieving its goals of "honest mirth" and "truth", and then identify the communicative strategies it resorted to when, under a new name, it attempted to resurrect what was a failing enterprise.

2.1 Wit and mirth in *The Welch Mercury* numbers 1–3

The humour throughout *The Welch Mercury* is primarily based around the fiction that the pamphlet has been written by a Welshman. This journalistic conceit was innovative in that although we find earlier occasional pamphlets purportedly written by a Welsh pamphleteer there had appeared no such newsbook.[7] The

---

5. It is probable that the "Diurnall" and "Informator" are references to *A Perfect Diurnall of Some Passages in Parliament* and *Informator Rusticus* respectively, whilst "*Brittanicus*" and "*Mercurius Cilicus*" are clear-cut allusions to *Mercurius Britanicus* and *Mercurius Civicus*.

6. This additional meaning is not only found with the word "wit" but also with the adjective "witty". In the first issue of *The Welch Mercury*, the writer refers to "witty Aulicus", a reference to the occasional raillery found in the royalist publication's commentary of parliamentary affairs.

7. Occasional pamphlets include *The Welch-mens Prave Resolution* (7 June 1642), *Newes from Wales or the Brittish Parliament* (1642), *The Welch-mans publike Recantation or, His Hearty*

implied Welsh author in *The Welch Mercury*, as indeed in the occasional pamphlets, is a stereotype, and as such falls within the anglocentric cultural tradition whereby the Welsh were generally considered comic, naïve, and incapable of escaping their rustic origins. This tradition, which had roots in medieval English culture, had been reinforced in late Elizabethan and early seventeenth-century plays and masques by Dekker (*Patient Grissil* 1600, *Satiromastix* 1601), Jonson (*For the Honour of Wales* 1619), and to a lesser extent by Shakespeare (*Henry V* 1599).[8] The fact that *The Welch Mercury* not only followed but further highlighted the negative characterisation is not surprising since the newsbook was parliamentarian in outlook and hence hostile to the Welsh, who had mostly sided with the king in 1642 at the outbreak of the Civil War.[9] In its reporting of news, what the newsbook foregrounds is not only the Welsh character and lifestyle but also Welsh English, for it is the implied Welsh author's language that most obviously characterises the Welshman in his folly and cultural backwardness. It is through his and his compatriots' inability to speak a standard English that the Welsh betray their rustic, primitive background which in turn explains their totally irrational decision to support the king in his misguided struggle against parliament.

The following passages, taken from the second number of the newsbook, exemplify the tone and features of the newswriter's mock Welsh English:

(2)   Her doe heare that a thousand Irish Tevils on foot, or Irish Rebells are coming over, to play her Tevlish pranks here in England [...]
(28 October 1643–3 November 1643)

(3)   Her doe understand that 300 Papists, and a creat many other Malignants are got into Dudley Castle, upon the edge of Shropshire, which is pigger than any of her Welch Villages, and pigge houses in Wales [...][10]
(28 October 1643–3 November 1643)

In this markedly oral presentation of news the English writer is foregrounding stereotypical Welsh English features. These are represented textually at an orthographic and morphological level, and in their divergence from standard English are designed to provide a very important part of the humour and mirth that the

---

sorrow for taking up of Armes against her Parliament (1642). Stoyle (2000) examines these and other occasional pamphlets, but not *The Welch Mercury*.

8.   See Bartley (1943, 1954) for an analysis of Welsh characterisation in early modern English drama.

9.   See Russell (1990) for a highly respected account of the causes of the Civil War and Royle (2004) for an acclaimed narrative history of the period.

10.   "Malignants" was the term used by parliamentarians to refer to royalists.

newsbook sets out to achieve. As regards non-standard orthography, and its representation of regional pronunciation, in (2) and (3) Welsh English pronunciation is represented by the substitution of devoiced plosive *c* (or *k*), *p*, and *t* for voiced plosive *g*, *b*, and *d*. Further substitution processes occur in the following passages where what is found is the plosivisation of the dental fricative:

(4) Her doe now plainly see with both her eyes, that awle te proceedings of te Kings army was mere delusions. (3 November 1643–11 November 1643)

(5) Of te prave resolutions of Flint-shire, and te like purpose of te Countie of Tenby [...] (3 November 1643–11 November 1643)

The marked frequency of non-standard orthography is therefore designed to represent non-standard pronunciation that in turn is generally indicative of substandard education and general foolishness. This correlation between cultural backwardness and non-standard orthography is a recognised feature of contemporary literature (Blake 1981:63–93), and even if it is not directly expressed in *The Welch Mercury* it is referred to in other mock Welsh publications.[11] Thus, in the occasional pamphlet, *The Welch-Mans Complements* (1643), Maudlin, a proud and upright English maiden, comments derisively on the language of her would-be Welsh suitor, saying that not only is native Welsh "mountainous [...] such as Goates would utter if they could speak", but that when he attempts to speak English all that he can manage is "so much false English, and Welch wit, which is no better then [sic] English nonsense" (*The Welch-Mans Complements* 1643).

Apart from non-standard orthography, the other main stereotypical Welsh English feature in *The Welch Mercury* is the use of *her*. The word has multiple referencing potential in that it can refer to both the singular and plural forms of first, second and third person pronoun, both subject and accusative, as well as to the whole range of possessive adjectives:

(6) The cessation of Armes with the Irish Rebells is somewhat dangerous to our Kingdome and Parliament, and her will come over to Bristoll and West-chester, and cut all her throats if her can, for her be thirsty after the ploud of the Protestants, and be notorious Papists, and her doe talke in her Irish language like her barking Foxes in Wales; and if her were hanged in a rope, yet her would make a wry month at the Parliament; for her be damnable Papists and Rebells. (21 October 1643–28 October 1643)

---

11. See also Taavitsainen, Melchers and Pahta (1999) for a wide-ranging analysis of the non-standard in literary and non-literary texts.

However, in his use of *her* the Welsh author is not only exposing his own comic ignorance of standard English, but more particularly he is betraying the essential femininity of his character, thereby belying the magniloquent bellicosity of much of his discourse for which he was stereotypically renowned. Bowen (2004: 365) aptly writes that "in feminizing the Welsh out of their own mouths, parliamentary commentators maintained their satirical treatment while also impugning Welsh pretensions to military expertise".[12]

Of course, given the multiple referencing potential of *her*, there could also occur problems of comprehension on the part of the reader in passages where it is not clear to whom or what the word refers, but no doubt this obscurity of meaning was also designed to create humour and ridicule in that it iconically reflected the disconnected garrulousness of so much presumed Welsh conversation.[13]

The mirth and comedy in the newsbook are therefore principally provided by the implied Welsh author's use of his regional dialect, which is not only found in the presentation of hard news and political comment but also more generally where the author digresses on aspects of Welshness. Not surprisingly, these authorial asides caricature supposed national traits. Thus, in (7) we read of the Welsh people's passion for leeks whose cultivation and consumption is identified as being the countrymen's principal reason for desiring peace:

(7)   if her [...] could have peace, but tere be no pease in her feeld, and no leek left,
       O Saint *Taffee*,[14] Saint *Taffe*, send her the happinesse of peace, that her may

---

12. Regarding the origins of *her*, Lord (1995: 38) suggests that its use in Welsh English could have arisen as a result of the Welsh word *hi*, meaning 'she' or 'her', looking and sounding similar to the English male pronoun. Thus, originally the English took the Welsh female pronoun or possessive adjective to have both female and male referencing, and once this initial conclusion had been reached the English writers satirised Welsh English further by extending the referencing range to all persons and cases. See Thomas (1994: 107–112) for further analysis of early Welsh English.

13. See, for example, the following passage: "Her told her formerly, that her intended to raise a creat Armie of peoples under ground called the Welch Ecchoes: and now her must tell her plainly that to make the Conjunctions and joining of Forces with the Ecchoes was fully resolved in awle her Countries to presse awle the loud talking womens to make another creat Armie; for her tink it cood policies to presse her women, and make her serve under Captain and Common souldiers too for her womens will not runne away at the sight of the longest weapon her warrant her. (*The Welch Mercury*, 28 October 1643–3 November 1643). Regarding Welsh English incomprehensibility in actual daily life, I would like to thank Laura Wright for bringing to my attention the online proceedings of eighteenth-century London Old Bailey criminal trials involving Welsh speakers. The obscurity of some Welsh English is exemplified in a trial of 1738 where we read of a London constable who said that a deceased Welshman "spoke such broken English that I could hardly understand him" (www.oldbaileyonline.org: t17381206-38).

14. "Taffee" or "Taffe" was the derogatory English name for the Welsh.

once againe see store of pease, and of te cood leek, which would be te best
news that ever came out of *Wales* [...]
(3 November 1643–11 November 1643)

Whereas in (8), what is ridiculed is the Welsh belief in their illustrious classical
ancestry:

(8) WHEN her creat captaine and Countrie-man, the Trojan, Sir Knight
     Aeneas was come to the Court of the faire Queen *Dido,* he told her such
     admirable stories of the long continued siege of *Troy* and awle the Trojan
     Warres, that the Queen was much delighted to hear the sad, but true dis-
     courses of her Countries: And the *Welch Mecurie* doth not doubt that her
     remarkable Intelligences of the present warre in her Countries, and in awle
     England, and other occasions, was for the truth of her exact and most cer-
     taine Relations gain the approbations and good wills of her Readers: For
     her brain being as hot with Newes as the creat Oven, *Aetna* in *Sicily* [...]
     (28 October 1643–3 November 1643)

Therefore, in *The Welch Mercury* the entertainment factor is based around the
mock newswriter's Welshness. In his linguistic and cultural embodiment of the
comic Welsh stereotype the newswriter cannot but amuse the English reader. Or,
rather, that was at least the editorial intention, but as we shall see in the later numbers of the newsbook there is a marked discontinuity in the foregrounding of the
Welsh element, and hence of the humour.

2.2   News in *The Welch Mercury* numbers 1–3

In the very first paragraph of the first number, *The Welch Mercury* underlines the
importance it gives to the quality of its news and information. Comparing com-
peting news pamphlets to his own, the newsbook writer declares:

(9) Her have read [...] that many writers, with their confederate Intelligencers, doe
     concur at the Wine-spring of taverns, to invent mis-begotten Pamphlets. Or
     indeed, monstrous Lies, but her will upon her credit give in no Informations,
     but such as shall be true and currant, which her will carry on in a fayre and
     even manner, and with her swords and daggers maintain all her Reports to be
     certaine verities and truths, whereupon her will with bold Confidence come
     forth among the other crowdes of *Mercuries*, whom her doe far exceed in
     ingenuity, and generous educations, and therefore her will be called *The new
     Welch Mr. Mercury*. (21 October 1643–28 October 1643)

The Welch Mercury is, therefore, not just intended to provide wit and humour but also to give, as indicated by the very sub-title of the publication, "remarkable Intelligences and true Newes to awle the whole Kingdome". I shall now examine the textual and rhetorical devices the news writer adopts in his presentation of news. As with the analysis of wit and humour, in this section I shall focus on the first three numbers of the publication.

Unlike other newsbooks of the period, *The Welch Mercury* has a separate title-page. In the first number the page reads as follows:

(10)
Numb.1.
Colonell *Vrrey* slaine   An Inventory of *Aulicus* her lyes.
by her Countrey-man.   Her affection to her King & Parliament.
The fidelitie of her
Countrey of *Tenby*.

The Welch Mercury,

Communicating remarkable Intelligences and true Newes to awle the whole Kingdome, from Saturday, Octob. 21. till Saturday 28. 1643.

1 *That the Queene and the Cavaliers do rule her King at* Oxford, *and the prave resolution of* Tenby, *and awle her country of Wales.*

2 *Of the entertainment of the French Embassadour by her King & the great hopes her hath to live in peace again, & to toast her cheese in her chimney corner.*

3 *The siege of* Plymmouth *raised,* Tewxbury *abandoned by her countrey-men, with a letter sent her from one of her slaine countrey-men.*

4 *The advancement of the cood Scots for* England, *with her Welch proiect to raise a create Army.*

5 Bristoll *cruelly plundered by the Kings Forces, with a defeat given to the Earle of* New-Castle, *and her countrey-men kill'd by Welch Goats.*

6 *A pacification of te English Irish rebels.*

[...]

10 *Her Kings Regiment verie ragged,* Prince Roberts *dog condemned by a Councell of War, and reprieved againe.*

11 *A long Inventory of Mr.* Aulicus *her lyes, with the Welch* Mercury *her answer to her lyes, and awle her false inventions.*

This is Licenced, and entred into the Hall Book,
according to Order.

LONDON,
Printed for *W. Ley,* and *G. Lindley.* 1643

The news element on this title-page is underlined in a number of different ways. At the top of the page, we find the minor sentences "Colonell *Vrrey* slaine by her Countrey-man", "The fidelitie of her Countrey of *Tenby*", "An Inventory of *Aulicus* her lyes" and "Her affection to her King & Parliament". Although containing the *her* feature of Welsh English, which thereby provides an intentional element of humour, these brief texts are essentially informative. Whilst it would be difficult to consider the minor sentences as anything other than proto-headlines in that they do not precede the texts to which they refer, and, with the exception of the first, lack the verbal element generally associated with headlines, they nevertheless play an important part in establishing the serious, informative role of *The Welch Mercury*.[15] What is more, as the usage of such proto-headlines in contemporary newsbooks was extremely rare, we must conclude that its use in the Welsh newsbook had the precise purpose of emphasising the news contents of a publication which otherwise could have been inadvertently misunderstood by the browser at a St Paul's stationer's as just generic anti-Welsh satire.[16]

However, apart from the proto-headlines, the numerated news items below the subtitle also serve an informative function. Sentences 1, 3 and 4 just provide hard news, that is, they summarise the "intelligences" found in the newsbook itself. Admittedly, the language is still characterised by stereotypical features of Welsh English, but this does not relegate the hard news element to a secondary role. Similarly informative are sentences 2, 5 and 10, even if these content summaries also contain a stereotypical anti-Welsh jibe at the end of the sentence. In these sentences, as in the proto-headlines, the writer is attempting to balance both the news and mirth.

In the first two numbers the news and wit are also intertwined by means of a form of continuous narrative expressed in the mock Welsh writer's regional dialect. The narrative is structured around quite short paragraphs of about 50–100 words, with little attempt to connect one piece of news with its textually adjacent item:

> (11)   Her be informed of the City of *Bristoll* having yielded unto the Kings forces, is continually plundered, creat taxations laid upon them, and their wives bodies

---

15. For a linguistic description of modern-day headlines, see Mårdh (1980).

16. We find similar proto-headlines in the newsbook *Certaine Informations*. Making use of either block language, or at most very basic declarative sentences, the writer draws the reader's attention to stories found in the publication. For example, in the issue of 29 May–5 June 1643 we find on the first page, top left-hand corner, the words: *Robbing by the knowme* [sic] *Laws. Treachery will raise Houses. The Scots sent for. Plots against the parliament and City. The Scotish Dove* also often highlights its news through the use of simple front-page news captions, though in the case of this publication the text is often in the form of verse.

are plundered; so that *Bristoll* hath more discontented Cuckolds in it, than any other City; for the Cavaliers would lie with the Tevill in a white smock.

Reports was given out, that the Earle of Newcastle was defeated; but know there was a creat deale of bloud spilt, and her know it to be extreame crueltie to sacrifice men to pretended Religion, and kill her sick Welch Goats; for none but her pudding wives get any thing by shedding of bloud.

It is reported that Prince *Rupert* was make awle her Townes in *England* as poore as a Welch Village; and that her shall go bare-foot and bare-legg'd as her doe in Wales […] (21 October 1643–28 October 1643)

In line with much news reportage at that time, the news item is introduced by a reporting clause. Typical reporting clauses include "Her be informed", "Her doe understand", "Her doe heare", "Her doe see", "Wee heare from", "It is reported that". The information is generally attributed to unspecified sources, and as Jucker (2006: 112) says in relation to this kind of information attribution in seventeenth- and eighteenth-century newspapers, the source "may be public opinion or rumours, or it may be a single informant who passed on the information".

In the absence of such a reporting clause the news piece simply begins with the narration of the news event:

(12)   At *Shrewsbury*, Sir *William Breerton*, and Sir *Thomas Middleton* have done very brave service, but not took the Town […]

The cessation of Armes with the Irish Rebells is somewhat dangerous to our Kingdome and Parliament, and her will come over to Bristoll and West-chester, and cut all her throats if her can […]

The Earle of *Lothian* being a creat Scotch-man going to Oxford was by his Majestie imprisoned, because her was appointed to be Generall of the Scotch Armie […] (21 October 1643–28 October 1643)

In contrast with the first two numbers, what one finds in the third number is a greater focus on the entertainment aspect of the publication. Hence, although the news is frequently introduced by a reporting clause, such a clause also contains an attribution source that is designed to amuse. Most frequently the source is a "Welsh Parret", presumably in comic contrast to the title of the serious newsbook *Scotish Dove*.[17]

The news element in the first three publications is further seen in the section at the end of each number devoted to the rebuttal of news found in the principal royalist newsbook, *Mercurius Aulicus*. As is characteristic of much animadver-

---

17.   For example, "But now her Welsh Parret tat doth live in te Cage in a great Lords house, and doth heare tem talk of divers matters, dis Parret doth tell her in breefe, words to dis effect: The Lord *Stapton* is Lord Marchall of te West […]." (3 November 1643–11 November 1643)

sion from that time, the rebuttal is so structured that the opposing camp's news is rebutted point by point, with the adversarial news item presented first and the rebuttal following immediately.

(13)   And first her will begin with Witty *Aulicus*; Her doth write awl false newes, her will make an Inventory of her Lyes. 1. Her say that the Brethren are going for *New-England* in a Ship called the *Roundhead: her doe indeed make round lies*. 2. Her call the honourable Houses of Parliament pretended Houses, *her be a base fellow of a House in Oxford; the fish House*, All Soules. [...] 4. Her call all that stand for the Parliament seditious Rebells: *Her self is known to be a Court Rebell in print*. (21 October 1643–28 October 1643)

In its rejection of the royalist's false news, the Welsh pamphlet adopts characteristic animadversion features to reinforce the argumentative force of its own rebuttal. For example, in the first two weeks the newsbook's exposure of royalist lies and misinformation is structured numerically so that each successive piece of false news is numbered. In so doing, the writer not only underlines the adversary's quantitative mendacity but also succeeds in reinforcing the argumentative force of his own position in that the reader is made aware that all the adversary's positions can be answered simply and unhesitatingly point by point, one after another.

Also characteristic is the way in which the adversary's news is distinguished typographically from *The Welsh Mercury*'s rebuttal. By representing the counter-argument in italics, as opposed to the roman type used in the royalist citation, the writer is emphasising his disassociation from what has been published by *Mercurius Aulicus*.[18] In this respect, the writer is ensuring that there is no "leakage" – the term adopted by Shuman (1993) to indicate the clear separation of content and communicative force between the "voices" of the current writer of a text and the cited source. One further point regarding the mock Welsh newsbook's rhetorical strategy is the writer's use of punning reformulation of some word or expression referred to in the citation. Thus, in (13) the Welsh newsbook puns on "round" in the first news item, and "house" and "print" in the second and third. In this respect the writer is once again allying wit with truth.[19]

---

18. In this I agree with Anderson who, in relation to the textual integration of verbatim citation, writes that "even an apparently routine surface feature such as typographical layout can be strategically exploited to influence reader perspective" (1997: 166).

19. For further analysis on the use of animadversion in English Civil War pamphlets, see Brownlees (2006).

2.3   Mirth in *The Welch Mercury* numbers 4–8[20]

Having set out the broad textual and linguistic features underpinning the intertwined elements of "mirth" and "news" in the first three numbers, I now wish to conclude my analysis by examining how this hybrid relationship (entertainment and information) changed over the last numbers as the editor experimented with aspects of this news presentation model in an ultimately vain attempt to find a commercially successful discourse.

The humour of *The Welch Mercury* in numbers 4–8 continued to revolve around its parodic representation of Welshness and in particular its use of Welsh English. However, whereas in the first numbers one finds a generally constant occurrence of the dialect and its stereotypical features, in numbers 4–8, as the figures in Table 1 show, this varies considerably.

Table 1. Occurrences of stereotypical Welsh English lexemes in *The Welch Mercury*. The number in brackets is the normalised figure per 10,000 words.

word	No. 1 (3,674 words)	No. 2 (3,553 words)	No. 4 (2,668 words)	No. 5 (2,957 words)	No. 7 (2,543 words)	No. 8 (1,155 words)
cood	5 (14)	21 (59)	3 (11)	2 (7)	1 (4)	1 (8)
creat	14 (38)	39 (110)	30 (114)	9 (30)	2 (8)	9 (78)
prave	1 (3)	2 (6)	2 (8)	2 (7)	1 (4)	2 (17)
te	1 (3)	8 (22)	72 (274)	128 (422)	2 (8)	46 (395)
her	342 (930)	269 (753)	170 (646)	120 (396)	69 (269)	38 (327)

What is most striking about Welsh English usage is, first, the much greater frequency of *te* (as substitute for *the*) in numbers 4, 5 and 8, and, secondly, the conspicuous reduction of dialectal items in the seventh number. Regarding *te*, the figures show that its increased occurrence results in a reduction in the frequency of *her*, which in the first numbers had stood out as the quintessential characteristic of Welsh English. This significantly increased prominence of *te* further underlines the lack of linguistic objectivity in the writer's use of the dialect. From almost one number to the next, the use of *te* increases exponentially in response to what one can only presume to be editorial necessity, that is, the need to come up with a new style, a new form of reproducing Welsh English so as to maintain the reader's interest.

However, apart from *te* the other interesting aspect highlighted by the table is the marked decrease in Welsh English features in the seventh number. This

---

20. As the ninth and final number of *The Welch Mercury* is in too imperfect a state to afford useful analysis, my examination finishes with the publication's penultimate issue.

number was published on 13 January 1644, more than five weeks after the previous number that had appeared on 5 December. What one must presume is that an editorial decision had been reached during the five-week interval to sacrifice much of the "mirth", as represented by the use of the regional dialect, in favour of significantly more conventional news expressed in standard English. In fact, in the January publication not only is the dialect much less evident but also references to Wales and the Welsh are notable by their almost total absence.

However, after this reduction of Welsh English in the seventh number, one is struck by an increase in the use of the regional dialect in the following publication of 24 January 1644. It would appear that in this number the mirth element has once again returned to the forefront. Yet, on closer inspection what one sees is that the highlighted dialect is most obviously evident when the news concerns events relating to the Royalist cause. Royalist news is narrated in Welsh English whilst occurrences dealing specifically with Parliament are generally communicated in standard English.

For example, the following passage is about Oxford, where Charles I had eventually set up his court after leaving London in early 1642, and the "creat papist" who is mentioned is most likely Charles I himself:

(14)   Her heare from Oxford tat te creat Papist followes hard to bee heyr of te Marquesse *Hamilton's* Estate, and terefore keep him, and his prudder te Lord *Lauricke* in prison: cause when tey dye, he may enjoy all; but te Lord *Lauricke* hath made an escape, and is come away: which may chance save the Marquesses life too; for the intent was, that if one dyed, both should dye: else te creat Papye was neer te better. (17 January–24 January 1644)

This passage in Welsh English can be compared with the following paragraph in standard English where, instead, the news is about parliament:

(15)   Yesterday, the Parliament met at the Thanksgiving Sermon at Christ Church, and afterwards dined with the Aldermen and Common Councell men at Merchant Taylors Hall in London, and went thither in great honour, and were welcomly received. (17 January–24 January 1644)

What we see in the eighth number of *The Welch Mercury* is a more focused exploitation of the regional dialect. In adopting it to refer to royalist matters, the writer is aiming to contaminate the royalist subject matter with some of the inherent comedy, if not derision, associated with such dialect.

In conclusion, the comic exploitation of Welsh English in *The Welch Mercury* can be broadly divided into three phases. In the first phase, numbers 1–6, the writer makes significant use of the dialect in his aim to highlight the comic quality of the publication. In the second phase, number 7, the pamphlet's humorous element is relegated to a much less prominent position as the writer attempts to refocus the publication around a more traditional means of news presentation, that is, hard news presented in more or less standard English. This second stage in the exploitation of Welsh English in turn gives way in the eighth number to a greater and more focused use of the regional dialect as once more editorial direction is changed in the face of what was probably ever greater uncertainty as to what could appeal to the pamphlet's actual and potential readers.

2.4   News in *The Welch Mercury* numbers 4–8

Some significant differences contrast the mode of news reporting in the second phase of *The Welch Mercury* with what is found in the first three numbers. The first difference is the absence of proto-headlines from the fourth issue onwards. In determining why they should have been omitted, I think one only needs to consider the graphic layout of the pamphlet under its new name. As the new title – *Mercurius Cambro-Britannus, the British Mercury, or the Welch Diurnall* – was considerably longer than the previous one, it took up more space on the page, thereby leaving little or no room for the proto-headlines. Thus, we see how a model of news presentation was directly influenced by the physical properties of pamphlet publication.

   Also absent from the fourth issue onwards was the final section of the pamphlet devoted to the rebuttal of news found in *Mercurius Aulicus*. In order to understand why this form of news presentation should have been omitted we probably have to consider the role of other contemporary newsbooks in the transmission of news. It is probable that the writer of *The Welch Mercury* decided that as other parliamentarian pamphlets, in particular *Mercurius Britanicus*, were already providing this kind of news, there was little commercial sense in reiterating what was found elsewhere.

   As for the textual structure of news transmission, one finds that much of the hard news continues to be presented within a continuous narrative divided into thematically unrelated paragraphs. However, in contrast to this default structure, in the eighth issue the writer experiments with the use of datelines. In this number, in one final attempt to find a successful mode of news presentation, the writer structures his news around the days of the week in which the news reached his office. This structure, which was characteristic of many newsbooks at that time, had the advantage of providing apparent chronological order to the succession of news events even if little attempt was made within the separate daily bulletins to link up one on-going news event with any previously-mentioned reference.

3.   Conclusion

In this paper I have explored some of the thematic, textual and rhetorical features of an English Civil War newsbook, which, though short-lived, nevertheless rewards examination. Innovatory in its clearly stated attempt to combine both news and entertainment, a form of proto-infotainment, *The Welch Mercury* offers the historical news analyst intriguing insights into how the provision of information and entertainment were conceptualised and presented in these early years of the English press.

Through an examination of the pamphlet's language and discourse it has been possible to see how the writer experimented both with different ways of news presentation and with the representation of mock Welsh English, the regional dialect which coloured the language of the pamphlet and which was designed to provide a significant part of the pamphlet's humour and entertainment. By tracing the development of this innovatory newsbook over its four-month existence, what has become clear is how much of the news discourse was on-going, ever changing and very much dependent on commercial considerations. The inherent mutability that characterises *The Welch Mercury* reaffirms the need to situate news transmission very firmly in the socio-historical context in which it occurred.

References

Primary sources

A Perfect Diurnall of Some Passages in Parliament, 1643–1649.
Certaine Informations, January 1643–February 1644.
Dekker, Thomas. 1600. *Patient Grissil.*
Dekker, Thomas. 1601. *Satiromastix.*
Informator Rusticus, 1643.
Jonson, Ben. 1619. *For the Honour of Wales.*
Mercurius Aulicus,1643–1645.
Mercurius Britanicus, 1643–1646.
Mercurius Civicus, 1643–1646.
Newes from Wales or the Brittish Parliament, 1642.
Shakespeare, William. 1599. *Henry V.*
The Proceedings of the Old Bailey, www.oldbaileyonline.org.
The True Informer, 1643–1645.
The Welch-Mans Complements, or the true manner how Shinkin wooed his Sweet-heart Maudlin after his returne from Kenton Battaile, 1643.
The Welch-mans publike Recantation or, His Hearty sorrow for taking up of Armes against her Parliament, 1642.

The Welch-mens Prave Resolution, 7 June 1642.
The Welch Mercury/ Mercurius Cambro-Britannus, 1643–1644.

Secondary sources

Anderson, Laura. 1997. Intertextuality and the creation of discourse communities: Verbatim citation in academic writing. In Francesco Gozzi and Anthony L. Johnson (eds.). *Scienza e Immaginario*. Pisa: Edizioni ETS, 159–184.

Bartley, James. 1943. The development of a stock character, iii: The stage Welshman (to 1800). *Modern Language Review* XXXVIII, 284–288.

Bartley, James. 1954. *Teague Shenkin and Sawney Being: An Historical Study of the Earliest Irish Welsh and Scottish Characters in English Plays*. Cork: Cork University Press.

Blake, Norman. 1981. *Non-standard Language in English Literature*. London: André Deutsch.

Bowen, Lloyd. 2004. Representations of Wales and the Welsh during the Civil Wars and Interregnum. *Historical Research* 77, 197 (August), 358–376.

Brownlees, Nicholas. 2006. Polemic and propaganda in civil war news discourse. In Nicholas Brownlees (ed.). *News Discourse in Early Modern England*. Bern: Peter Lang, 19–42.

Jucker, Andreas H. 2006. "but 'tis believed that …": Speech and thought presentation in early English newspapers. In Nicholas Brownlees (ed.). *News Discourse in Early Modern England*. Bern: Peter Lang, 105–125.

Lord, Peter. 1995. *Words with Pictures. Welsh Images and Images of Welsh in the Popular Press, 1640–1860*. Aberystwyth: Planet.

Mårdh, Ingrid. 1980. *Headlinese. On the Grammar of English Front Page Headlines*. (Lund Studies in English 58). Malmö: CWK Gleerup.

Raymond, Joad. 1996. *The Invention of the Newspaper. English Newsbooks 1641–1649*. Oxford: Clarendon.

Raymond, Joad. 2003. *Pamphlets and Pamphleteering in Early Modern Britain*. Cambridge: Cambridge University Press.

Royle, Trevor. 2004. *Civil War: The Wars of the Three Kingdoms*. London: Abacus.

Russell, Conrad. 1990. *The Causes of the English Civil War*. Oxford: Clarendon.

Shuman, Amy. 1993. "Get out my face": Entitlement and authoritative discourse. In Jane H. Hill and Judith T. Irvine (eds.). *Responsibility and Evidence in Oral Discourse*. Cambridge: Cambridge University Press, 135–160.

Stoyle, Mark. 2000. Caricaturing Cymru: Images of the Welsh in the London press 1642–46. In Diana Dunn (ed.). *War and Society in Medieval and Early Modern Britain*. Liverpool: Liverpool University Press, 162–179.

Taavitsainen, Irma, Gunnel Melchers and Päivi Pahta (eds.). 1999. *Writing in Nonstandard English*. Amsterdam and Philadelphia: John Benjamins.

Thomas, Alan. 1994. English in Wales. In Robert Burchfield (ed.). *The Cambridge History of the English Language* Volume 5. Cambridge: Cambridge University Press, 94–147.

Religious language in early English newspapers?

Thomas Kohnen

1. Introduction

Religious language is often seen as a conservative, archaic and even unintelligible register in contemporary English. Apart from functions in its proper religious domain, its use in contemporary English is mostly limited to literary or humorous purposes (see Crystal and Davy 1969). This "archaic peculiarity" of religious language is mainly due to features which can be traced to the Early Modern English period, when the basic patterns of a vernacular religious language were created. These features seem to have been retained during the following centuries.[1]

But has religious discourse always been felt to be "archaic"? Were vernacular religious texts always supposed to conform to a separate and principally conservative kind of language use? There is some evidence that many authors and translators in the religious domain were extremely cautious and traditional with regard to language right from the start.[2] But this does not necessarily mean that the language employed in the liturgy and in prayers was felt to be conservative and archaic by a majority of language users.

One way of finding an answer to the above questions is to look at religious language in a different genre in a period which is close enough to the Early Modern period but distant enough from contemporary English. In this paper, I will compare a corpus of prayers which covers the sixteenth and the seventeenth centuries with the early English newspapers contained in the ZEN Corpus (covering the

---

1. Many of these typical features are analysed with regard to liturgical language in Crystal and Davy (1969).

2. On this see, for example, Partridge (1973) and McGrath (2001: 269), with reference to Bible translations.

period from 1661 to 1791).[3] My aim is to find out whether there is any religious discourse in the news texts and, if so, how religious language is presented and how it is used. The results may allow an initial answer to the question of whether the religious discourse found in prayers was felt to be conservative and archaic one or two hundred years later in newspapers and whether religious language had already acquired a separate status as a "special" register.

In the following section, I will compare the two corpora by means of a keyword analysis. Section 3 will then be devoted to a closer examination of selected keywords. In the first part of Section 3, I will look at the distribution of the most prominent keywords in the sub-genres of the news texts and their typical uses. In the second part of Section 3, I will examine the most common collocations of another set of keywords in prayers and in news discourse. In the concluding section, I will briefly discuss the archaic and detached nature of religious discourse in seventeenth- and eighteenth-century news texts.

2.   Comparing two corpora: Keywords

How can we find out whether the texts of the ZEN Corpus contain religious language? And where, in the 1.6 million words contained in this corpus, do we find people engaged in religious discourse? One way of finding out is by means of the so-called keyword analysis. "Keywords" is a function contained in the computer program WordSmith (Scott 1999). The term keyword is here used as a technical term which does not necessarily have our everyday meaning of a keyword. A keyword in the technical sense is a word which appears in a given text or text collection with an unusually high (or unusually low) frequency when compared to another, larger text collection. For example, when I compare the wordlist of a prayer text with the wordlist of a (larger) newspaper text, the keywords would be those items that are unusually frequent in the prayer text against the background of the newspaper text, or, in other words, the keywords would be those items whose frequency in the newspaper is fairly low.[4] If we assume that the religious language typical of prayers is rather rare in news discourse, the keywords might just show us where religious language can be found in the larger news corpus.

In my keyword analysis I kept to the following procedure. I started with a lemmatised version of my prayer corpus (which is part of the *Corpus of English*

---

3.   On the prayer corpus see Kohnen (2006); on the ZEN Corpus see Fries and Schneider (2000) and Lehmann, auf dem Keller and Ruef (2006).

4.   For a more detailed account of keywords and how keyness is calculated see Dunning (1993) and McEnery et al. (2006: 208–320).

Religious Prose). This corpus contains about 309,000 words, covering the time between 1527 and 1666. I compared this corpus by means of the keywords function of WordSmith with the ZEN Corpus, which served as a reference corpus. In order to find out possible diachronic developments, I split the ZEN Corpus into two (unequal) parts: ZEN1, containing roughly 475,000 words, covering the time between 1661 and 1711; and ZEN2, containing about 1,125,000 words, covering the time between 1721 and 1791.

Table 1 shows the first 23 keywords from the two comparisons, their incidence in the corpora and their "keyness value" against the background of the respective comparison. The keywords listed here are only lexical keywords (except for the item *oh*, which is included because it is so typical of prayers). Keywords that are function words were excluded from the analysis because the aim of this study is to approach religious discourse from the perspective of typical lexical items.

Table 1. Keywords (List 1 and List 2, with incidence and keyness, and incidence in the prayer corpus) based on comparisons between the prayer corpus and ZEN1 and ZEN2

Prayers (incidence)	List 1	ZEN1 (incidence)	Keyness	List 2	ZEN2 (incidence)	Keyness
3.069	Oh	12	5.610,9	Oh	74	9.068,8
3.225	Lord	277	4.386,7	God	233	5.628,0
2.228	God	109	3.402,1	Lord	1.315	5.367,3
1.506	Holy	39	2.494,7	Holy	78	4.185,4
1.256	Jesus	5	2.290,9	Jesus	19	3.789,8
978	Christ	19	1.661,0	Amen	12	2.643,0
873	Amen	0	1.633,5	Christ	74	2.595,7
872	Mercy	10	1.532,1	Beseech	9	2.554,9
837	Beseech	3	1.529,3	Mercy	40	2.451,3
998	Father	52	1.505,5	Father	149	2.343,1
806	Grant	46	1.195,8	Glory	34	1.981,3
679	Blessed	22	1.096,6	Blessed	21	1.970,8
708	Glory	36	1.072,1	Grant	116	1.907,8
552	Sins	1	1.018,9	Sins	15	1.615,9
840	Life	106	1.013,6	Grace	184	1.415,5
762	Son	94	926,7	Love	131	1.347,4
530	**Spirit**	7	923,7	Son	279	1.330,7
572	Heart	19	920,9	Soul	63	1.325,9
627	Love	52	857,6	Let	263	1.304,6
738	Let	107	845,2	Praise	27	1.238,6
537	Soul	26	819,7	**Merciful**	6	1.237,8
707	Grace	104	805,0	Heart	140	1.169,3
453	Praise	9	767,5	Life	513	1.099,6

It is quite striking that the two lists in Table 1 basically contain the same lexical items, although in slightly different order. There is almost no word not found in both lists. The only exceptions are "spirit" in ZEN1 and "merciful" in ZEN2. It should be noted, however, that both items follow very soon in the other list, respectively, which would be seen if both lists were expanded here beyond the (arbitrary) 23rd position. Both lists are nearly identical.

So the evidence produced by the keyword analysis is quite consistent: the keywords showing the highest keyness in the prayer corpus are identical with regard to both ZEN1 and ZEN2. That is, in both sub-corpora of news discourse the same lexical items are relatively infrequent and there is very little change across time. In addition, many of the lexical items carry straightforward religious meanings or connotations (*Lord, God, holy, Jesus, Christ, Amen, mercy* etc.).

In the next step, I compared the two keyword lists with the frequency list of the prayers. Again, in the frequency list of the prayer corpus all function words were excluded. Table 2 contains the two keyword lists and the frequency list.

Table 2. Keywords (List 1 and List 2) and frequency list of the prayer corpus

List 1	ZEN1 (incidence)	List 2	ZEN2 (incidence)	Prayer corpus (incidence)	
Oh	12	Oh	74	Lord	3.225
Lord	277	God	233	Oh	3.069
God	109	Lord	1.315	God	2.228
Holy	39	Holy	78	Holy	1.506
Jesus	5	Jesus	19	Jesus	1.256
Christ	19	Amen	12	Father	998
Amen	0	Christ	74	Christ	978
Mercy	10	Beseech	9	Amen	873
Beseech	3	Mercy	40	Mercy	872
Father	52	Father	149	Life	840
Grant	46	Glory	34	Beseech	837
Blessed	22	Blessed	21	Grant	806
Glory	36	Grant	116	Son	762
Sins	1	Sins	15	**Good**	760
Life	106	Grace	184	**Give**	751
Son	94	Love	131	Let	738
Spirit	7	Son	279	Glory	708
Heart	19	Soul	63	Grace	707
Love	52	Let	263	Blessed	679
Let	107	Praise	27	**World**	664
Soul	26	Merciful	6	**Things**	656
Grace	104	Heart	140	Love	627
Praise	9	Life	513	Heart	572

The data presented in Table 2 show that the most frequent content words in the prayers are basically identical with the top keywords in List 1 and List 2. The only items which do not occur in the two keyword lists shown are "good", "give", "world" and "things". Quite interestingly, these do not follow immediately when the two keyword lists are expanded, that is, their keyness values are not so high, and, in addition, they do not seem to bear as straightforward and exclusively religious connotations as the top keywords do. In particular, "good" and "give" have relatively low rankings, ranging in both keyword lists around position 100. This means they are relatively frequent both in prayers and newspapers ("give" has 526 occurrences in ZEN1 and 999 in ZEN2, "good" 445 in ZEN1 and 1,088 in ZEN2).

Apart from these exceptions, the data imply that the most frequent, typically religious lexemes in the prayer corpus are those which have an unusually low frequency in news discourse. According to their keyness, they would be rather unlikely to occur in news discourse. Thus, the present analysis suggests that, in terms of top-ranking lexis, prayers and newspapers are nearly complementary. Judging from the most frequent, typically religious lexical items, we cannot expect too many examples of religious discourse in seventeenth- and eighteenth-century news discourse.

On the other hand, some of the prominent keywords (like "Lord", "God", "father" and others, see Table 1 above) do show a reasonable number of items and we might look here first if we want to find examples of religious discourse in the ZEN Corpus.

3.   Linguistic analysis

The present study can only give an illustrative investigation of the most salient keywords. It will focus on two different sets of selected keywords contained in Table 2. The first set includes items which are among the twelve top-ranking keywords ("Oh", "Lord", "Jesus", "God", "Christ", "holy", "mercy", "blessed"). From a semantic point of view, they are typically linked with religious discourse,[5] and they occur with an incidence of at least 20 in ZEN1 and ZEN2.[6] In my analysis, I will look at the distribution of these items in the sub-genres of the ZEN Corpus and their typical uses.

---

5.   One could argue, though, that "oh" is not exclusively indicative of religious discourse. But in terms of frequency of lexemes, it is the second most frequent item in the prayer corpus.

6.   More precisely, these lexemes are among the twelve top-ranking items in List 1. "Amen" and "beseech" have less than 20 occurrences. "father" and "grant" are not exclusively religious and thus belong to the second set (see Section 3.2).

The second set includes items which, from a semantic point of view, are not exclusively religious and which occur in the ZEN Corpus with a relatively high frequency (more than 100). These are "father", "grant" and "life".[7] In this set I also include "give", as an example of an item which is fairly frequent in both prayers and the ZEN Corpus und thus ranks lower in the keyword lists. In the second set, I will contrast typical collocations both in the prayers and in the ZEN Corpus.

3.1   Selected keywords in the ZEN Corpus: Distribution across sub-genres and typical uses

Some of the keywords in the first group occur with a fairly high frequency in the ZEN Corpus (for example, "Lord", "God", "holy" and also "oh"; see Table 2 above). However, the corpus search produced quite a few irrelevant items here. For example, with "Lord", as could be expected, quite a few secular proper names were found. "Lord" is also often used with reference to a year (*the year of our Lord*). The item *oh* (or *o*) often turned out to be a shortened form of *on* or *of*, an abbreviation or part of a proper name. If we leave out these and other mismatches, the typical uses of the items fall into four classes.

The first class comprises fixed expressions which usually involve the terms "God" or "Lord". They include expressions like *God be thanked, blessed be God, God knows, God forbid, God preserve, in the name of God, the Lord deliver me, the Lord have mercy* etc. These expressions may occur in all kinds of sub-genres, but they typically occur in news reports. Here they express the writer's attitude that some favourable unexpected turn of events is due to God's interference (example (1)), or they occur in reported speech, where they invoke God in some wish or reproach (example (2)).

(1)   We have many Pickaroons on our Coast, but they have done no harm of late. We are here (**blessed be God**) clear of the Plague, though some of our Neighbours have been afflicted.

    (1671, *The Current Intelligence*, home news)

(2)   But it is my duty to pass the sentence of the law upon you, which is, That you, JOHN DONELLAN, be taken from hence to the place from whence you came, and on Monday next that you be carried to the place of execution, there to be hanged by the neck until you are dead: and that your body be afterwards given to the Surgeons to be dissected and anatomized; and **the Lord have mercy on your soul**! During the whole of the trial,

---

7.   Here the point of departure is the 15 top-ranking keywords in List 1. "Sins" and "glory" do not have more than 100 items in the ZEN Corpus.

which lasted near twelve hours, the prisoner stood, to all appearance, totally resigned to the fate that he must expect. The Correspondence referred to in Sir William Wheeler's Evidence will appear in our next.

(1781, The London Chronicle, home news)

These examples might be considered religious discourse in a general sense. But I think their fixed nature and repetitive use reveals their real character as standardised formulae which do not really betray a genuine religious attitude but rather comply with a kind of conversational (or textual) routine.

The second class comprises titles or citations from songs or poems which are mentioned in reviews or announcements (example (3)).

(3) Song, Mr. Spence – **O** come let us worship. Grand Chorus – Hallelujah, for the **Lord God** Omnipotent reigneth – Messiah. No Money to be returned. Books of the performance to be had at the Theatre.

(1791, The Public Advertiser, advertisement)

Here the items cannot qualify as religious discourse proper because they comprise only short citations from religious works which are being announced or reviewed.

The third class comprises those examples which occur in advertisements for religious books. Here we find that many of the top-ranking religious keywords, in addition to other typically religious words and phrases, co-occur, reflecting a "religious" style which differs significantly from the rest of the news text, in particular the sections which serve the function of advertising. In fact, there is often a marked contrast between the textual act of advertising and the act of naming (or describing) the object which is advertised (which involves quoting from the title or from chapters). In example (4) this religious section comprises the relative clause "in which are delineated all the Travels of our Saviour and his Apostles. THE History of the Incarnation, Life, Doctrine and Miracles; the Death Resurrection and Ascension of our blessed Lord and Saviour JESUS CHRIST". The rest of the passage contains typical words and phrases used in advertisements, that is, formulations which praise the usefulness, quality and attractiveness of the object that is to be sold. The advertisement part thus forms a frame which gives the religious section almost the nature of a citation from a different world.

(4) This day is publish'd, (Price neatly bound and letter'd, 1 l. 5 s.) Beautifully printed in one large Volume, Folio, being the cheapest and most useful Book on the Subject extant. Necessary for all Families. Adorn'd with thirty-three Copper-Plates, representing the most remarkable Historical Passages; and two very useful Maps, in which are delineated all the Travels of our Saviour and his Apostles. THE History of the Incarnation, Life, Doctrine and Miracles;

the Death Resurrection and Ascension of our **blessed Lord** and Saviour **JESUS CHRIST**. In Seven Books. Illustrated with Notes and interspers'd with Dissertations, Theological, Historical, Geographical and Critical. To which are added, the Lives, Actions and Sufferings of the Twelve APOSTLES; also of St. PAUL, St. MARK, St. LUKE, and S:. BARNABAS. Together with a Chronological Table, from the Beginning of the Reign of Herod the Great, to the End of the Apostolick Age. The Whole collected from the Books of the New Testament, the most judicious Commentators, the best Ecclesiastical Historians, and other eminent Writers. By a Divine of the Church of England. Printed for Charles Hitch, at the Red Lion in Paternoster-Row.

(1741, *The Daily Post*, advertisement)

The titles of the books and their tables of contents clearly reflect religious discourse. But their status as advertised objects and the stylistic difference from the rest of the advertisement mark them as specific sections which do not really form part of the news discourse but belong to a different domain.

The fourth class of items stems from texts which obviously represent genuine religious discourse. These are mostly essays, stories and letters dealing with religious topics. As in the third group, many of the items under discussion co-occur in these texts. So it seems that the top-ranking keywords, taken together, are indeed good indicators of religious language.

However, the texts which belong to the fourth group are indeed very few. They show serious restrictions in terms of distribution. There are only 15 different texts, which belong to the years 1761 and 1771. The seven texts from 1761 are found in *The London Gazette* (two essays, one entry from the home-news section), in *The London Evening Post* (one essay, one letter, one entry from the home-news section) and in *The London Chronicle* (one essay). The eight texts from 1771 all belong to the *Westminster Journal* (eight letters). Given the fact that the ZEN Corpus comprises 349 complete newspaper issues, the four issues with which we are dealing here make up slightly more than one per cent. This supports the initial assumption that religious discourse is peripheral in news texts.

In addition, there are restrictions in terms of presentation in these religious texts. Quite often the religious texts are set apart from the proper news discourse by special text frames. These may take the form of introductory notes or fictional settings. For example, there are two prayers which are given as complete, separate documents, headed by a short introduction (see examples (5) and (6)) and, in one case, followed by a short commentary (example (6)).

(5)   A Prayer of Prince EUGENE; which all the Officers under the Duke of MARLBOROUGH had by heart. I Believe in Thee, **O** my **God**! Do thou strengthen my faith: I hope in thee; confirm my hope: I love Thee; inflame

my love more and more: I repent of all my sins; but do thou increase my repentance! ... That it may please thee, **O Lord** to guide and lead me, by thy Providence, to keep me in obedience to thy justice, to comfort me by thy **mercy**, and to protect me by thy almighty power. ... I will nothing, but what thou willest, **O God**, because it is agreeable unto Thee. **O** give me grace that I may be attentive in my prayer, temperate in my diet, vigilant in my conduct, and immoveable in all good purposes. Grant, most merciful **Lord**, that I may be true and faithful to those who have intrusted me with their secrets; ... Assist me, good **God**, in subduing lust, by mortification; covetousness, by liberality; anger, by mildness; and lukewarmness, by zeal and fervency. ... Finally, **O God**, make me sensible how little is the World, how great thy Heavens, how short time, and how long will be the **blessed** eternity! **O** that I may well prepare myself for death; that I may dread thy judgments; that I may avoid the torments of hell; and obtain of thee, **O God**, eternal life, through the merits of **Jesus Christ** our **Lord**. Amen.   (1761, *The London Gazette*, essay)

(6)   A Prayer composed by Queen Elisabeth, to be used daily in each Ship of the Fleet, sent against Cadiz, under the Earl of Essex, in 1596. Most Omnipotent Maker and Giver of all the world's mass, ... we humbly beseech thee with bended knees, prosper the work, and with the best forewinds guide the journey, speed the victory, and make the return the advancement of thy glory, the triumph of their fame, and surety of the realm, with the least loss of the English blood. To these alone petitions, **Lord**, give thou thy **blessed** grant. Amen.
Dr. Hawkins, the English Resident at that time at Venice, translated the above prayer into Italian, and dispersed it abroad, tho' with some danger of the Inquisition; as it was conceived, in those parts, that in England there was neither prayer, nor knowledge of Christ, nor indeed any religion: whereas this being read, was highly commended by all for true Christian devotion.
                    (1761, *The London Evening Post*, home news)

Both prayers, of course, represent genuine religious discourse, but the way these texts are presented shows that they are objects which stem from a different world, a world which, in the case of Queen Elizabeth I, has long passed or, in the case of Prince Eugene (1663–1736), is fairly distant. In this they are similar to the advertisements of religious books: they are set within a framework which is very unlike the prayer texts themselves. Thus, they are not seen as part of the news discourse proper.

A similar text frame is found in the prayer contained in the will of Sir William Petty, which is presented as a document from a past century in *The London Evening Post*.

(7)   To the EDITOR of LLOYD'S EVENING POST.
       SIR, In reading your last, I met with an account of the death of the Earl of
       Shelburne. On this I was curious to turn to the Irish Peerage, by which I find
       the late Earl was great grand son to Sir William Petty. Your inserting the Will of
       that great man, which contains the history of his life, and great rise in the world,
       cannot fail of being as agreeable to your readers, as it was to, Your's & c.
       IN the name of **God**, Amen. I Sir William Petty, Knt. born at Rumsey in
       Hantshire ... and expressing my love and honour to Almighty **God**, ... I will-
       ingly resign my soul into his hands, relying only on his infinite **mercy** and the
       merits of my Saviour, for my happiness after this life; where I expect to know
       and see **God** more clearly, than by the study of the Scriptures, and of his works
       I have been hitherto able to do. Grant me, **O Lord**, and easy passage to thyself,
       that as I have lived in thy fear, I may be known to die in thy favour. Amen.
       [In 1667 he married Elizabeth, daughter to Sir Hardress Waller, of Castletown,
       ... and dying at his house in Piccadilly-street, Westminster, ... 16th December
       1687, was buried in the Church of Rumsey, near the bodies of his father and
       mother].   (1761, *The London Evening Post*, letter)

The text frame may also take the form of a fictional setting. Here the prayer sections or devotional invocations are embedded in a fictional world which is explicitly introduced by the author, for example in the *MEMOIRS OF the last Hours of
a Man of Pleasure* (example (8)).

(8)   I am about to represent to you the last hours of a person of high birth, and
       high spirit; of great parts, and strong passions, every way accomplished, nor
       least in iniquity. ... The death-bed of a profligate is next in horror to that
       abyss, to which it leads. ... –   **Oh**, Thou blasphemed, yet most indulgent,
       Lord God! hell itself is a refuge, if it hides me from thy frown.
       Soon after, his understanding failed.   (1761, *The London Gazette*, essay)

Examples (5) to (8) show the special status of religious texts in news discourse.
The fictional or documentary nature of the texts, together with the separate or
even isolated position of the religious section, attest to the fact that religious discourse is either not part of the world of news discourse or that it is relegated to
specific niches.
     There remain eight letters, stemming from the year 1771, and one essay, stem-
ming from 1761, which do not show the special documentary or fictional frame
encountered in the other examples. These texts discuss religious topics (e.g. pre-
destination) and they seem to have been written in part as reactions to previous
letters of a similar nature. It is true that in these texts we find religious discourse
proper. But here, as well, the sections marked by combinations of the top-ranking
keywords seem to have a special character. These sections, in many cases, comprise

citations from the Bible or invoke Biblical formulations (see example (9)), which are sometimes meant in an ironical or even cynical way (see example (10)).

(9) Excuse me, if I am of a different Opinion, but my Thoughts are as follows: ... Now, since we are assured, that the whole of our Redemption is founded on what **Christ** hath done for us; and that he hath entered into the **Holy** of Holies as our Forerunner, Head, and Representative, what Reason I ask, has he to confine those for whom he hath thus acted, in a Prison on Earth, after they had lived their appointed Time in the Body? He saith, Where I am, ye shall be also. Again, Rev. vi. 9, 10, I saw under the Altar the Souls of them who were slain for the Word of **God**, and for the Testimony which they held. – – – And they cried with a loud Voice, saying, **O Lord**! **holy** and true, dost not thou judge and revenge our Blood on them who dwell on the Earth. ... But least I should be writing in vain to undeceive you, let me conclude for the present. I am, Your humble Servant, THOMAS OSBORNE.

(1771, *Westminster Journal*, letter)

(10) I am sorry, I can say, I know this to be too true, from general Observation. From these Considerations, I hope you will pardon me, if I give you the same Advice which you gave the Inspector – – – fall upon your Knees before **God** with your hand upon your Breast, and this Cry in your Lips, Search me, **O Lord**, and try me; prove me also, and examine my Thoughts; shew me to which Clay I belong. Give me solid Proof that my Name is written in the Lamb's Book of Life, by making it clear to me, that I am in the Faith, and that I avoid giving Occasion for Sin. I am, SIR, Your Friend, and humble Servant, M. &c.

(1771, *Westminster Journal*, letter)

In example (9) the author makes his point by presenting (or invoking) citations from the Bible. Example (10) also employs a section with citations from the Bible (*fall upon your Knees ... giving Occasion for Sin.*). One could argue that in both examples the religious keywords are mostly associated with quotations, quotations from works which are stylistically different from the rest of the text and which belong to the distant world of the Bible. This becomes particularly clear in the second example, where the Biblical section not only stands out as different from the rest of the text, but is meant in a rather cynical way: it is twice distanced from the news text, because, as a Biblical citation, it is also a citation (or repetition) of the addressee, which, however, is now turned against him.

3.2   Selected keywords: Collocations in prayers and news discourse

The second set of keywords comprises four items: "father", "grant", "life" and "give". These items are relatively frequent both in prayers and in the ZEN Corpus.

Since they are not exclusively religious, both prayers and newspapers might use them in the same co-texts, that is, with similar collocations. I looked at the most frequent collocations of the words in prayers and in the ZEN Corpus, using the collocation display in the concord function of WordSmith (Scott 1999). My aim was to see whether these items show different or similar collocations in prayers and newspapers.[8]

Table 3. Major collocations preceding *father* in the ZEN Corpus and the prayer corpus[9]

L1 in ZEN		L1 in prayers	
his	69	our	102
her	23	merciful	97
my	7	heavenly	84
		oh	59
		dear	34
		my	33
		thy	30
		loving	25
		almighty	16
		gracious	17
		his	12
		her	7

Table 3 contains the major collocations immediately preceding *father* (L1) in the ZEN Corpus and the prayer corpus. In the news texts, *father* is typically preceded by third-person possessive pronouns (*his, her*), whereas in the prayers we are dealing mainly with first-person and second-person possessive pronouns (*our, my; thy*), a number of positive adjectives (*merciful, heavenly, loving* etc.) and the item *oh*. Here the possessive pronouns typical of news discourse are relatively rare. The data suggest that in news discourse the term *father* is often used to indicate a family relationship with regard to a specific (mostly third) person (see example (11)), whereas in prayers it is typically used as an address term which, in addition, may specify the relationship to the persons praying and include positive features (see example (12)).

(11)   King WILLIAM was the Posthumous Son of **his Father** William II. Prince of Orange, by Princess Mary, eldest Daughter to King Charles I of Great Britain.
(1701, *The Flying Post*, home news)

---

8.   In collecting the collocates, articles and demonstratives were excluded from the analysis.

9.   L1 designates the position immediately preceding *father*.

(12) **O father**, I thanke thee for the good and prosperous successe, which thou in thy mercie hast giuen my husband.

(1582, Thomas Bentley. *The fift lampe of virginitie*)

Table 4. Major collocations of the verb form *grant* in the ZEN Corpus and the prayer corpus[10]

| ZEN Corpus | | | Prayers | |
L2	L1	R1	L1	R1
pleased 40	to 90	to/unto 46	to 24	that 119
		me 5		me 101
		that 1		to/unto 99
				us 86

Table 4 shows the major collocations of the verb form *grant* in both corpora. In the ZEN Corpus the most prominent left collocates are *pleased* and *to*, which yields the pattern *pleased to grant*. The most frequent item following *grant* is *to / unto*, which suggests the beneficiary (see example (13)).

(13) His Majesty has been **pleased to grant to** Dr. John Joachim Becher, and Henry Searle Esq; the sole Benefit of making Pitch and Tarr out of Sea-Coal.

(1681, *A New News-Book*, home news)

In the prayers this pattern of *grant* is not found. By contrast, the most frequent items following *grant* are *that* and the first-person pronouns (*me, us*). This may be said to reflect the basic pattern of a petition (see example (14)). *To / unto* may indicate the beneficiary of the petition (see example (15)).

(14) Have mercy upon me, and forgive me all that is past: and **grant that** I may always study to serve thee, and please thee.

(1666, *The Countess of Morton's Daily Exercise*)

(15) **Grant vnto** vs we beseech thee, that ... we may liue togither therein in thy faith.   (1582, Thomas Bentley. *The fift lampe of virginitie*)

Thus it seems that the collocation patterns associated with *grant* are quite distinct in the two corpora. Although the item is fairly common in both genres, it is linked to separate uses. Whereas in the news texts we usually find a report about an act of granting (typically associated with an eminent person, thus constituting a noteworthy piece of information), in the prayers *grant* is used as an imperative in a petition.

---

10. L1 designates the position immediately preceding *grant*, R1 the position immediately following *grant*. L2 immediately precedes L1.

Table 5. Major collocations of *life* in the ZEN Corpus and the prayer corpus

ZEN Corpus		Prayers	
L1	R1	L1	R1
his 105	of 88	my 133	everlasting 35
of 90		of 119	in 23
her 24		our 61	of 20
for 19		everlasting 26	eternal 6
human 12		eternal 23	
high 9		his 11	
private 8			

Table 6. Major collocations of *give* in the ZEN Corpus and the prayer corpus

ZEN Corpus			Prayers		
L1	R1	R2	L1	R1	R2
to 774	notice 688	that 494	to 93	me 218	grace 77
hereby 122	him 40	account 30		us 98	
	us 28	leave 20		to/unto 85	
	me 29			thee 38	
	them 26			them 30	
	you 12			thanks 24	
	her 10			him 10	
	to 10				

Table 5 shows the major collocations of *life* in the two corpora. In the ZEN Corpus *life* is mainly used together with third-person possessive pronouns (above all *his*) and prepositions (mainly *of*) in the position immediately preceding it (L1). Adjectives which are found in L1 are *human*, *high* and *private*. *Life* is followed most frequently by the preposition *of*. In the prayers we find mainly possessive pronouns relating to the first person (*my*, *our*) and the preposition *of*. Prominent adjectives in L1 and R1 are *everlasting* and *eternal*. The preposition *of* is not nearly as frequent as in the news texts.

Again the data suggest that the collocations are mainly disparate in the two genres: in prayers the emphasis is on the first person, suggesting that the persons praying are mostly concerned with their own lives or with "life everlasting". In the news texts *life* is mostly used in connection with the description of the life of a specific (third) person. The adjectives associated with *life* are also quite different in the two corpora.

The item *give* is different from the three above-mentioned lexical items in that it occurs even more frequently in both prayers (751) and the ZEN Corpus (1525). The data of the ZEN Corpus suggest a clear collocational pattern of *give*, which is "(to) give notice that" (see Table 6). This pattern reflects an essential function of news texts since it makes explicit the major aim of news discourse, namely making things known (see example (16)). The explicitness of the formulations also explains why *give* is used quite often together with the performative marker *hereby* (see example (17)).

(16)   WHereas there hath been a great want of good Water at this place, this is **to give notice** that Mr. William Warner and Partners, have at great expence brought Water here.   (1701, *The Post Man*, advertisement)

(17)   The Court of Assistants of the Corporation for making Hollow Sword Blades in England do **hereby give Notice**, That a General Court of the Members of the said Corporation will be held at their House in Birchen-lane, London, on Thursday the 22d Instant, at 10 in the Forenoon.
                    (1711, *The London Gazette*, announcement)

The prayers show a different picture. The frequency of *to* in L1 is significantly lower. In R1, we find mostly personal pronouns relating to the first person (note the low frequency of personal pronouns in R1 in the ZEN Corpus). Another frequent collocate in R1 is the preposition *to / unto*, and there is one particular noun, *grace*, which is found quite often in R2. All this suggests again the pattern of a petition, which is so typical of prayers (see example (18)).

(18)   O Lorde **gyue me grace** to forgyue myne aduersaryes frely for thy sake.
                    (1546, *A boke of prayers called ye ordynary fasshyon of good lyuynge*)

Thus, the disparate collocational patterns of *give* in the two corpora show how the same lexical items are used for completely different purposes, purposes which in this case nicely illustrate the different functional profiles of the two genres.

   In all, the four case studies have demonstrated that prayers and newspapers show quite different and genre-specific collocational patterns. Although the case studies cannot be taken to be representative of the two corpora, they provide additional support for the assumption that religious language and the language of news discourse are quite distinct. Prayers may show the same lexical items as news texts, but they are used for different purposes in markedly different combinations. In fact, the analysis of the four keywords implies that the language of sixteenth-century prayers is quite far away from the language used in news discourse about 100 years later.

4.   Conclusions

The aim of this short contrastive study of prayers and news texts was to give an initial answer to the question of whether the register of religious language, which is still characterised by many features reaching back to the Early Modern period, has always been felt to be conservative and archaic. The keyword analysis of the prayer corpus and the ZEN Corpus clearly showed that the most frequent and typically religious lexemes found in prayers are consistently rare in eighteenth-century news discourse. This reflects the fact that religious language typical of prayers is rarely found in newspaper texts of the period.

In addition, a closer analysis revealed that the keywords, if they were found, showed peculiar restrictions in terms of use and presentation. Religious keywords appear in fixed formulae representing set conversational or textual routines; or the sections containing them are set apart as separate quotations or separate parts which are not felt to be part of the news discourse proper.

The analysis of the collocations of four more neutral lexical items showed that the two genres, although to a certain extent sharing many lexemes, use them in completely different combinations. All this seems to point to the fact that the "otherness" of the specialised religious register as pointed out by Crystal and Davy (1969) in their analysis of liturgical language was already preserved in the eighteenth century. Thus it is quite likely that religious language was felt to be conservative and archaic during the eighteenth century and that it had already acquired a separate status as a "special" register.[11]

If this result should turn out to be correct, that is, if it can be corroborated by data from other eighteenth-century genres, the focus of further analyses investigating the archaic nature of religious language should shift (back) towards the Early Modern period. If the "otherness" of the religious language is already clearly visible in the eighteenth century, one should raise the question of whether this register was not felt to be archaic from the start. In order to test this hypothesis, secular genres from the sixteenth and seventeenth centuries should be contrasted with the prayer corpus.

On the other hand, this short study has clearly shown that news discourse is indeed far removed from religious discourse and seems to reflect a purely secular domain.

---

11. The present study has, of course, only revealed the lexical side of this archaic nature. Crystal and Davy (1969) list both lexical and morpho-syntactic features in their description of religious language. In fact, morphology and syntax also contribute significantly to the archaic nature of religious language.

References

Crystal, David, and Derek Davy. 1969. *Investigating English Style*. Harlow: Longman.

Dunning, Ted. 1993. Accurate methods for statistics of surprise and coincidence. *Computational Linguistics* 19, 61–74.

Fries, Udo, and Peter Schneider. 2000. *ZEN*: Preparing the *Zurich English Newspaper Corpus*. In Friedrich Ungerer (ed.). *English Media Texts – Past and Present. Language and Textual Structure*. Amsterdam and Philadelphia: John Benjamins, 3–24.

Kohnen, Thomas. 2006. Historical corpus linguistics: Perspectives on English diachronic corpora. *Anglistik* 17.2, 73–91.

Lehmann, Hans Martin, Caren auf dem Keller, and Beni Ruef. 2006. ZEN Corpus 1.0. In Roberta Facchinetti and Matti Rissanen (eds.). *Corpus-based Studies of Diachronic English*. Bern: Peter Lang, 135–155.

McEnery, Tony, Richard Xiao, and Yukio Tono. 2006. *Corpus-Based Language Studies. An Advanced Resource Book*. London: Routledge.

McGrath, Alister. 2001. *In the Beginning. The Story of the King James Bible and How It Changed a Nation, a Language, and a Culture*. New York: Random House.

Partridge, Astley C. 1973. *English Bible Translation*. London: André Deutsch.

Scott, Mike. 1999. *WordSmith Tools*. Oxford: Oxford University Press.

"As silly as an Irish Teague"

Comparisons in early English news discourse

Claudia Claridge

1. Introduction

News discourse is a register comprising various journalistic text types and, as such, it is characterised by a certain combination and recurrence of formal and linguistic features which particularly fit and/or reflect its purpose(s) and its production situation. Historical news discourse is a register in the making, but relatively few of its formal and linguistic features have been studied in detail to date. Among its features are, for example, headlines, modality and argumentation, speech reporting, and newspaper advertising, all of which are of fairly obvious interest for the emergent register. The present contribution may at first sight seem a less obvious choice of feature by dealing, as it does, with comparisons in the seventeenth- and eighteenth-century press. So why comparisons in *news* discourse and why in *historical* news discourse?

One of the writers in the *Zurich English Newspaper Corpus* (ZEN) wrote the following: "For as all Things are more clearly distinguish'd, so they are more sensibly felt by Comparison" (*Read's Weekly Journal*, 1731). The first part of this quotation refers to an ideational function of comparisons: by distinguishing and – conversely – associating things, these become clearer to the reader. Comparisons can thus have a clarifying or explicating function, making previously unknown or vague aspects more accessible and easier to understand. Newspapers, almost by definition, will carry a considerable amount of information that is entirely or partly new to their readers. This was true then as it is now but, with regard to foreign news at least, this aspect might have been even more relevant for past newspaper readers. Comparisons fulfil their task "clearly" by being explicit in contrast to metaphors, which means that they are easier to understand and comparatively unambiguous in their interpretation, that is, writer intention and reader interpretation have a reasonable chance of coinciding. Research by Fishelov (2007: 76) has shown that fairly conventional similes, i.e. those based in pre-existing linguistic and cultural networks,[1] are understood by the majority of people in exactly the same way and are rated as "easy" by most people. According to Schneider (2002), metaphors were apparently not at all common in news writing before 1800, so that the question arises as to whether news writers perhaps preferred the less striking form of comparison precisely because of its clarity. The second part of the above quotation ("sensibly felt") refers to the emotional or attitudinal response of the reader as being triggered by clearer categorisation and comparative evaluation.[2] In this sense, comparisons may be one means of increasing reader involvement and of doing so in a "predictable" direction, thereby also potentially drawing the reader over to the side of the writer.

Journalistic writing can be said to be characterised by two functional dichotomies: the relationship between 1. information and persuasion, and 2. information and entertainment (Burger 2005). What has been noted above about comparisons fits the first of these: clarifying, explanatory comparisons are informative, while comparisons with overt or covert attitudinal content overtly contribute to persuasion. Furthermore, there is a link between comparisons and entertainment in the second dichotomy. Any comparison, if it is imaginative and striking enough, can of course be entertaining. Furthermore, comparisons in the typical form of the simile belong to rhetorical figures, which always have an aesthetic function in addition to their content. An eighteenth-century rhetorician, Hugh Blair, identified two types of comparison: those that explain and those that embellish, the latter especially adding beauty to a discourse (Blair 1783). In his view, (embellishing) comparisons do not convey strong passion, but belong to a kind of middle style, lying between the highly pathetic and the extremely humble – which may fit news discourse, although Blair neither mentioned nor probably thought about this type of writing. The reason for bringing in rhetoric here may not be immediately obvious, but it is connected to 1. the seventeenth and eighteenth centuries being a period when rhetorical interest and training in education were still commonplace (McIntosh 1998:146–155), 2. the fact that journalism then was not yet a separate, unified profession (Bonham-Carter 1978:5) or was only gradually emerging, and 3. the apparent non-existence of house-styles and style manuals for early newspapers.[3]

---

1.   That is, neither 'poetic' nor very opaque similes. His examples for the conventional type are *Dan is like a snake / Dan is as dangerous as a snake* versus non-conventional *Dan is like the State of Israel / Dan is as restless as the State of Israel.*

2.   Fishelov (2007:76, 78–80) also found high agreement among subjects on whether a given simile contained a positive or a negative evaluation.

3.   Schneider (2002) mentions that the first newspaper style-guide is the one drawn up by *The Times* in 1913.

Language usage in newspapers may thus have been influenced to a greater extent than today by both period styles and by individual stylistic preferences. Many professional authors, i.e. those writing for money, had, or had been trained for, other occupations (e.g. in the clergy or as schoolmasters) (Feather 1988:104), and they did not necessarily only write journalistic prose. Defoe is a case in point here; similarly, Jonathan Swift and John Gay wrote occasionally for *The Craftsman* and Richard Steele was at one time the editor of the *London Gazette* (Siebert 1965:340; Sommerville 1996:127f.).[4] Linguistic practices from other professions and other discourses, partly rhetorically inspired ones, might therefore have leaked into the emerging register of news discourse to a certain extent.

The aim of this paper is, then, to investigate the use of comparisons in historical newspapers, as represented in the ZEN Corpus (1661–1791), with particular emphasis on the functions they fulfil and their connection to the macro-functions mentioned above. While Sommerville (1996: 122f.) maintains that pre-1700 newspapers leaned more heavily towards the function of providing (pure) information, it seems clear that, at least from 1700 onwards, the periodical press were not only covering facts, but were active in creating political opinion and debate (Downie 1987:115; Feather 1988:85). The historical results will be contrastively evaluated with the help of the press sections of the 1991 F-LOB Corpus.

2.   Comparison

Comparison is found when a term or proposition A and a term or proposition B are set in relation to each other in such a way as to highlight their (degree of) similarity or dissimilarity. Both A and B share certain properties, i.e. they are equivalent or equal to each other in some respect, as otherwise the comparison might appear obscure. What respect this is can be explicitly expressed by the standard of comparison, e.g. *tall* in *Bill is as tall as his father*. Many comparisons, like the one just cited, involve positioning on a scale or grading, e.g. on a scale of size (cf. Quirk et al. 1985:1127ff.; Huddleston and Pullum 2002:1099ff.). Comparisons can be literal or figurative, with the latter type often going by the label of simile (e.g. Ortony 1979).

There is a great variety of formal means for comparing, such as the comparative and superlative degree; comparative prepositions or conjunctions (e.g. *than, as (… as), like, as if / as though*); specific lexical forms (e.g. *same, identical to, different from*) including those of a (quasi-)metalinguistic nature (e.g. *compare,*

---

4.   Issues of both papers (*The Craftsman* and the *London Gazette*) are included in ZEN.

parallel); and derivational morphology (e.g. -*ish*) (cf. Wikberg 1999: 95f.). Not all serve the purpose of comparison equally well (e.g. -*ish* is neither monosemous nor very explicitly comparative) and not all are equally amenable to semi-automatic searching (e.g. the possible lexical items are too diverse). Indications of their behaviour in modern news contexts can be found for only some. Biber et al. (1999: 524) found that the superlative and the comparative degree (synthetic types) are very common in the news register and, in the case of the former, more frequent than in any other register. The construction "*as* adjective *as*" can be as frequent as in conversation (American English) or somewhat less so (British English), and is less frequent than in fiction, but more so than in academic writing (Biber et al. 1999: 528). No statistics involving comparative *like* are available.

In this study I will concentrate on only two items or constructions, namely on comparisons using *like* and *as...as* with one, two or three intervening items. Both are frequently used, typical comparative items, and are fairly unambiguous semantically. They allow more textual elaboration than the superlative and the comparative and are thus textually more interesting. Furthermore, it is these two items that are usually included in the rhetorical concept of simile, and conscious rhetoric may play a role in public texts such as newspapers, in particular in the period under consideration. Both *like* and *as...as* emphasise equality rather than difference, with the latter also including the scalar notion. Whereas *like* can easily accommodate comparisons without an explicit standard of comparison, this is automatically present in *as...as* comparisons. *As...as* also allows potentially more explicit comparisons than *like* because of the ease of clausal complementation.

3.   The data

As mentioned above, the data for this study is taken from the ZEN and F-LOB Corpora. ZEN contains 349 complete newspaper editions published between 1661 and 1791, representing 52 different papers. Most of the papers occur in only one, or few, of the corpus decades, perhaps reflecting a short period of publication for many papers. ZEN amounts to about 1.6 million words. The Sections A, B and C of the 1991 F-LOB Corpus represent three press genres, namely reportage (A), editorials (B) and reviews (C). Together they come to 177,155 words.

Before proceeding to the two comparative constructions which are the focus of this study, a few remarks about other realisations of comparisons are in order. Superlatives are indeed extremely common (27.3 / 10,000 words in ZEN, 26.0 / 10,000 in F-LOB), and, as also noticed by Biber et al. (1999: 524), most adjectives involved are evaluative or can easily be used in an evaluative manner. The three most common superlative adjectives in ZEN are *best*, *greatest* and *highest*; others include *choicest, deepest, finest, fullest, largest, lowest, richest, slightest,* and *weakest,* to mention just a few. The comparative followed by *than/then,* in contrast, is strikingly less common in the past than in modern press writing (1.9 / 10,000 versus 8.2 / 10,000) – a difference which may merit a closer look in the future. An explicit lexical realisation is found in example (1) below, involving the word *resemble* and a fairly elaborate explanation or spin.

(1) The promises of Mr. PITT **resemble** the trick of a showman, who went about the country, and after having collected some money, and performed a few feats of legerdemain in the view of the gaping rustics, said that he would exhibit still greater wonders, provided they would shut their eyes, and trust to the description which he should give them. It is needless to add that while the ignorant boobies, with their eyes shut, were greedily devouring the imposture, he made use of the opportunity to pick their pockets.
(*The Morning Chronicle*, 1791)

In contrast to most simple superlatives or comparatives, instances like this create a vivid mental image, which transports a very clear evaluation and is also potentially entertaining for the reader. Other similar cases found involve such items as *resemblance, compared with, in comparison to, equal to, parallel,* and *difference between.* All involve a lexeme that is an overt, metalinguistic, marker of comparison, even if the item can of course also be used otherwise. That comparisons need not necessarily contain such an explicit or typical comparative word is shown by the italicised parts in (2):

(2) Bourdalou [...] preach'd before the King and the whole Court, upon this Text, 'Tis not lawful for thee to have thy brother's wife, with such vehemency and boldness, as did amaze his Hearers, who immediately concluded, that this would be his last Sermon before his Most Christian Majesty, if nothing worse happened to him; and the rather, because he made use of the following **Comparison**, so obvious to every common understanding, that the meanest capacity could not but see clearly the meaning of it: *If a Star, by the interjection of an opacious Body, happen to be eclips'd, few are either concern'd, or observe it; whereas the Sun is no sooner darkned by the interposition of the Moon, but we all lift up our eyes to the Heavens to gaze upon it, as if it were a real Miracle, and not the natural product of the general Laws of Motion*: He fail'd not to make the application of this **Simile**, tho clear enough, of it self, by saying, *That the Faults of private men being commonly talk'd of but in the Neighbourhood, scarce ever reach'd the utmost Limits of the Kingdom; but that Crime of Scandal committed by the Sovereign Magistrate, drawing upon him the eyes of all his Subjects, did so far influence the weaker sort, as to give them occasion either to think it lawful*

> *to do what was authoriz'd by the example of their Prince, or that they might gain*
> *his favour by complying with, and imitating his greatest Imperfections.*
> (*The Pacquet of Advice from France*, 1691; italics original)

Such cases are of course normally hard to find, so that instances which attain comparative force by sheer contrastive juxtaposition will usually go unnoticed in analysis.[5] What (2) also illustrates is that some comparisons are newsworthy, that is they are reported and even quoted more or less verbatim (and here also labelled with the rhetorical term *simile*). There are other such cases in the ZEN Corpus, for example in the *Evening Mail*, 1791 and the *Daily Courant*, 1731, with the latter including a criticism of a perceived comparison (*If the Writer means by this to insinuate any Parallel, or hint at any Resemblance between the Patriot of the last Age, and the Malecontent of this, he was certainly in the Wrong*), a usage one finds not uncommonly in the modern media.

Let us now turn to the structures involving *like* and *as...as*. The results from the two corpora indicate that these are more frequent today than in the past.[6] *As...as* occurs with a frequency of 2.7 instances per 10,000 words in ZEN versus 3.3 in F-LOB. The difference with *like* is more striking, with 0.9 (ZEN) versus 5.5 (F-LOB).[7] Also, the numerical relationship between the two variables has been reversed between the two periods, *like* being the more common item nowadays. Lumping the data together in this way may obscure interesting aspects, however. Split according to decades for ZEN and to genres for F-LOB, the picture as shown in Figures 1 and 2 arises. Decade representation for ZEN means that each point on the graph represents newspapers published in one year (e.g. 1681, 1701), which

---

5.   The adversative *whereas* here serves to highlight the contrast, but this is not an element one would look for with regard to comparisons.

6.   A note on the data selection process is in order here: verbal instances of *like* were excluded easily. The only fuzzy area occurred with *like* with respect to cases which are paraphrasable by 'such as'. While these retain traces of comparison semantics, they nevertheless have a different function and were thus discarded. In the case of *as* (with a frequency of 8,697 in ZEN), including the single form would have meant dealing with a major case of polysemy involving a considerable number of unclear cases, so that the *as...as* option, which includes *so...as* for ZEN, was chosen. Lexicalized or grammaticalized instances of *as...as* (*as soon as, as far as, as long as, as well as*) were also discarded, as were *so...as to* sequences. All remaining cases used in the statistics represent true comparisons. While this gives a good overview of one segment of comparisons, the true overall incidence of comparative structures, including cases like example (1) for instance, would only be revealed by reading through parts of the corpus.

7.   The difference for *like* is statistically significant with the chi-square test ($\chi^2 = 244.84$, $p < 0.0001$, df = 1), in contrast to *as...as* ($\chi^2 = 1.78$, $p < 0.2$, df = 1). *Than*-comparisons go along with *like* by also exhibiting a clear rise, from 8.5 occurrences per 10,000 words in ZEN to 17.4 in F-LOB.

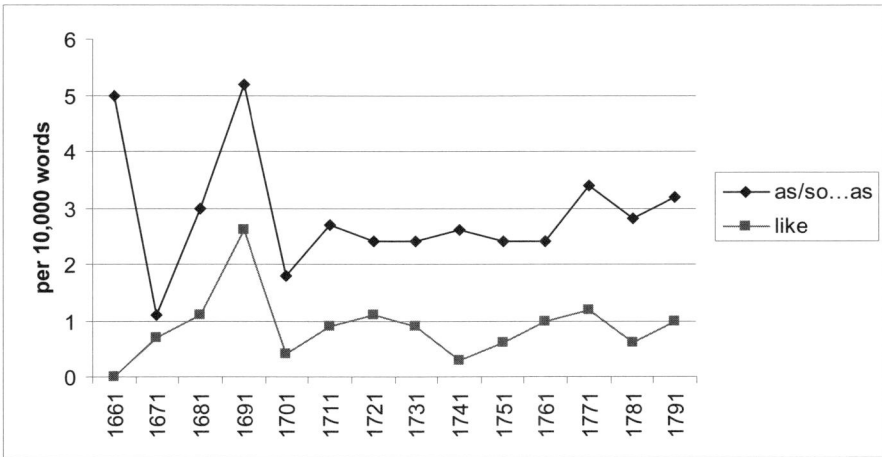

Figure 1. ZEN by decades

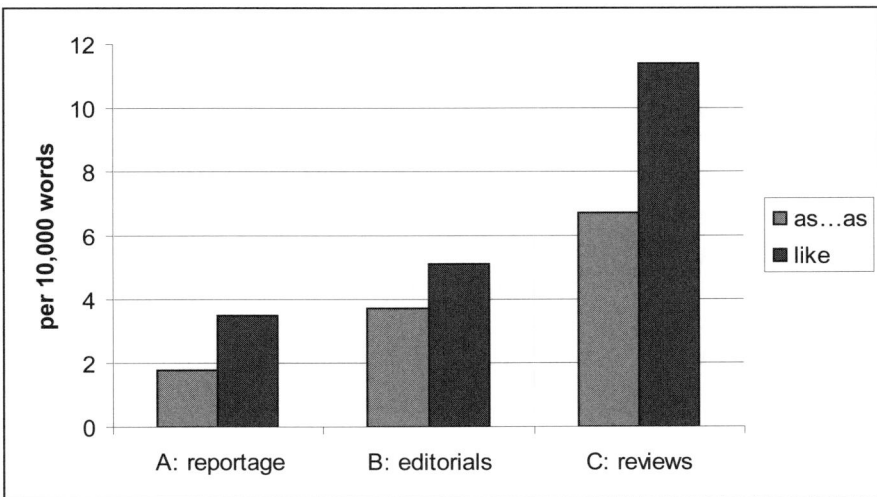

Figure 2. F-LOB by genre

makes the data more comparable to F-LOB as a whole, which also represents one year (1991). A direct comparison of genres is not possible, as ZEN's text classes[8]

---

8. The text classes of ZEN are the following (cf. Fries and Schneider 2000): foreign news, home news, ship news, crime, accidents (most of which will contain reportage, but the presence of some editorial-like material cannot be excluded), reviews (only eighteen of which are found

contain neither reportage nor editorials, reflecting the fact that these modern text categories developed only at a later time.

As...as shows a fairly stable and consistent result of between two to three instances per 10,000 words in the middle decades of the corpus, increases in the last three decades, and is fairly erratic at the beginning. The distribution of *like* seems on the whole to have more ups and downs throughout the entire corpus period. This may indicate that *like*-comparisons could be more prone to influence by topic or idiosyncratic stylistic preferences. While the very striking results for 1661 have to be disregarded due to insufficient data, the steep rise for both items in 1691 is in need of explanation.[9] According to the ZEN compilers, this decade contains a certain amount of pamphlet material, which might account for the difference to the rest of the corpus. A search of the *Lampeter Corpus*, which contains only pamphlets, confirms this suspicion, as the use of comparative structures is considerably more frequent there (*as...as*: 619 instances = 5.2/10,000; *like*: 447 instances = 3.7/10,000). As the most salient difference between newspapers and pamphlets is that the latter are even more geared towards discussion, persuasion and polemic, comparison is revealed as a construction that is apparently more useful for argumentative text types.

The specialisation in argumentative contexts is also supported by the evidence from F-LOB as visible in Figure 2.[10] Comparison is least frequent in reportage, i.e. in the prototypically information-heavy newspaper texts. Both editorials and reviews are persuasive text types, so that the question arises of how the rather striking difference between them can be accounted for. Reviews presumably realise their persuasive aim through overt evaluation much more than editorials do, while the latter may opt for a wider range of different argumentative structures. The answer therefore may lie in the functions that comparative structures fulfil – and this is what the next section will deal with.

---

in the corpus, all in the 18th century); births, weddings, deaths; letter, essay (potentially of an editorial-like nature), address, proclamation, announcement; advertisement, lost and found.

9. There is only one newspaper issue of about 4,000 words in 1661. In contrast, there are 28 issues or texts amounting to 83,000 words in 1691.

10. The differences between the genres are generally significant (chi-square), with the exception of the difference between A and B for *like*, which is not. The result in Figure 2 is also confirmed by the distribution of the overall more frequent *than*-comparisons: reportage has 14.4 occurrences per 10,000 words, editorials 19.3 and reviews 21.9.

4.   Functions of comparisons in newspapers

Attributing functions to specific constructions in text is not easy and always has a subjective touch to it. The functions to be identified here have arisen inductively out of an analysis of the data, paying attention to as much of the surrounding cotext as possible. In many cases particular comparative uses seem to be serving more than one function. In such instances, multiple functions were attributed in the analysis, but only the apparently dominant function counted for the statistics given in Table 1 below. In the process, as many as fourteen different functions were attributed at least once, many, though not all, of which have been mentioned in the literature before. Leaving aside more specifically literary functions (cf. Addison 2001), one finds the following rather diverse aspects mentioned in the literature: comparing similarities, *clarification*, illustration by an analogue (i.e. presumably more vivid) mode of description, persuasion, *evaluation* through connotations, provoking thought, *intensification*, ornamental and humorous use (based on Norrick 1986; Harris and Mosier 1999). The functions italicised in this listing are, together with providing information, the most common ones in the present data, as Table 1 shows:

Table 1. Functions of comparisons in ZEN

Functions	as...as	like
Intensification	181 (41.2%)	9 (6.2%)
Evaluation	127 (28.9%)	50 (34.2%)
Providing information	76 (17.3%%)	27 (18.5%)
Explanation/clarification	6 (1.4%)	24 (16.4%)
Other[11]	49 (11.2%)	36 (24.6 %)

Providing information is a function[12] which is used for instances where the comparative construction carries important factual information that would not otherwise – or not as easily – be conveyable in the text (cf. discussion and examples below). The three functions of intensification, evaluation and information account for 85 per cent of all *as...as* instances, while 69 per cent of *like*-comparisons are covered by the functions evaluation, information and explanation. There is a clear difference between *as...as* and *like*, with the former disfavouring explanation and

---

11. 'Other' includes: generalisation, contrast, comparing, humour, hedging, imprecision, cohesion, vivid description, ornamentation – with a greater variety being found for *like* than for *as...as*.

12. Cf. also Claridge (2006) for this and other functions as realised in nineteenth-century scientific prose.

the latter intensification. It could be argued from the present data that *as…as* specialises in intensification and *like* in evaluation. This would also account nicely for the high frequency of *like* in modern press reviews (cf. Figure 2). These correlations, while present, are not nearly as strongly developed in scientific prose of the nineteenth century, however (cf. Claridge 2006). Thus, it is possible that the preferences attested here are a characteristic of newspaper language. A comparison with the F-LOB data confirms this for *like*, where the evaluation function is even more strongly attested (43 per cent of all cases), but not for *as…as*, in which case the intensification (20 per cent) and evaluation (47 per cent) functions are reversed in importance. The explanation function is also much reduced in F-LOB, at five per cent for *like* and zero for *as…as*. The information function is more or less stable for *like* (20 per cent), but is diminished somewhat with *as…as* (ten per cent). From this one can conclude that the situation as presented in table 1 is partly typical of newspaper language as such, and partly characteristic of seventeenth- and eighteenth-century newspaper style only.

Let us now have a closer look at these functions, starting with intensification. Many *as…as* instances are of the kind found in (3) and (4):

(3) To allow a people to return to their Country and Estates, whom he forc'd some years ago to abandon, and look't upon as his greatest happiness in this World, and his most prevailing Merit to gain another; I say, to do all this now, or but to offer to do it, *speaks out* the necessity of his Affairs, **as much as any thing can do**. (*Mercurius Reformatus*, 1691)

(4) Mean time the Curate returned to the Vestry, promised not to Celebrate Mass, and *went home* **as fast as he could** thro' the Crowd of People, which had like to have stifled him. (*The Flying Post*, 1721)

The comparative clause contains indefinite pronouns and modals, which (together) produce a proposition denoting an extreme or outer limit, similar in effect to forms like *as x as ever / as possible*, which are also found realising the intensifying function. It is this, albeit vague, extremity which gives emphasis to the main proposition. An alternative to this method is choosing an item for the B-term which is considered to be an extreme or a prototype of the point to be illustrated, as we find it in the following two examples.

(5) THE very first Dose of which (a few Drops only) instantly penetrates the innerst Recesses of the minutest Nerves, and *darting* almost **as quick as Lightening** thro' the whole Human System, diffuses kindly Warmth and general Comfort to the weakned Limbs and all Parts of the Body, (*Daily Post*, 1731)

(6) Lord Rawdon insisted that what he advanced was a fact, and he again repeated, if the House permitted him by appointing a Committee, he should

prove to a demonstration **as clear as any problem in Euclid,** that our outgoings from January 1786 to Jan. 1789 exceeded our income by 765,000l.
(*Evening Mail*, 1791)

Lightning, in (5), is proverbially, and thus prototypically, fast, so that it can be used to intensify other processes. Similar cases can be found with intensifying *like*-comparisons, such as *thin/pale like death, rush like a torrent, slippery like an eel.* All such cases can be assumed to be clear to the reader, whereas the B-term in (6) is a less obvious choice and thus potentially prone to misunderstanding. First, it presupposes a certain amount of knowledge, here of a classical and scientific nature, which not all the readership might necessarily have (cf. also Section 5 below). Secondly, this usage also assumes an evaluation of Euclid's writing that is shared between author and reader, which, even given common knowledge, might be problematic. A further point of interest about (6) is that it is presented as an indirect quote, as a statement produced originally by Lord Rawdon. This is fairly common in the F-LOB data, in particular in the reportage section, but it is apparently rare in ZEN.[13]

The above examples, in particular (5) and (6), also contain an element of evaluation, which has been rated as being of secondary importance here. In the following examples, however, evaluation is the major aspect. Example (7) works with the connotations of the B-term (statue of Parian marble), but gives them an interesting twist. The usual and dominant connotations of (neo-)classical statues are certainly positive and this is taken up in the attribute *polish*, but this is followed by a negative characteristic, that of lack of warmth and emotionality.

(7)   Of those finer feelings which are the very life of sociability, Bolingbroke *was* **as unsusceptible as a statue of Parian marbles. Like that,** a polish he had, but **like that** too, not a spark of sentimental animation. (*Public Advertiser*, 1791)

---

13. In F-LOB-A, quotes (all but one in direct speech) make up half of all *like*-instances. Only seven historical instances are found within quotes marked as such in ZEN, i.e. by quotation marks (tagged in the corpus with <qb>, <qe>; tag evidence reveals 953 such quotes in the whole corpus; they are much more frequent in the last four decades than in those up to 1751). However, not all these marked cases are typical quotes, while some real quotes are unmarked in the original texts and thus also in the corpus. The following example is contained in one of these latter cases:

I answer'd, that I must justify the Duke of Marlborough to be no Impudent Fellow: He insisted for to Morrow, I told him, the Moon Shines, no Time **like the Time present**. (*The Flying Post*, 1711)

It is thus not possible to ascertain the precise number of quoted comparisons.

While the structure of the whole three-fold comparison makes for an overall negative assessment (the negative part is found in end position!), the particular choice of B-term here nevertheless allows for an ambivalent evaluation, which may be useful for the writer. In contrast, (8) and (9) are unequivocal in their negative assessments.

(8)   Well may we call a Man disguised that has got too large a Brimmer in his head, for it makes a Fool of the wisest man in the World, it turns the Politician inside out, and makes him vomit out all his stinking Secrets, till he *looks* **as silly as an Irish Teague**. (*Athenian Mercury*, 1691)

(9)   The Spaniards are of a different disposition; – they have a long tongue, but a short arm: timid, pusillanimous, unsteady, and have nothing to recommend them but their gold; – **like the Jews** – it is their only protection: – They are, in short, unworthy of our friendship. (*Public Advertiser*, 1791)

These also employ connotations, or, more precisely, national and racist stereotypes. In contrast to (7), the grounds for comparison are not as clearly and exhaustively spelt out, thus leaving more room for free association. They are found within larger evaluative contexts, in which the comparison could be seen either as superfluous or as re-enforcing and emphasising, as a kind of culmination of the surrounding assessments. Apart from their immediate point, such comparisons also transport a larger ideological subtext, such as the pervasive (in the Western world) ideology of anti-Semitism shining through in (9). The parenthetical form of the comparison in (9) is also important: it is, strictly speaking, not necessary to the discussion of the Spaniards and could easily have been left out, which makes its inclusion all the more noteworthy. The evaluative comparisons in (10) and (11) are more explicit than the preceding instances in so far as they leave less to be inferred by the reader.

(10)   It has been generally understood, that he was ever extremely averse to hostile measures with England, *thinking*, **like a wise and an honest Minister**, how little is ever procured by the most successful war, but an increase of taxes, and decrease of population and of commerce. (*London Chronicle*, 1791)

(11)   Of these, the principal was Mrs. POPE, who met with a share of applause **as warm and persevering as her talents are exalted and diversified**. (*Morning Post*, 1791)

Both employ overtly evaluative adjectives within the comparative constructions. Example (10), which is about the Spanish Minister for Foreign Affairs, furthermore combines evaluation with generalisation (of what counts as wise politics), thus putting the present case into a larger perspective.[14] In (11), the reporting of an evaluation (applause) is coupled with an assessment of the object of the applause, probably by the journalist, but presented in such a way in the interlinked comparison as to make it sound like the audience's appraisal. In this way, writers can present their own views as sentiments which are generally shared, which potentially makes for stronger involvement of the reader and for greater credibility.

Examples (3) through (11) all contain more than is necessary for the simple reporting of news, although they do this to varying degrees. They highlight certain parts of the information given as more or less noteworthy and give more or less clear indications of how facts could (or should) be interpreted by the readers. In some instances they also increase reader involvement. In that respect they are a feature of argumentative or persuasive writing, i.e. argumentation is one overarching or resulting function of comparison. Therefore, it is not surprising that such cases are often found in the text category 'advertisement' (cf. Footnote 8 for ZEN's text classes), illustrated by examples (5) and (11) above, as this text type is geared towards persuading the reader to some course of action (usually buying the product). It is probably also not by chance that potentially argumentative examples are more commonly found in foreign news (e.g. (3), (4), (9) and (10) above) than in home news (e.g. (6)). It is less risky for the press to evaluate and critically discuss foreign politics than to make assessments of the actions of the British Government, a course of action which could often have been interpreted as libellous. Example (7), although with a British context and politician (Bolingbroke), is unproblematic as it refers to the past and is, furthermore, a safe option as it is (said to be?) a piece quoted from a twenty year-old newspaper. In this respect, (12) is also of interest, in that it overtly argues, also with the help of comparisons, against libelling one's own government – a plea which I assume must ultimately be read as ironic.

(12)   Libelling a Government, is a kind of Pen and Ink Rebellion; to attack the Soveraign, or the Administration, or the Legislature in Print, is **as real as attacking them, and as positive as raising War against them, as that of attacking them with Sword and Gun**; and therefore whether you will allow it to be legal or no, you must expect, that all Governments will exert themselves in proportion as much to punish it. (*Applebee's Original Weekly Journal*, 1721)

---

14. Another example for generalisation usage and one which also involves the readers is the following quote:

> To err is human, and we have no Right to laugh at the most accomplished Character for falling into it: Our Raillery, if we rightly understood it, is in this Case not directed against the particular Person, but against human Nature, and **ourselves, as much as he**, are the Subjects of it: (*London Daily Advertiser,* 1751)

The comparatively greater reluctance of the seventeenth- and eighteenth-century press to provide argumentative and opinion-driven treatments of political events, even though diminishing over the time span represented by ZEN, leads to a less extensive use of comparisons than in the modern press. Nevertheless, the potential was already present, as the above instances show.

The remaining two prominent functions, information and explanation (which often shade into one another), serve the purpose of fact-centred reporting, as will be shown. Examples (13) and (14) both provide important pieces of factual information, which in the given cases is more easily conveyed in a comparison than by any other means. The writer of (13) could have given the sizes of both armies and then drawn a conclusion (or let the readers work it out themselves), which would have been textually cumbersome, while the author of (14) could have offered a numerical measurement, which would have been harder to imagine for the reader.

(13)   Six Thousand Germans have lately joined Prince Eugene, so that now he is reckoned to be **as strong as the French**. (*London Gazette*, 1701)

(14)   They farther add, that a great Storm, accompanied with Thunder and Lightning happened at that time, and that there fell Hail-stones **as big as Pidgeons Eggs** in divers places, (*The Domestick Intelligence*, 1681)

In both cases we are concerned with newsworthy and relevant information, which is given in the most precise manner possible. While these instances deal with foreign (13) and home (14) news, information-providing comparisons are also often found in the non-news sections of the papers. Example (15) is found in the crime section, which is of course partly news reporting, but in this case it is also instructive, as a reward is offered for anybody reporting on the whereabouts of John Catchmead.

(15)   JOhn Catchmead, about 24 or 25 years of age, of a middle stature, something haughty in speech and carriage, with very light coloured hair, **more like a short Perrewig than his own hair**, little or no beard, his face somewhat redish by reason of the small Pox, but a chearful Countenance; he used to wear a gray Hat, and a sad coloured cloath Coat, and travel the Countreys to sell Ruggs, Coverlids, Bed-Ticks, Curtains, &c. (*The Protestant Intelligence*, 1681)

The reader is supposed to become involved by looking out for the wanted person, for which s/he needs detailed information about the appearance of Catchmead. This is provided, partly by the *periwig* comparison, probably on the assumption that everybody is familiar with the typical appearance of wigs. Similarly, reader action is required in the advertisement and lost-and-found sections, of which (16) and (17) respectively are instances.

(16) And that the Publick may no longer be impos'd upon by the spurious Counterfeits of the Town, they are desired to try the very Bottle they buy, by putting a Spoonful into a Glass of Water; if it *turns* the Water **as White as Milk**, it's good; if a Sky Colour or Bluish, 'tis nought. (*The Post Boy*, 1721)

(17) LOst the 28th instant, about 5 in the Evening, in St. Paul's Church-yard, a Gold Watch with two Movements, having a black Filagreen Case *studded* **like Shells**, and a Steel Hook and Chain, made by Abel Gold; (*London Gazette*, 1691)

In (16), we additionally find a sort of instruction for the reader, where again it is very important to provide a precise description, a condition which *white as milk* clearly fulfils.

It is somewhat surprising that the last function to be treated here, explanation, was not more common. One might have assumed that newspapers contained a considerable amount of information unfamiliar to their readers, in particular in reports from foreign and far-away places, and that therefore comparisons as a simple familiarisation strategy might have been used more frequently. Examples (18) to (20) represent this strategy. Example (18), found in the foreign news section, explains a French legal document by comparing it to the English Magna Charta, a document about which every reader can be assumed to have some, however vague, knowledge, at the very least about its general importance. This is presumably enough to make the reader understand the larger context without the author having to go into too much detail.

(18) According to the Joyeuse Entree (an Act consisting of fifty-five Articles, *containing* different privileges much **like our Magna Charta**) every person serving in a civil or military capacity, must be a Burgundian, that is a native of one of those Provinces, all which belonged formerly to the House of Burgundy. (*Evening Mail*, 1791)

(19) Several cart loads of fat were *cut off* them [= "sea swine", i.e. dolphins, CC], **like that of bacon**, which was sold at 12s. a cart, and, upon the whole, they were thought to be worth 50l. (*The Craftsman*, 1771)

(20) They are computed by all Gentlemen that ever saw them to be half Birds and half Beasts; and when they are at their full Growth, by the Report of all those that ever have seen any of them in that Country, they are computed to *be* **as big as an English Horse**. (*Daily Post*, 1731)

Examples (19) and (20) are both contained in the home news sections, but they deal with facts that the great majority of readers cannot be thought to be familiar with. Example (19) is about dolphins stranded in Scotland, whose fat is likened to pork bacon, something well-known to everybody. The creatures described in (20) are from India, but were then on show in London. Thus, the comparison works both as explanatory information for those readers not able to go and see them, as well as an interest-rousing advertisement for Londoners, who were able to go to the show.

Examples (13) to (20) are clearly concerned with making things more easily comprehensible for the reader. They are all fairly concrete comparisons, in contrast to the intensifying and evaluative ones treated earlier, and thus potentially verifiable. That is, they are grounded in fact and (apparently) as little influenced by the writer as possible. Where the comparison is only approximate, the reader is provided with a signal, such as *reckoned to be* (13), *more like* (15) and *much like* (18); in other instances we find *something/somewhat like* equally indicating a degree of imprecision. The style of these comparisons is thus rather sober or plain, and they are accordingly well suited to a reporting and fact-centred type of writing.

There are exceptions, of course. Explanatory examples, such as (21), which is found at the beginning of an essay assessing the situation in France, can also be used to provide or prepare argumentative points. The courses of the 'map' mentioned here stand for the alternative actions of the French aristocracy, about which the author has definite views as expounded in the text that then follows.

(21)   History is **like a map**, which describes the course which one may safely steer, and the rocks, promontories, shoals, and sand-banks which ought to be avoided. (*Evening Mail*, 1791)

Note also that in contrast to the preceding instances this is a metaphorical comparison, and one which paves the way for further metaphors (*promontories, sand-banks* etc.).

5.   Further aspects of comparisons

History is like a map in (21) represents a classical copular simile, of a quasi-literary and aphoristic quality. It is certainly noteworthy that (21) is found in the text category "essay", which is not the most prototypical newspaper text class. The majority of *like*-comparisons (70 per cent) do indeed contain verbs other than "be", as well as a certain amount (approximately 14 per cent) of, strictly speaking, verbless instances (parenthetical as in (9) and (10) or in nominal post-position as in (6)).[15] While a few of the verbs found are copular ones such as "become", "appear" or "seem", the overwhelming majority can be illustrated by such items as "shake", "look", "cry", "turn", "dress", "swell", "reign", "torment" etc. Many comparisons are thus adverbial in form adding a manner component, but while one could accordingly expect them to add precision this is not borne out by the data. Example (22) does not say much about the precise method of tying employed (which many readers might not know about), but uses the comparison more for its connotational values.

(22)   the French *tied* them two and two *together* **like Galley Slaves**, and so forced them to march, which has extreamly incensed all the Italians. (*London Gazette,* 1691)

(23)   If a Prince amasses Wealth, to *hoard* it *up* **like Henry the seventh**, it is useless to Himself, and lost to the Publick; (*The Craftsman,* 1731)

Similarly, (23) is not about the manner of hoarding but about Henry VII being a good example of this course of action and its effects. Instead of adding precision or detail in adverbial manner, these comparisons call up an analogous case, often working with an assumed prototype (e.g. *like a thorow-pac'd Politician, like Alexander the Great, like a Christian Hero*) and use the verb as the explicit grounds for the comparison. The most important point here is, therefore, that the reader is rarely left to work out the point of the comparison on his or her own, this is provided in more or less detail by the writer. As (21) above illustrates, the authors usually add the grounds or explication also after copular comparisons.

Another interesting question connected both to the ease of understanding and to the aesthetic (or entertainment) value of comparison is that of the frequency of literal versus figurative types. While the more factual orientation of newspapers speaks for a preponderance of literal instances, the fairly common evaluative function, linked to persuasion, might also favour the use of figurative comparisons. On the whole, literal realisations are more common, with 97 per cent of all *as...as* and 67 per cent of all *like*-comparisons,[16] cf. the following two examples.

---

15. The situation with *as...as* is comparable, but as the grounds are already (partly) contained in the adjective or other form within the *as*-frame these comparisons are more explicit, so that the distinction is of somewhat less importance in this case.

16. This is paralleled almost precisely by the F-LOB data, 97 per cent literal for *as...as* and 71 per cent for *like*.

(24)   In the article of India goods the Dutch will be considerable losers, for their
trade to that part of the world, although **as great as ours**, yet did not furnish
more than half what was sufficient for their market:
(*The Morning Herald*, 1781)

(25)   The same Evening about Nine o'Clock, a Gentleman was attacked by three
Fellows dress'd **like Sailors**, in the Bird Cage Walk, armed with Bludgeons and
Pistols: (*General Advertiser*, 1751)

As literal comparisons involve no semantic clash, they are presumably clearer,
leave little to no room for misinterpretation and are thus easier to understand. In
(24) and (25) like is compared with like (amount of trade, human dress), so that
no complicated semantic transfer is necessary, nor any explanations on the part
of the writer. Literal instances like those above can carry information in an unambiguous way, which may often be a writer's primary intention.

If literal instances are in principle better suited to the conveying of information, figurative occurrences have a clear preference for evaluation, and also
tend to be more useful for ornamental/rhetorical and humoristic functions. Example (7) above, comparing Bolingbroke to a marble statue, is an evaluative case
in point, as are (26) and (27). Example (26) likens humans to mythical creatures
and combines this with the metaphor of *swallowing* the law. Here the comparison
contains nothing factually new; the information, or rather assessment, has been
given already in literal form and the figurative comparison, climax-like, sums up
the situation in an evaluation (cf. preceding *in a word*).

(26)   That the people are under terrible apprehensions that the law is perverted, that
Juries are deprived of their constitutional powers, that the Courts of Justice
are not sound and untainted; in a word, that the Judges have, **like a dozen of
monstrous Patagonian giants**, either swallowed, or are going to swallow up
both law and gospel. (*General Evening Post*, 1771)

(27)   The Famous King Philip the Second saw it possessed of an incredible
Grandeur, and yet upon the declining hand in his own Reign; and after a
Baulk in the Netherlands, and a Defeat at Sea, it was quickly ravish'd of a great
many of the richest and beautifullest of its Provinces, and Kingdoms, and now
remains **like a vast, insipid, and unuseful Trunk**.
(*The Weekly Remarks*, 1691)

We find the same sequence of literal information plus figurative evaluation in
(27), which points to a pattern. The figurative finish is stronger and more memorable than the points already unambiguously made, and thus makes for an overall
more convincing effect. An example of the fact that comparisons can also simply
be used for playful and humorous purposes is found in (28). Comparing a lady

and a weapon, this instance draws its special humour from the punning use of the verb "go off".

(28)   A PISTOL in the hands of CLEMENTINA PERRY would be absolutely a very dreadful weapon – were that same PISTOL at all **like the lady in its readiness to GO OFF**! (*Evening Mail*, 1791)

It is such uses as in (26) and (28), for instance, that contribute to the entertainment function of news discourse and that I would intuitively have expected to be more prominent. However, while individual examples are highly memorable – and thus may give the wrong impression as to their frequency – they are in fact rare in newspapers both in the past and the present.

There are also figurative instances which are almost literal, in the sense that they are conventionalised. Among these are *quick as lightning* in (5) above; *is not this Tenet, as dark as Pitch, as dead as Death*? (*Westminster Journal*, 1771); *as gentle as a lamb* (*Bingley's Journal*, 1771) and the intensifying *like*-cases quoted above (Section 4). This leads to the general question of how common conventional, non-creative usage of comparisons is in newspapers. Truly idiomatic instances, i.e. fixed phrases with a usually metaphoric origin, are in fact very rare (as textual uses of idioms seem to be in general, cf. Moon 1998). With *like*, only eight cases in all are found which may be called conventional, e.g. *like (flocks of) sheep, like fire*. Conventional items like these encapsulate to a certain extent the world-view and beliefs of a speech community and contain vehicles of high cognitive value (Norrick 1986: 40), which means that they could be used to present something as mutual knowledge or as a given, unquestionable assessment. One writer exploits the stable (and here negative) connotations of such items when he attacks a politician as someone who is "resolved to evade my question, and to slip out of my hands like an eel" (*The Craftsman*, 1771). With *as...as*, there are as few as nine cases, all with one intervening item which is part of the idiom, e.g. *as black as ebony*. The latter is used in an advertisement in conjunction with the contrasting *white as ivory* (*London Post*, 1701), to highlight the amazing workings of a dental cleaning powder. Again, standardized connotations are exploited. Clichés, or "stock similes" (Norrick 1986), are nevertheless fairly uncommon, which may be due to stylistic decisions.[17] Additionally, however, there are also a great number of *as...as* instances which will strike the reader as highly familiar as they are usages with an "everyday", almost colloquial flavour to them. These are cases like: they went *as far as place X*, they did *as much as they could*, it will be done *as fast as possible*, and something is *as good as any*. Such instances make up the bulk of the intensifying

---

17. Some modern press style guides include such cases in their lists of expressions to be avoided, e.g. *spread like wildfire* in the BBC style guide.

comparisons. Conventional cases of whichever kind could be said to make for easier, "undisturbed" reading, because nothing out of the ordinary is encountered to potentially make the reader pause. This type of easy reading is provided to a certain extent. Creative, or nonce-usages, in contrast, at least potentially make for more interesting and entertaining reading, as can be said of the figurative instances above. And, at the very least, they offer some new(ish) content, in contrast to many emphatic *as...as* comparisons.

As was mentioned in Section 4 above in the context of example (6), some comparisons require a degree of knowledge that might go beyond that commonly prevailing. These are somewhat risky because if the reader lacks the necessary knowledge s/he will also not fully understand the point of the comparison. There are a number of such comparisons found in the present data, much more commonly with *like* (15 per cent of all instances) than with *as...as* (1.8 per cent). The quote in (29), marked by rhetorical parallelism, presupposes that the reader knows (something about) these six persons from classical antiquity. Of course, one can argue that Brutus and the others simply stand as prototypes of the virtue expressed already by the adjective, so that all readers will get the gist. But some part of the comparison will nevertheless be lost for less knowledgeable readers. As (29) is a piece of argumentative prose, full comprehension would certainly be preferable.

(29)   In like Manner should, in any future Times, a like Crisis arise, for the Punishment of our Sins, [...] should then any Patriot *arise* **as moderate as Brutus, severe as Cato, eloquent as Cicero, temperate as Scipio, honest as Fabricius, and just as Aristides**, this great and excellent Person, would be instantly libell'd for the worst of bad Men, (*The Champion*, 1741)

(30)   But at present, it seems, they are in a posture **somewhat like that of Hobse's State of War**, and what will be the Upshot, we expect by another Post. (*The Impartial Protestant Mercury*, 1681)

The knowledge required in (30) is much closer to home, both in terms of time and space, as the work referred to, Hobbes' *Leviathan*, was published in 1651. The slightly toned down (cf. *somewhat*) hyperbole of (30), which deals with a household refusing to pay certain rates, is only understandable if one knows that Hobbes was describing the "natural" state of all mankind in the absence of any constraining governmental power ("warre, as if of every man, against every man").[18] The references in both (29) and (30) require a certain breadth of reading and level of education. As to reading capability, literacy levels during the period

---

18. Example (30) refers apparently to this quote and the surrounding passage in Part 1, Chapter 13 of the *Leviathan*.

in question were certainly on the rise. Around the middle of the seventeenth century, about 30 per cent of men and 20 per cent of women could read, while at the end of the eighteenth century more than 60 per cent of men and about 40 per cent of women were literate, according to Cressy (1980: 177). These figures may also imply a greater number of "good" readers, i.e. (far) beyond the elementary stages. Nevertheless, it cannot be assumed that everybody who could read (and did read newspapers) also had a high standard of education.

Some press writers paid attention to the fact that their readers might require more background information in order to understand some points. The comparison in (31), which likens poverty as a result of speculation and financial loss to killing, follows in the text only after the author had explained the story of the inhabitants of Capua killing their families and then themselves in the face of a Roman attack.

(31)   Was not this cutting the Throats of Wives and Children **as effectually as the Cipoans** (= the Capuans, CC) **did with their Daggers and Swords?** (*Post Man*, 1721)

(32)   We can only suppose that Mr. PITT means to settle the peace of Europe in detail, and, **like the Plasterer in Jot Miller,** *never to finish one job till he gets scent of another*; (*The Morning Chronicle*, 1791)[19]

In other cases, the necessary background knowledge is provided as the grounds for comparison in the same sentence as the *like-* or *as*-construction, as in the italicised part of (32). If one looks at all comparisons involving cultural knowledge, it turns out that as many as half of them make reference to aspects of classical antiquity (e.g. *Pelius's spear, the iron race of Cadmus, the archer in Diogenes*), perhaps reflecting what was seen as a common standard in education. If one takes this together with the relative rareness of the explanation function (cf. Table 1), it seems that newspapers were expecting their readers to be quite knowledgeable. Alternatively, or additionally, the classical comparison could also denote a certain pretentiousness on the part of newspaper writers, who were trying to emulate what they thought of as good writing. What is also noteworthy in this context is that, not uncommonly, something fairly trivial or something very modern (e.g. (30) and (31)) is graced with a far-removed classical or philosophical allusion. Furthermore, there are also references to English history and culture (e.g. *King Richard*; *Shakespeare's Apothecary*), to the Bible (e.g. *the man's five talents*), and to

---

19. The reference here may be to a book called *Joe Miller's Jests*, first published in 1739, borrowing the name from a then well-known actor but authored by somebody else. If this assumption is correct, the Plasterer will have been a character in one of the jokes in this book. Many such jokes will of course also have been part of every-day oral culture.

miscellaneous items (e.g. *the ancient Swedes*; *the Aetna*), but none of these groups is individually very frequent.

6.   Conclusion

What this paper has shown is that comparisons have a role to play in argumentative, persuasive news discourse, often in an unobtrusive, supportive role (cf. the many unspectacular *as*-comparisons) but sometimes also in a more prominent way (e.g. figurative and culturally-loaded comparisons with greater rhetorical force). Partly, this is due to the fact that many comparisons highlight or create common ground between the writer and the reader. Argumentative functions, in the widest sense, even dominate in news writing, thus contributing to debate and the creation of public opinion rather than to the imparting of information. Many comparisons are, moreover, found in constructions and contexts where they are not, strictly speaking, "necessary", that is they represent a conscious (stylistic or content) choice on the part of the journalist. Nevertheless they are not as frequent as they are nowadays, so that the suggestion, made at the beginning of the paper, that a rhetorically conscious age might employ similes to a greater extent, has not been supported. An explanation for this might be found in a point neglected so far, namely a certain "anti-oral" attitude noticeable in the eighteenth century (McIntosh 1998: 34ff.; Biber and Finegan 1989). Many comparisons have an oral flavour, as witnessed by the examples provided above (and also by their similar or identical frequency in modern conversation and press language), which may lead to their less frequent use by writers with more "literate" tendencies. Furthermore, newspaper language was a new, emerging register, and registers tend to "evolve to become even more distinct from speech over the first 100–200 years of their history" (Biber 1995: 297). In Biber (2001), a multi-dimensional analysis of eighteenth-century texts, news figures on Dimension 1 as the most 'informational' type next to legal prose. Whether this was in fact de-oralization of press language would of course need further research (Schneider 2002 points to increasing sentence and word length during the eighteenth century).

Sources

F-LOB, Freiburg 1991 clone of the LOB Corpus, compiled by Christian Mair et al. In Knut Hofland, Anne Lindebjerg and Jørn Thunestvedt (eds.). *ICAME Collection of English Language Corpora* (CD-Rom), 2nd edition, the HIT Centre, University of Bergen, Norway.

Lampeter Corpus of English Tracts. 1999. Compiled by Claudia Claridge, Josef Schmied and Rainer Siemund. In Knut Hofland, Anne Lindebjerg and Jørn Thunestvedt (eds.). *ICAME Collection of English Language Corpora* (CD-Rom), 2nd edition, the HIT Centre, University of Bergen, Norway.

ZEN, *Zurich English Newspaper Corpus*, Version 1.0. 2004. Compiled by Udo Fries, Hans Martin Lehmann et al. Zürich: University of Zürich.

References

Addison, Catherine. 2001. "So stretched out huge in length": Reading the extended simile. *Style* 35.3, 498–516.

Biber, Douglas. 1995. *Dimensions of Register Variation: A Cross-linguistic Comparison.* Cambridge: Cambridge University Press.

Biber, Douglas. 2001. Dimensions of variation among 18th-century registers. In Hans-Jürgen Diller and Manfred Görlach (eds.). *Towards a History of English as a History of Genres.* Heidelberg: Winter, 89–109.

Biber, Douglas, and Edward Finegan. 1989. Drift and the evolution of English style: A history of three genres. *Language* 65, 487–517.

Biber, Douglas, Stig Johansson, Geoffrey Leech, Susan Conrad and Edward Finegan. 1999. *Longman Grammar of Spoken and Written English.* London: Longman.

Blair, Hugh. 1783. *Lectures on Rhetoric and Belles Lettres.* Dublin Whitestone etc. (accessed via Eighteenth Century Collections Online, URL: http://galenet.galegroup.com).

Bonham-Carter, Victor. 1978. *Authors by Profession.* Volume I. London (n.p.).

Burger, Harald. 2005. *Mediensprache.* 3rd edition. Berlin: Mouton de Gruyter.

Claridge, Claudia. 2006. Comparison in 19th-century non-fictional prose. In Christoph Houswitschka, Gabriele Knappe and Anja Müller (eds.). *Anglistentag 2005 Bamberg: Proceedings. Proceedings of the Conference of the German Association of University Teachers of English*, Volume XXVII. Trier: Wissenschaftlicher Verlag Trier, 501–514.

Cressy, David. 1980. *Literacy and the Social Order. Reading and Writing in Tudor and Stuart England.* Cambridge: Cambridge University Press.

Downie, J. A. 1987. The development of the political press. In Clyve Jones (ed.). *Britain in the First Age of Party, 1680–1750: Essays Presented to Geoffrey Holmes.* London and Ronceverte: The Hambledon Press, 111–127.

Feather, John. 1988. *A History of British Publishing.* London and New York: Croom Helm.

Fishelov, David. 2007. Shall I compare thee? Simile understanding and semantic categories. *Journal of Literary Semantics* 36, 71–87.

Fries, Udo, and Peter Schneider. 2000. ZEN: Preparing the Zurich English Newspaper Corpus. In Friedrich Ungerer (ed.). *English Media Texts Past and Present: Language and Textual Structure.* Amsterdam and Philadelphia: Benjamins, 3–24.

Harris, Richard Jackson, and Noah Jacob Mosier. 1999. Memory for metaphors and similes in discourse. *Discourse Processes* 28.3, 257–270.

Huddleston, Rodney, and Geoffrey K. Pullum. 2002. *The Cambridge Grammar of the English Language.* Cambridge: Cambridge University Press.

McIntosh, Carey. 1998. *The Evolution of English Prose, 1700–1800.* Cambridge: Cambridge University Press.

Moon, Rosamund. 1998. *Fixed Expressions and Idioms in English. A corpus-based approach.* Oxford: Clarendon Press.

Norrick, Neal. 1986. Stock similes. *Journal of Literary Semantics* 15.1, 39–52.

Ortony, Andrew. 1979. The role of similarity in similes and metaphors. In Andrew Ortony (ed.). *Metaphor and Thought.* Cambridge: Cambridge University Press, 186–201.

Quirk, Randolph, Sidney Greenbaum, Geoffrey Leech and Jan Svartvik. 1985. *A Comprehensive Grammar of the English Language.* London: Longman.

Schneider, Kristina. 2002. *The Development of Popular Journalism in England from 1700 to the Present.* PhD thesis: Rostock University.

Siebert, Fredrick Seaton. 1965. *Freedom of the Press in England, 1476–1776.* Urbana: University of Illinois Press.

Sommerville, John. 1996. *The News Revolution in England. Cultural Dynamics of Daily Information.* New York and Oxford: Oxford University Press.

Wikberg, Kay. 1999. The style marker *as if (though).* In Hilde Hasselgard and Signe Oksefiell (eds.). *Out of Corpora: Studies in Honour of Stig Johansson.* Amsterdam: Rodopi, 93–105.

"Place yer bets" and "Let us hope"

Imperatives and their pragmatic functions in news reports

Birte Bös

1. Introduction

As experienced newspaper readers, we are familiar with headlines like "Place yer bets" (2006 *Sun*) or "Let us hope" (1930 *Daily Mirror*), which are apparently directed individually to us. With their oral tone, headlines like these are supposed to both grab readers' attention and set their expectations.

The examples show that the use of imperatives in news writing is no invention of the twenty-first century. More than 40 years ago, Leech, in his seminal book on advertising, pointed out that (just like interrogatives) imperatives are "stimuli which normally require an active response from the addressee" (1966: 111) and are thus very useful in establishing rapport. Even earlier, imperatives were listed by Flesch (1949: 94f.) among what he called "personal sentences" and described as "really nothing but a one-sided conversational exchange between author and reader". That the communicative situation is definitely more complex than indicated in this quotation is one of the aspects discussed in this paper.

The use of imperatives is obviously in line with the trend to personalization in mass media communication (cf. e.g. Fairclough 1989: 195). A random investigation of 60 modern British newspapers[1] shows an abundance of imperatives in the service section, which has apparently become increasingly important in the

---

1. The collection, which I assembled for comparative purposes, consists of ten samples each from the following national newspapers: *The Times, The Guardian, The Daily Mail, The Daily Express, The Sun, The Daily Mirror* (2003–2006).

past decades.[2] Here, the reader is given advice on a range of topics. For example, regarding financial matters, it is recommended that the reader:

(1)   Make certain your capital is guaranteed / Preferably stick to a well-publicised index… / Check the growth being offered / Stick to bonds lasting five years… (2004 *Daily Mail*)

The illocutionary force of such imperatives differs clearly from examples such as "Place yer bets", which introduces a news story on Britain's first super-casino and does not function as a real instruction.

Leaving aside the rather straightforward imperatives in the service section, the question arises whether the use of imperatives in the news section goes back further than the twentieth century. In order to investigate tendencies in the development of imperatives, the *Rostock Newspaper Corpus* (RNC), a collection of news reports from 1700 to 2000, will be analyzed. First, some quantitative results will be provided. However, the major focus will be on the qualitative analysis of the corpus data.

Furthermore, the material retrieved from the RNC will be used for the discussion of some questions of a more general nature. An investigation of the relevant literature has given rise to the impression that there is a terminological muddle regarding the characterization of imperatives, often resulting from a confusion of formal and functional aspects. Trying to tackle this problem, I will provide a brief formal description of imperatives in Section 4. The detailed pragmatic discussion in Section 5 will focus on the diverging illocutionary forces of imperatives and take account of the various communicative constellations observed in the corpus.

2.   Preparing the analysis: The communicative situation in newspapers

In order to prepare the pragmatic analysis of imperatives in newspapers, Figure 1 provides a basic model of the communicative situation (cf. also Bös 2007).

As the simplified model shows, three major parties are involved. Authors and editors both take part in the relatively complex production process of news. In some cases, the personal correspondence style of early news reports allows for a distinction of authorial and editorial voice. However, especially in the more modern newspapers, it is mostly not possible to distinguish them. In these cases, they

---

2.   "Reader-friendliness" was already a buzz-word in the 1990s (cf. Kurtz 1993:65). A stronger service orientation is considered part of the newspapers' reaction to the ever-growing competition in the media market.

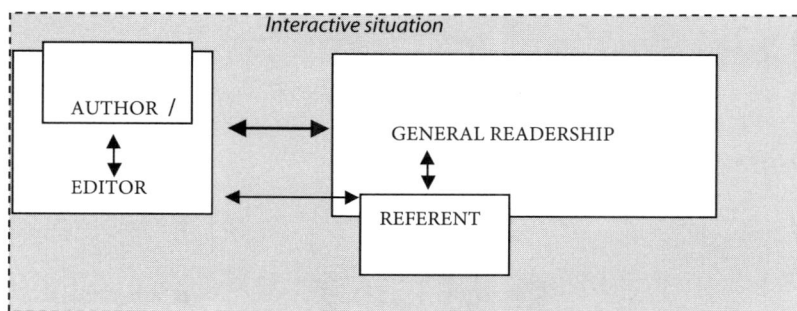

Figure 1. Basic model of newspaper communication

are represented as one entity (Author/Editor) in this paper. Generally, the major target of newspapers is the readership, which undoubtedly is a heterogeneous group. It is clear that newspapers, just like other texts, aim at a kind of model reader, i.e. the average reader according to readership profiles, who represents the General Readership. The third entity in this model is the Referent, i.e. those people involved in news events, described and cited in the news stories. As Figure 1 shows, the Referents are often part of the potential readership.

The arrows illustrate that General Readership and Referents can also be taken as participating in, or influencing, the news production process, either indirectly (e.g. by playing out their purchasing power) or directly (e.g. by launching news via spin doctors and press agencies). What is relevant in the context of this paper is that General Readership and Referents are also given a voice at times, with imitated first-person quotations.

3.   Imperatives in the RNC: Quantitative results

The RNC comprises 600,000 words; it consists of ten 60,000-word samples taken in 30- or 40-year-intervals from six British newspapers per period (i.e. 10,000 words per paper).[3] My working hypothesis is that the frequency of imperatives would have steadily increased through the centuries owing to a rising portion of direct quotations and the growing tendency of personalization. The actual findings are presented in Figure 2.

In the 1700 and 1730 samples, no imperatives were found. The first imperative in the RNC dates back to the 1760 edition of the *Morning Post*. Figure 2 shows that from that time, until the middle of the nineteenth century, the number

---

3. For more details on the corpus size and compilation cf. Schneider (2002: 48–58).

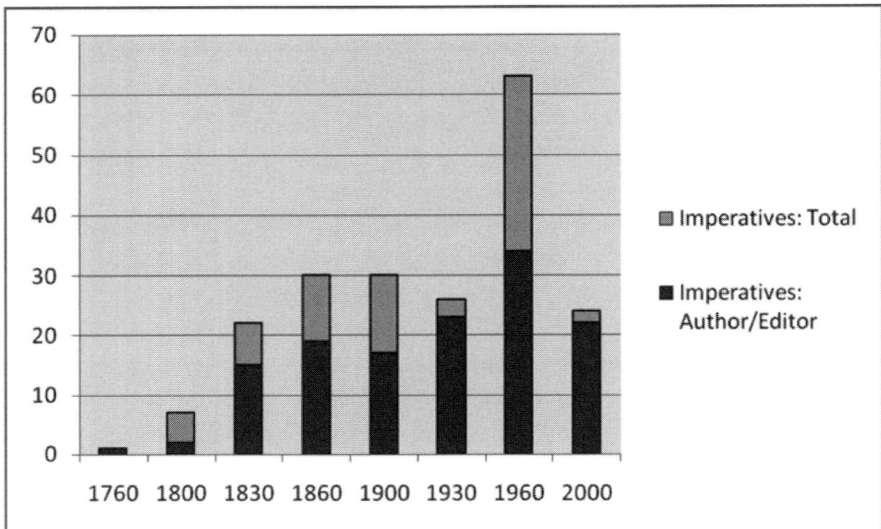

Figure 2. Imperatives in the RNC

continually increased, but the rise which was expected for the twentieth century could not be confirmed. In fact, the figures are even decreasing slightly, with the exception of the sample from 1960. There, however, 17 of the 63 instances were found in one article which has to be regarded as a borderline case of soft news and service information as it presents various pieces of advice to the reader.

Considering the cotext of our examples, we find that – as expected – most of them actually appear in direct quotations whose number has multiplied over the centuries (cf. Bös forthc.). The following extract from an early crime report illustrates this usage:

(2)   The man immediately said, "I must have that watch and your money, Sir, so don't make a noise". (1800 *London Evening Post*)

However, the usage of imperatives in quotations is certainly not representative of news reports in general. If we focus exclusively on the authorial/editorial material, as represented in the darker shaded part of the column, and sort out the instances of imperatives which represent spoken utterances from quotations, the picture changes to some extent[4]. Here, the number of imperatives increases slowly, but steadily (with the exception of 1900), but it drops in 2000. Thus, the apparent

---

4.   Additionally, these figures have been cleared from some minor exceptions like song or film titles, and compounds such as *get-well-soon messages*.

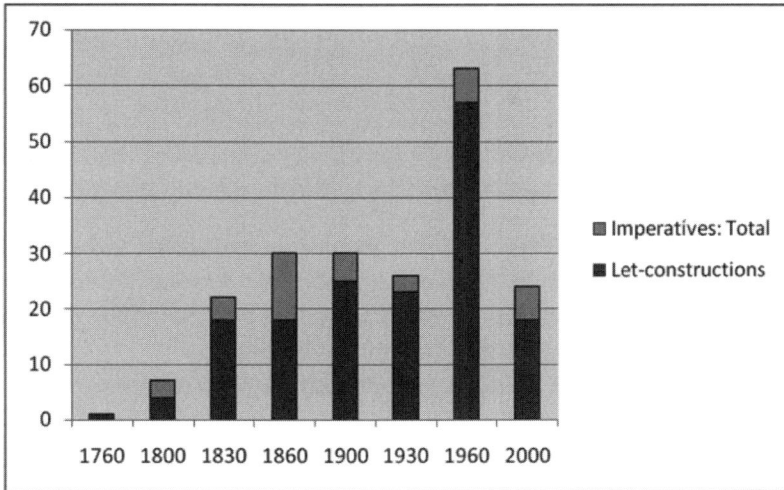

Figure 3. *Let*-constructions in the RNC

ubiquity of imperatives in modern newspapers is not supported by our findings. Imperatives may seem so frequent to modern readers because they tend to occur in prominent positions (predominantly headlines) and in genres other than news reports.

Looking at the examples from the RNC more closely, another finding proves interesting: roughly 20 per cent of the instances are constructions of the following type (cf. Figure 3):

(3) Let us hear no more of French generosity. (1800 *London Evening Post*)

(4) Let the reader mark the enthusiasm with which certain great French families have rallied about Lamoricière… (1860 *Lloyd's Weekly Newspaper*)

(5) …let me say that I am as pleased as they can be. (1960 *Daily Mirror*)

Let-constructions have been treated very ambiguously in the literature, and they are certainly worth some further examination. In the following sections, I will therefore provide a more differentiated account of "ordinary" imperatives and *let*-constructions, and their forms and functions in the RNC.

4.   Formal aspects: "Ordinary" imperatives and *let*-constructions

There seems to be agreement about the basic formal characteristics of imperatives of the following kind:

(6)   "Follow me". (1930 *Daily Mail*)

They lack a surface subject (apart from occasional uses of *you*), use the base form of the verb, and contain no modals, tense or aspect markers (e.g. Davies 1986: 5ff.; Biber et al. 1999: 219; Quirk et al. 1985: 827; Swales et al. 1998: 100). This can be considered the prototypical form of imperatives in English.

The question is how to categorize and describe constructions involving *let* (cf. examples (3)–(5)). Although they do not in all cases fit the formal definition of imperatives in the narrow sense, i.e. "sentences with an understood second person subject" (cf. König/Siemund 1985: 21), they are commonly listed under "Imperatives". Very often, they are considered "special types" within that category.

Constructions with *let* and *let's* have been analyzed in diverging ways. In early studies, *let* is, for example, considered a full lexical verb (e.g. Costa 1972) or modal auxiliary (Seppänen 1977). Later contributions focus on the usage of *let's* as invariant pragmatic particle (e.g. Quirk et al. 1985; Biber et al. 1999). Here, a more fine-grained classification appears necessary.

Huddleston and Pullum (2002: 924f.) differentiate two subtypes of *let*-constructions: first-person inclusive versus open *let*-imperatives. The former type is presented by instances like:

(7)   Let's have a rollover in the hay! (2000 *Sun*)

(8)   Shameful, but don't let's be unjust to Germans. (1960 *Daily Express*)

Examples like these are also called *let's*-constructions (cf. Clark 1993: 188), and they are grammatically distinguishable from ordinary imperatives. They allow for the contraction of *us* to *'s*, *you*-insertion is not possible, tag questions are formed with *shall we?/will we?* (instead of *will you?/won't you?*), and negation can be formed either with *do not/don't* or just with *not* without changing the semantic scope (cf. Huddleston and Pullum 2002: 934f.). Hopper and Traugott (2003: 10ff.) present *let's*-constructions as typical cases of grammaticalization, pointing out that *let us* has shifted to monomorphematic *lets* and thus functions as invariant pragmatic particle in some varieties. In other varieties, however, it "still shares a number of syntactic properties with the lexical *let* in its fossilized syntax but is semantically moving away from it" (De Clerck, 2004: 217).

In the RNC, cliticized forms only start to occur in the 1960 editions, and their use is restricted to direct quotations (or imitated ones, as in (7) and (8), both headlines from popular newspapers). More commonly, the more formal *let us* is applied, as demonstrated by the headline presented in the title of this paper:

(9)   Let us hope. (1930 *Daily Mirror*)

These non-contracted *let*-constructions are ambiguous in that their surface structure is not distinct from ordinary imperatives with *let* + second person addressee (in the sense of: 'Allow us to hope, will you?').

Open *let*-imperatives, the second subtype postulated by Huddleston and Pullum (2002), comprise examples of the following kind (cf. also example (4)):

(10)   Let the Italians think more of their strength than of their weakness…
       (1860 *Times*)

(11)   Justice has been done, let clemency begin with the New Year.
       (1900 *Daily Mail*)

(12)   …let it be plainly understood… (1960 *Daily Express*)

They mostly involve third-person reference, but cases involving first-person reference are also possible, though rather rare (cf. Collins' (2003: 4) findings on open *let*-imperatives, and Kohnen's (2004) study on *let me*-constructions)[5]. These *let*-constructions share some characteristics with the first-person inclusive type (no insertion of *you* as subject, similar negation patterns, but no interrogative tags). In contrast to ordinary imperatives and first-person inclusives, there seems to be a greater acceptance of stative and passive verb phrases (cf. Collins 2003: 5). However, generally speaking, the distinction of open *let*-imperatives from ordinary imperatives appears to be "a matter of meaning and use rather than form" (Huddleston and Pullum 2002: 937).

5.   Pragmatic analysis of imperatives

5.1   General characteristics

Generally, imperatives are attributed a wide range of illocutionary forces. They conventionally realize directives, i.e. they count as "attempts […] by the speaker to get the hearer to do something" (Searle 1976: 9). As Leech puts it, "they all, in

---

5.   Both studies are corpus-based. Collins analyzes *ICAME* materials (cf. 2003: 1, Fn. 3 for a complete list) and ICE-AUS. Kohnen's diachronic study (2004) is based on the *Helsinki Corpus* and backed up with data from the *Middle English Dictionary*, the *Oxford English Dictionary*, and a sampler version of the *British National Corpus*.

some respect or other, present the propositional content as a candidate for fulfill-
ment by [the hearer]" (1983:117). However, they can display varying degrees of
strength. For example, orders and commands strongly call for compliance, whereas the force gradually decreases in requests, recommendations, instructions and
invitations.

 Let-constructions display a more narrow range of functions. They can be used
in the prototypical way described above, as the following plea by the victim of a
spouse murder illustrates:

> (13)   She said, "Joe, you let me alone and do no more; I'll go all the way with you,
> and I'll not punish you". (1860 *Lloyd's Weekly Newspaper*)

However, for the most part, let-constructions are not directives aimed at a
second-person addressee, but rather marginal members of the directive class
(cf. Huddleston and Pullum 2002:936). First-person inclusive *let*-imperatives
(*let us/let's*) are commonly considered as proposals for joint action by speaker
and addressee, but there are some cases which diverge from the cohortative usage. Thus, *let's* can also be speaker-oriented and function e.g. as a (self-)exhorta-
tive announcement. Or it can be addressee-oriented, carrying a "second person
quasi-imperative meaning" (Biber et al. 1999:1117; cf. De Clerck 2004:218f.).

 The force of open *let*-imperatives is often optative or "deontic-assertive" and,
in such cases, they are roughly paraphrasable as 'may' or 'should', respectively
(Collins 2003:5f.). Although they define some future action and call for compliance, they often do not have a specific addressee, or the referent is not present in
the context of the situation (cf. Huddleston and Pullum 2002:936). This feature
probably facilitates their usage in written communication.

 As Swales et al. (1998) point out in their study on academic texts, imperatives
fulfill a range of functions in written discourse which go beyond that of bald-on
record directives. They are seen as "complex textual signals by which academic
writers manipulate various rhetorical strategies" (Swales et al. 1998:99). The data
from the RNC indicate that newspaper communication shows an even more varied use of imperatives, which results from the various possible communicative
constellations. Thus, before the functions of imperatives are presented in detail, it
appears necessary to list the major communicative combinations observed in the
use of imperatives in the RNC.

5.2   Communicative constellations

Basic constellation (A) includes only speaker and addressee; it thus represents the
relevant communicative roles in the case of ordinary imperatives (including ordi-

nary imperatives with *let* + second person addressee) and *let*-constructions which contain a first-person pronoun in the slot after *let* (for ease of reference, this slot will henceforth be called the "*let*-entity"). The interesting question is who fills the roles of speaker and addressee in our examples of newspaper communication. Table 1 summarizes the combinations found in the RNC.

Table 1. Distribution of speaker and addressee roles in the RNC

Communicative constellation	Examples
AUTHOR/EDITOR → READER	(14) Find Death Wish Fiend (2000 *Sun*)
	(15) …let me say… (1960 *Daily Mail*)
	(16) Let us hope (1930 *Daily Mirror*)
AUTHOR/EDITOR → REFERENT	(17) Arise Sir 1965 (1960 *Sun*)
REFERENT → (CO-)REFERENT	(18) "Give the poor devil something"
	(1900 *Daily Mail*)
	(19) "Let's kill the bastard" (2000 *Daily Mirror*)
REFERENT → AUTHOR/EDITOR	(20) "Tell the British People…" (1900 *Daily Express*)
	(21) "…let's face it…" (2000 *Daily Mail*)
REFERENT → READER	(22) "Look," he would say… (1900 *Daily Sketch*)
READER → REFERENT	(23) Sign here, please (1960 *Daily Mail*)
	(24) Let's have a rollover in the hay! (2000 *Sun*)

That the Author/Editor addresses the General Readership is certainly the most prototypical pattern in newspaper communication (cf. examples (14)–(16)). However, it is not uncommon that the Author/Editor directs to the Referent (17). This is particularly frequent in soft news and – as the comparison with the modern corpus (cf. Fn. 1) shows – in personal columns. With this usage, the Author/Editor feigns a personal relationship with the Referent, which often appears notably intimate (as implied, for example, by the use of endearment terms and nicknames, cf. Bös 2007). In a wider sense, however, the intention is to draw the reader's attention to the respective article, of course. Thus, communication takes place on two levels.

Examples in which the Referent takes over the role of the speaker usually occur in quotations. As quotations often reflect spoken discourse between Referents, a wide range of directives can be found which are addressed to co-referents of the article ((18) and (19), cf. also Table 3 in the next section). Additionally, a few of the instances discovered in the corpus can be related to the interview situation, in which Referent and Author interacted with each other (cf. (20) and (21)). Of course, imperatives in quotations are only (more or less faithfully) reproduced and not generated by the Author/Editor. However, they are often consciously selected for certain stylistic purposes and thus they contribute to the specific quality of the news report (cf. Bös forthc.).

This effect shows particularly in quotations which are not genuine. In some cases in the corpus, it is quite obvious that the voice of the Referent is an imitated one. Example (22), for instance, represents the speech of a fictitious Martian who talks to the Reader (cf. the discussion in 5.3.3). Other cases are more ambiguous.

Clearly, the instances in which the Reader directs to the Referent are fabricated by the Author/Editor. Example (23) makes reference to a picture which shows the comic Harry Secombe signing autographs. Again, this is a case of multiple addressing, since also these imitated first-person quotations are effective attention getters for readers, particularly when used in headlines.

The cases covered by basic constellation (A) display varying orientations when it comes to the question of who is responsible for the realization of the future act defined in the propositional content. Obviously, ordinary imperatives are addressee-oriented. The *let's*-examples found in the corpus illustrate the prototypical inclusiveness of that construction, although, generally, the focus is variable and speaker- or addressee-orientation is possible as well (as pointed out in the previous section). *Let*-constructions which involve a first-person singular pronoun are naturally speaker-oriented.

Basic constellation (B) is special insofar as it introduces a third party in addition to speaker and addressee. This communicative constellation represents open *let*-imperatives, more specifically, cases where the *let*-entity contains some third-person reference. The *let*-entity can either be realized by a concrete entity, or (an occurrence that is more frequent in the RNC) an abstract one, i.e. an "entity strictly incapable of actualizing a potential situation" (Collins 2003: 6).[6]

Interestingly, speaker/addressee-variation is less common here than in constellation (A). Mostly, this kind of *let*-construction is applied by the Author/Editor and directed to the Reader. Rarely, examples from quotations display the Referent as the producer. Thus, a further differentiation of speaker and addressee roles does not appear necessary here. Instead, Table 2 provides some examples with various realizations of *let*-entities.

---

6. Additionally, at least spoken communication allows for further differentiation, depending on whether the party represented in the *let*-entity is present in the actual communicative situation (and thus able to realize the future act proposed) or not. As the differentiation is not as clear-cut in written mass media communication, it is neglected here.

Table 2. Realizations of third party *let*-entities

Let-entity	Examples
Concrete	(25) Let the reader mark the enthusiasm with which certain great French families have rallied about Lamoricière… (1860 *Lloyd's Weekly Newspaper*)
	(26) Let the Temps speak for itself (1900 *Times*)
Unspecified	(27) "Let any person, familiar with the constitution of the Catholic community in the metropolis, look over this document and say whether it does not faithfully represent the sentiments of the Catholics of Dublin". (1860 *Morning Post*)
Abstract	(28) Justice has been done, let clemency begin with the New Year. (1900 *Daily Mail*)

Returning to the question of agentivity, these *let*-constructions diverge. Obviously, concrete entities are, at least hypothetically, able to fulfill the propositional content. Example (25) presents a special case, in that the third party specified in the *let*-entity and the addressee of the speech act are identical. So, technically, the construction displays basic constellation (B), pragmatically, however, there are only two parties involved. After all, it is the reader who is asked in an indirect way to pay attention to a certain fact. This usage creates some polite distance between the Author/Editor and Reader, and, contradicting the tendencies for personalization and direct address, it appears rather archaic from a modern perspective.

Example (26) introduces a quotation from a French newspaper and is also special, involving personification. However, this construction is perfectly common in everyday interaction (e.g. "Let Peter speak for himself"), and the responsibility for the future act lies clearly with the third party given in the *let*-entity. The same is true for the (hypothetical) agent represented by the unspecified entity in example (27). Cases with abstract *let*-entities (cf. (28)) illustrate that agentivity is not always clear in open *let*-imperatives. Here, it is not the third party which is capable of the realization of the desired future act, but – in the case of our example – the addressee again.

When it comes to passive constructions, the *let*-entity definitely denotes a "patient". Again, concrete and abstract entities are possible, and often dummies such as *it* occur:

(29) Let however the main question be decided – let it be understood that the Colony is to be given up, a Colony fertile only in disease, vice and death… (1830 *Morning Post*)

5.3   Detailed account of pragmatic functions

The examples provided so far illustrate that, in newspapers, imperatives are not always applied as real calls for action, but often as stylistic or text structuring devices. In the following section, I will present evidence for both groups and discuss some borderline cases.

5.3.1   Calls for action (non-text-related)

As pointed out earlier, the widest range of genuine calls for action, which are not text-related, is represented in quotations reflecting spoken interaction. Accordingly, Referent-(Co)Referent interaction contributes the largest group of examples. Table 3 provides selected examples from the RNC. As far as form is concerned, the list includes both ordinary imperatives and *let*-constructions. The data are classified according to their illocutionary force.

Table 3. Illocutionary range of calls for action (non-text-related)

Orders/commands/ demands	(30)	"Soldiers, repair to your quarters instantly, and prepare for an immediate march!" (1800 *Morning Post*)
	(31)	"Let me go, I'll do for him yet!" (1860 *Manchester Guardian*)
Pleas/requests	(32)	"Daddy, please don't leave me" (2000 *Daily Mail*)
	(33)	"Joe, you let me alone and do no more" (1860 *Lloyd's Weekly Newspaper*)
Advice/recommendations	(34)	"Do not walk home alone". (1960 *Daily Express*)
Invitations	(35)	"Do sit down, and I will tell you about it". (1860 *Lloyd's Weekly Newspaper*)
Permission	(36)	"Never mind us to-day; attend to the poor bairns; they need more attention than we do. Don't trouble about us for the next 24 hours. We are alright". (1930 *Daily Sketch*)
Warnings	(37)	"Just be very careful with what you are going to do". (2000 *Daily Mirror*)
Challenges	(38)	"Don't you think another row would be desirable? Just attempt one!" (1860 *Lloyd's Weekly Newspaper*)
Insults	(39)	"Stick your award up your jacksie". (2000 *Sun*)
Proposals for joint action	(40)	"Let's kill the bastard" (2000 *Daily Mirror*)

The examples in Table 3 display various illocutionary forces. The directive force is very strong in the command postulated in a military context (30) and the outcry of a murderer in example (31). The Referents who are the producers of (32) and (33), a child and a victim of crime, are apparently in a less powerful position than the producers of (30) and (31), and they strongly appeal to their co-referents, the father or husband, respectively. However, they are not in a position to control the future activities of the addressees.

The advice presented in (34) is special, again, insofar as it is attributed rather generally to the "police" and directed to "[t]housands of young girls and women at New Year's Eve parties in Birmingham". We could conclude that this is another case of multiple addressing, since there are probably many readers who would feel directly addressed and take this as a piece of advice for their own good. This is supported by the graphical presentation of the quotation, which is set apart from the rest of the body copy by capitals. The example aptly illustrates the fact that quotations are often cleverly selected and the illocutionary force of cited imperatives is not exclusively limited to the original speech situation.

Example (35) presents the prototypical case of a bald-on-record imperative functioning as a polite invitation. Here, Leech's Tact Maxim (1983: 107) with its cost-benefit considerations comes into play, which indicates that the higher the benefit to the addressee, the less problematic are direct speech acts like (35). The speaker-oriented counterpart of the Tact Maxim, the Generosity Maxim, proves useful in the interpretation of the directives in (36). They display a considerable degree of munificence on the speaker's part and could, in fact, be specified as "altruistic permission". The quotation comes from a group of hospital patients who generously step down in favor of the young victims of a disastrous cinema fire.

The groups warnings (example (37)) and challenges (example (38)) are distinguishable from the directives discussed so far in that they search for non-compliance of the proposed act. Likewise, an insult such as (39) is highly unlikely to be realized by the addressee, a co-referent of the producer.

Finally, the list in Table 3 includes an example of a first-person inclusive imperative which represents a proposal for some joint future action. Depending on the relation of the participants and the communicative situation, directives like these can again exert a varying force of compliance.

5.3.2 Borderline cases

Author/Editor-generated imperatives (including imitated quotations) display a rather different range of functions which is certainly more restricted than that of imperatives in quotations. As mentioned above, there are some cases of real advice, which have to be mostly attributed, however, to borderline cases of soft news and service information (cf. the interpretation of quantitative results in Section 3).

What is more typical is that the Author/Editor produces some kind of pseudo-advice, as illustrated by the following headlines:

(41)   Sniff before you buy. (1960 *Sun*)

(42)   Have a day by the sea in London. (1960 *Daily Express*)

Number (41) precedes an article on the use of odorants as a marketing instrument in shops; example (42) introduces a report about the opening of a national boat show. Although they still display some qualities of genuine calls for action and could be taken as instances of advice to the Reader, their status appears ambiguous. Since, as headlines, they occur in isolation, it is not exactly clear from the beginning who addresses whom. This ambiguity is, of course, intentional. The detachment of such utterances facilitates their function as an attention getter, as the Reader will probably be keen to figure out who is addressed and what the headline relates to.

In fact, there are many cases in which not only the addressee, but also the speaker is unclear. The corpus yields a considerable number of imitated or at least modified quotations which can only be interpreted after reading the article.

(43)   Passports, please. (1960 *Sun*)

(44)   "Make room". (1960 *Daily Express*)

In (43), an elliptic example, the Author/Editor imitates the voice of a publican who had sent some misfits away, claiming "[t]he way things are going nowadays, you soon won't be able to get into some pubs without a visa" (1960 *Sun*). The heading presented in (44) is generated from a Referent's quotation ("we have to make room for new subjects") in the body copy of an article propagating the elimination of Latin as a school subject. As with many other examples, this heading is, by intention, semantically and pragmatically opaque.

5.3.3   *Imperatives with textual functions*
Many of the imperatives found in the RNC take over textual functions. A part still display some directive force, others can be considered as non-directive examples. Starting with the former, some cases of expository directives are presented in (45) and (46).

(45)   Consider the heating arrangement of the ordinary, comfortable house... (1900 *Daily Sketch*)

(46)   "Look," he would say, "you have in two or three rooms of your house a little fire..." [...] "Think of the amount of heat which is going away up your chimneys. Why is not that used? Why are you so wasteful?" (1900 *Daily Sketch*)

Example (45) shows a construction which is also commonly found in academic writing (cf. Swales et al. 1998): it asks for compliance in following a certain exposition. The communicative constellation is quite easily recognizable here: it is the Author/Editor who develops the argument for the Reader. Obviously, expository directives like these are used to achieve the active participation of the Reader.

What is interesting in examples (45) and (46) is that they both come from the same article. After the initial sentences, the Author/Editor changes his/her stance and takes the perspective of a fictitious Martian, as we saw earlier (cf. (22)). By resorting to this special Referent's voice the Author/Editor takes the opportunity to avoid responsibility for the argumentation. Next to some more expository directives, the Martian asks the Reader a number of rather challenging questions. With its combination of imperatives and interrogatives and its specifically constructed communicative constellation, this article provides an example of exceptional directness at the start of the twentieth century. In the following cases, the directive force is considerably weaker or even non-existent:

(47)   Let there be free competition between East and West. (1960 *Daily Express*)

(48)   Take, we say, what can be got; but endeavour, at the same time, to get as much as possible… (1830 *Bell's Life in London*)

Here, the addressees remain unclear. Example (47) is a formulaic expression of a wish or hope of the Author/Editor; *let* can easily be replaced by *may*. Example (48) expresses the Author/Editor's opinion rather than asking for compliance with respect to certain acts. In seeking agreement and creating common ground with the Reader, first-person inclusives appear particularly suitable (cf. (49)).

(49)   But while the penalty of death remains, let us summon to our assistance enough of common sense to carry the law into effect with as much dignity and decency as it is possible under the circumstances. Let us cease to fatten murderers for the gallows as oxen for market... (1860 *Lloyd's Weekly Newspaper*)

However, imperatives are also applied for stylistic variation, for example, in order to avoid "(yet) another conditional sentence" (Swales et al. 1998: 115). These are what Jespersen called "imaginary imperatives" (1992: 315), and they are clearly used non-directively (cf. (50) and (51)). Notably, there seems to be a preference by quality newspapers for this usage.

(50)   Put on your waterproof and walk through the camp, on this, a wet Sunday, on the hills of Ceuta, and you shall hear no complaint… (1860 *Times*)

(51)   …let there be men to stand up for the country, and the cause of the country will triumph. (1860 *Times*)

Another quite prominent function of imperatives in the corpus is that of thematic structuring. In initiating new topics or introducing comments or quotations, often *let*-constructions are applied (cf. examples (52)–(54)):

(52) Let us now advert briefly to the performances themselves.
      (1860 *Manchester Guardian*)

(53) Let us endeavour to make a sensible and free remark on this event.
      (1800 *World*)

(54) ...let me say that I am as pleased as they can be. (1960 *Daily Mail*)

With the choice of *let us*-constructions ((52) and (53)), the Author/Editor presents the text as a "joint enterprise", although the "illocutionary force as a proposal for joint action is fairly weak and secondary to their use as idiomatic overtures, hesitation markers and pragmatic formatives" (De Clerck 2004: 227).

With the construction presented in (54), the Author/Editor displays audience sensitivity, marking his/her comment and involving the Reader. As Kohnen (2004: 166f.) points out, this combination of *let me* with a representative speech act verb has become quite frequent since it was introduced in the Early Modern English period. It can be considered a strategy of politeness, a conventionalized way of paying respect to the Reader's negative face.

My account of textual functions of imperatives in news reports will be closed with some metapragmatic applications. Formulaic in character, they provide clues to the interpretation of the utterance as a whole, or parts of it ((55)–(57)).

(55) ...but far more than, say, the computer, they are a fundamental resource.
      (2000 *Daily Mail*)

(56) ...because, let's face it, Diana was married... (2000 *Daily Mail*)

(57) It is Japan's opportunity, but we have no interest in the Far East sufficient to justify our attacking Russia, let alone the fact that the "helping hand" on our part would inevitably bring France into the struggle. (1900 *Daily Mirror*)

While *say* marks examples, approximate guesses and hypothetical cases, *let's face it* and *let alone* provide metapragmatic comments in the sense of 'honestly speaking' and 'not to mention', respectively.

6.   Conclusion

Although imperatives in the RNC are less numerous than originally expected, the material retrieved from the corpus yields interesting insights into the structure and pragmatic functions of imperatives in newspapers.

As far as formal characteristics are concerned, two major patterns could be observed in the corpus: the prototypical "ordinary" imperatives which are directed to a second-person addressee, and *let*-constructions with different *let*-entities (first person singular or plural pronouns and third-party references varying from concrete to abstract). Interestingly, *let*-constructions constitute a relatively high percentage of the material (cf. Figure 3); and while ordinary imperatives occur predominantly in quotations, *let*-constructions are often part of the authorial/editorial material.

The corpus data also indicate that the use of imperatives goes beyond a "one-sided conversational exchange between author and reader" (Flesch 1949: 94f.). Although Author/Editor-Reader interaction is certainly the major dimension in written mass media communication, other communicative constellations are possible as well. Six different combinations of speaker- and addressee-roles could be observed in the corpus, involving not only the Author/Editor and the Reader, but also the Referents of a news story (cf. Table 1). The Referents not only speak through authentic quotations, but also through faked versions. Likewise, as a special part of audience design, the readers are given a voice at times with simulated direct speech. And although the major target of newspapers is the General Readership, communication is not always direct and cases of multiple addressing are quite common.

With respect to the pragmatic functions of imperatives in news reports, it does not come as a surprise that quotations, mirroring spoken interaction, display the widest range of non-textual calls for action. Clearly, the functions of quote imperatives are not representative of the genre of news reports as such, however, their selection generally contributes to the conversational tone of the news report, and it is even possible that their illocutionary force is extended beyond the original speech situation.

In contrast, the imperatives in the authorial/editorial material are mainly text-related. Some of them, especially the expository directives, still display a certain directive force. With others, the text-structuring and stylistic functions dominate, and their directive force is weak or even non-existent. At least for the recent past, it can be claimed that popular newspapers show a stronger preference for imperatives as attention getters (especially in headlines as "stand-alone units" (Bell 1991: 187)), whereas in the quality papers, imperatives are generally more rare and tend to be applied with textual functions.

As for the diachronic dimension, it can be claimed that in the late eighteenth and early nineteenth century, imperatives either occurred as directives in quotations or – mainly in the form of *let*-constructions – functioned as comments and text-structuring devices. It was only in the middle of the twentieth century that imperatives, as pieces of (pseudo-)advice from the Author/Editor to the Reader, became popular attention getters in the headlines.

As pointed out earlier, the data gained from the news reports in the RNC cannot be generalized for all newspaper genres. For example, it seems highly likely that, in the opinion copy and the service section, imperatives occur in far greater numbers and the dominant pragmatic functions and communicative constellations vary according to genre. Further diachronic and synchronic research could contribute to a more comprehensive account of imperatives in newspaper language.

References

Bell, Allan. 1991. *The Language of News Media*. Oxford: Blackwell.
Biber, Douglas, Stig Johansson, Geoffrey Leech, Susan Conrad and Edward Finegan. 1999. *Longman Grammar of Spoken and Written English*. London: Longman.
Bös, Birte. 2007. Dispensation in contemporary British newspapers: Informal reference to persons. In José Mª Bernardo Paniagua, Guillermo López García, Pelegrí Sancho Cremades and Enric Serra Alegre (eds.), *Critical Discourse Analysis of Media Texts*, Valencia: Universitat de València, 127–141.
Bös, Birte. forthc. *People's voices* – Eine diachrone Betrachtung persönlicher Zitate in der britischen Presse. In Martin Luginbühl and Stefan Hauser (eds.). *MedienTextKultur – Linguistische Beiträge zur kontrastiven Medienanalyse. Beiträge zur Fremdsprachenvermittlung*, Band 16, Landau: Verlag für empirische Pädagogik.
Clark, Billy. 1993. *Let* and *let's*: Procedural encoding and explicature. *Lingua* 90, 173–200.
Collins, Peter. 2003. *Let* and *let's*. In Christo Moskovsky (ed.). *Proceedings of the 2003 Conference of the Australian Linguistic Society*, http://www.als.asn.au/proceedings/als2003/collins.pdf, 1–8.
Costa, Rachel M. 1972. Let's solve let's! *Papers in Linguistics* 5, 141–144.
Davies, Eirlys. 1986. *The English Imperative*. London: Croom Helm.
De Clerck, Bernard. 2004. On the pragmatic functions of *let's* utterances. In Karin Aijmer and Bengt Altenberg (eds.). *Advances in Corpus Linguistics: Papers from the 23rd International Conference on English Language Research on Computerized Corpora (ICAME 23)*. Amsterdam: Rodopi, 213–233.
Fairclough, Norman. 1989. *Language and Power*. London: Longman.
Flesch, Rudolf. 1949/1974. *The Art of Readable Writing*. New York: Harper&Row.
Hopper, Paul J., and Elizabeth Closs Traugott. 2003. *Grammaticalization*. 2nd ed. Cambridge: Cambridge University Press.
Huddleston, Rodney, and Geoffrey K. Pullum. 2002. *The Cambridge Grammar of the English Language*. Cambridge: Cambridge University Press.
Jespersen, Otto. 1992. *The Philosophy of Grammar*. Chicago: University of Chicago Press.
Kohnen, Thomas. 2004. "Let mee be so bold to request you to tell mee". Constructions with *let me* and the history of English directives. *Journal of Historical Pragmatics* 5.1, 159–173.
König, Ekkehard, and Peter Siemund. 1985. Speech act distinctions in grammar. In Timothy Shopen (ed.). *Language Typology and Syntactic Description*. http://www.unipv.it/wwwling/koenig3.pdf, 1–42.
Kurtz, Howard. 1993. Yesterday's news: Why newspapers are losing their franchise. In Frank Denton and Howard Kurtz. *Reinventing the Newspaper*. New York: Twentieth Century Fund, 59–112.
Leech, Geoffrey. 1966. *English in Advertising*. London: Longmans, Green and Co.

Leech, Geoffrey. 1983. *Principles of Pragmatics*, London: Longman.

Quirk, Randolph, Sidney Greenbaum, Geoffrey Leech, and Jan Svartvik. 1985. *A Comprehensive Grammar of the English Language*. London: Longman.

Schneider, Kristina. 2002. *The Development of Popular Journalism in England from 1700 to the Present*. Rostock: Unpublished dissertation.

Searle, John R. 1976. A taxonomy of illocutionary acts. *Minnesota Studies in the Philosophy of Science* Volume 6, reprint, 1–19.

Seppänen, Aimo. 1977. The position of *let* in the English auxiliary system. *English Studies* 58, 515–529.

Swales, John M., Ummul K. Ahmad, Yu-Ying Chang, Daniel Chavez, Dacia F. Dressen, and Ruth Seymour. 1998. Consider this: The role of imperatives in scholarly writing. *Applied Linguistics* 19.1, 97–121.

Pamphlets

Comparing seventeenth-century news broadsides and occasional news pamphlets

Interrelatedness in news reporting

Elisabetta Cecconi

1.   Introduction

When investigating the issue of news circulation in the seventeenth century, our modern perception of its exponential increase in terms of production and demand echoes the comments made by contemporaries that their age was the era of news. In 1622, Robert Burton wrote: "I hear news every day & those ordinary rumors of war, plagues, fires, inundations, thefts, murders, massacres, meteors, comets, prodigies, apparitions. [...] News books every day, pamphlets, corantos, stories. [...] Thus I hear daily, and suchlike, both private and public news, amidst the gallantry and misery of the world" (1622:4). In that same decade a cleric voiced a complaint which has become paradigmatic of people's contagious devotion to news: "What news? Everyman asks what news? Every man's religion is known by his news" (Zaret 2000:102).

The Stuart period was characterised by an impressive variety of news transmitted in the oral, manuscript and printed mode. Though oral communication remained the main source of news circulation and consumption, this was increasingly complemented by a conspicuous distribution of official and unofficial newsletters, commercial separates, pamphlets, broadsides, periodical news publication and, from 1640 onwards, serial newsbooks which paved the way for the modern era of information. Despite the apparent heterogeneity of news formats, recent studies on seventeenth-century news networks have documented their considerable degree of confluence and overlap (e.g. Fox 2000; Zaret 2000; Woolf 2005). Zaret's *Origins of Democratic Culture* (2000) is particularly relevant in this respect, as it scrupulously accounts for the way in which news circulated from the oral to the written/printed realm and back again. Nodal points for the intersection of different modes of news transmission were taverns, inns and bookstalls in the area of St. Peter and the Royal Exchange. Here, the boundaries between realms were easily blurred: rumours told by carriers and travellers could be written down and committed either to newsletters and private correspondence or to pamphlets and broadsides. In their turn, pamphlets and ballads attached to the walls of taverns, as well as newsletters and periodicals posted in prominent positions, could be read aloud and thus return to the oral sphere from which they originated.

This stimulating environment of news transmission determined a fruitful co-presence of different news genres which was one of the factors responsible for their inner dialogism. In this paper, I shall provide a comparative analysis of seventeenth-century news broadsides and occasional news pamphlets. Indeed, these two forms of cheap print shared socio-cultural features – ranging from the tenor of discourse to the low price, from the places of production to the venues of distribution – which have inevitably influenced their rhetorical structuring of the news event. On the basis of the mutual relation existing between text and context I shall account for the various forms of linguistic interrelatedness as they occur at the level of news presentation on the front page and at the level of the body of the news in the two genres. In particular, I shall be considering the news values responsible for common lexical choices and discourse constructions and whether, and to what extent, broadsides and pamphlets anticipate text-organising principles of modern journalism.

By referring to van Dijk's (1988) persuasive content features of modern jour-nalism and to his news schema categories, I shall concentrate on providential news about natural disasters and prodigies, which was one of the major themes of seventeenth-century broadsides and occasional pamphlets. The analysis of the discourse fluctuation existing between the two genres will eventually shed some light on the ideology and priorities held in Protestant England and on the com-munal strategies adopted to have them accepted by people.[1]

2.   "Strange and Wonderfull Newes" in broadsides and occasional pamphlets

As happens in modern-day news market, also in Tudor and Stuart England, dra-matic storms, bizarre prodigies, disastrous earthquakes and bloody crimes were what readers commonly craved and what publishers were willing to supply for commercial interests. Although some of the prodigy news amounted to blatant

---

1.   The news broadsides selected for analysis are taken from *The Bodleian Allegro Catalogue*, and amount to approximately 11,680 words. The occasional news pamphlets are drawn from EEBO and amount to approximately 25,430 words.

fraud – such as the famous case of Dorothy Mattley who was swallowed up by the earth for her imprecations against God[2] – there were many people of the period, and not only among the uneducated, who believed in marvels and had familiarity with practices of magic. Disregarding the notorious prejudices against the reliability of cheap print, they accepted the strange news as true and seriously pondered its providential meaning (Capp 1988: 225; Levy 1999: 17). The edifying aspect of news was crucial in the seventeenth century and the journalistic reportage of natural disasters intermingled with references to Divine Providence and human salvation. Readers were instructed to interpret wonderful events not only as fact but – far more important to their lives – as divine signs of spiritual disorder, or as providential manifestations of God's warnings to mankind. The entertaining purpose of the text highly contributed to the effectiveness of the moral lesson, as the more thrilling and shocking the news, the more persuasive was its call to repentance.

The main vehicles for the wide diffusion of sensationalism were broadside ballads and occasional news pamphlets. The first were verse narratives printed on one side of a single sheet of paper and sold for a penny or half a penny. Flourishing from the mid-sixteenth to the mid-seventeenth century, the genre combined in simple forms the elements of poetry, music and drama. Occasional pamphlets, on the other hand, were short quarto "books" typically consisting of between one sheet and a maximum of twelve sheets and they were sold for a few pennies from the sixteenth century. Unlike broadside ballads which were essentially vocal performances printed to aid private imitation of the musical rendition, pamphlets were prose texts printed to be read either silently or aloud, individually or collectively. Both genres are considered forerunners of modern newspapers and as such they anticipate some of the essential constituents of modern journalism.

As stated above, broadsides and occasional pamphlets shared the context of production, distribution and reception in the seventeenth century. Though we know little about the authors of these flimsy leaflets and sheets, it seems very likely that a balladeer could also write pamphlets and vice-versa (Raymond 2003: 59).[3]

---

2. See the broadside *A Most Wonderful and Sad Judgement of God upon one Dorothy Mattley* (1660) and the pamphlet *The Great and Grievous Punishment* (1660). Both texts present the news event, foregrounding its extraordinariness and truthfulness. The author conveys the factuality of the prodigy through precise reference to people, place and time of the happening. Particular attention is given to the didactic function of the wonder either through references to the Holy Scriptures (opening section of the pamphlet) or through a more general commentary on the divine significance of the event (closing section of the broadside and pamphlet).

3. The similarities in terms of event structure and choice of reported details in those broadsides and pamphlets narrating the same event would seem to suggest that the same author had

Hired by printers, these semi-professional authors wrote for financial profit and, when something newsworthy happened, the same writer could be employed to supply both a pamphlet and a ballad rendition of the same event. It was often the printer then who drafted the title page blurb and selected woodcuts. Once published, the two texts entered the market place.

Pasted on the walls of taverns, theatres and other habitual meeting spots or displayed for sale in shops and bookstalls near St. Paul's Churchyard, broadsides and pamphlets easily spread from London to the provinces and countryside. Their long-range distribution was ensured by the relentless activity of itinerant minstrels, who recited them at markets and fairs, and petty chapmen, who peddled them together with pins and needles in remote rural areas.

In the hands of peddlers the two genres had the power to reach a heterogeneous cross-section of English society. This was possible not only thanks to their low price but also as a result of their marked visibility and easy circulation among people. Rather than personal possessions, broadsides and pamphlets were often considered a sort of common property and were continuously exchanged, borrowed, shared and passed on (Walsham 1999: 34). In seventeenth-century England, it was not uncommon to see illiterate men buying printed news to have it read by literate friends and neighbours at home or in local centres of sociability (Watt 1990: 12–13; Walsham 1999: 36; Fox 2000: 44). This explains the mixed nature of the cheap-print audience where the humble receiver merged with the middle and even upper ranking consumer.

3.   The rhetoric of news discourse:
Schema categories and persuasive content features

In order to analyse the news discourse of cheap print I shall refer to van Dijk's news schema categories of modern journalism (1988).[4] According to van Dijk, each news item is composed of a summary section and the episode. The summary section contains the headline and the lead, the first always preceding the latter. The lead corresponds to the first paragraph of the news text. It is a sort of micro-story which provides information about the actors, the place and the time in

---

worked on both texts. See also the comparative analysis, in Section 4, of the broadside *Newes from Hereford* (1661) and the pamphlet *A Strange and True Relation* (1661).

4.   Since the basic constituents of seventeenth-century news broadsides and pamphlets are not essentially different from those characterising twentieth-century news discourse, the schema categories identified by van Dijk can be equally applied – though with a slight adjustment – to early modern cheap print.

which the event occurred. In some cases it can even offer a nucleus of evaluation by supplying the lens through which the remainder of the news story is to be read. The headline, on the other hand, is just an abstract of the lead. Together, they introduce the episode, which consists of a set of sub-categories arranged in different ways. Van Dijk identifies them starting from the main event (e.g. an earthquake). From there we can move backwards and discover the previous events (another earthquake one year ago) and the history (regular earthquakes over the last decades) or, alternatively, we can move forward and inspect the consequences (the rescue operation), the reaction of people (inhabitants, authorities) and the comment (future preventive measures, evaluation). In the first part of my analysis, I shall focus on the summary section of broadsides and pamphlets (i.e. their news presentation), whereas in the latter, I shall take into consideration their conceptual structuring of the episode (i.e. their news reporting).

Once I have identified the role and functions of seventeenth-century news categories, attention will be drawn to the use of persuasive content features (van Dijk 1988: 84). As happens in modern press, in fact, the ideologically biased propositions of seventeenth-century news were not just to be understood by the consumers but also accepted and believed. Persuading people of the truthfulness of the event and of its divine meaning was fundamental in encouraging them to perform the actions requested (e.g. repent, make amends) and change their dissolute lives. The big challenge for the early modern author of cheap print was precisely that of invalidating the prejudices against the authenticity of his sensational report, to obtain people's confidence in the news and in its moral message. Van Dijk (1988: 84–85) identifies a number of standard strategies to promote the persuasive process of assertion which is pervasively found in the news discourse of both broadsides and pamphlets, starting with their title page:

1. Emphasise the factual nature of events;
2. Build a strong relational structure for facts;
3. Provide information that also has an attitudinal and emotional dimension.

4. **News presentation on the front page:**
   Major headlines, proto-leads and woodcuts

The first instances of interrelatedness between broadsides and pamphlets occur at the level of news presentation on their title pages. Below is a comparison between the front page of the broadside *Newes from Hereford* (1661) and that of the pamphlet *Strange Newes from the North* (1650), both reporting earthquakes.

Figure 1. Title pages of the news broadside *Newes from Hereford* (1661), The Bodleian Library, University of Oxford, Wood 401(179) and the news pamphlet *Strange Newes from the North* (1650), (c) British Library Board. All rights reserved E.603.(3).

In both texts, the front pages are organised in such a way as to attract the potential buyer's attention and arouse his interest in the news from the very beginning. Unlike other early modern newspapers like the *London Gazette* (1665), the broadside and the pamphlet present a major topic-headline, an introductory prose section which I shall refer to as a "proto-lead" and a woodcut, followed by the body of the news which in the broadside occurs on the same page.[5] It is interesting to see how news discourse in early modern cheap print is predicated on the borrowing of different text types. This is particularly evident in the news broadside where we find a conjunction of: 1. prose style; 2. visual form; and 3. verse. But also in occasional news pamphlets we may see the coexistence of: 1. the prose narrative style of the proto-lead; 2. the visual mode of the woodcut; and – in some cases – 3. the epistolary structure of the news event (on the next page) intended to lend authenticity and credibility to the news (see Figure 2).

---

5. I use the term "proto-lead" because seventeenth-century leads are still quite different from modern ones in terms of length and discourse construction. Indeed, most are quite long (more than 30 words) and generally ignore van Dijk's macro-rules of deletion, generalisation and construction (Bell 1991: 162).

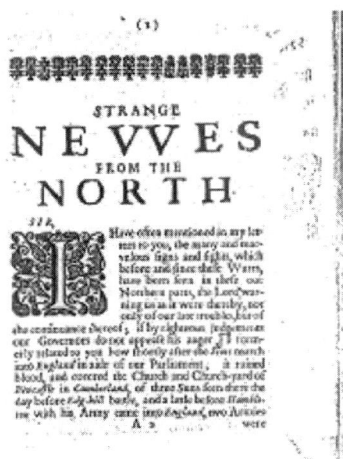

Figure 2. First page of the news pamphlet *Strange Newes from the North* (1650), (c) British Library Board. All rights reserved E.603.(3).

In both genres, the printer's choice of inserting a woodcut in the written text is dictated by his willingness to reach a wider audience. Thanks to the visual aid, in fact, even uneducated people could make sense of the text and be tempted to buy it.

In seventeenth-century news broadsides and pamphlets, the heading and proto-lead constitute the essential part of the news story presentation. Unlike what happens in modern journalism where the major heading is a completely stand alone unit, in the two genres topical headlines and leads, though graphically distinct, are syntactically linked through punctuation and connectors. In news broadsides, the two categories are usually joined together by the colon and the conjunction *or,* whereas in news pamphlets the connectors may vary and can include: *containing, whereby, committed on, in, with, which, that (happened).*[6] In both cases, the heading is written in larger characters and is aimed at informing/ attracting the reader by highlighting the reporter's claim for truth and authenticity. As we can see, "the degree of information and intended textual appeal strongly interacts with type-setting and layout" in both texts (Studer 2003: 29). Below is a comparison between headlines used in occasional pamphlets and broadsides.

Topic headlines in news pamphlets:

(1) *Strange Newes from the North* (1650); *A Strange and True Relation of a Wonderfull and Terrible Earthquake* (1661); *Strange and fearfull newes from Plaisto* (1645); *A Strange and True Relation of Several Wonderful and*

---

6. These are called sub-heads and have a mere structural function in the news-text (Studer 2003: 36).

> *Miraculous Sights* (1660); *A Full and True Account of the sad and dreadful Storm* (1689).

Topic headlines in news broadsides:

(2)   *Newes from Hereford* (1661); *A New Wonder* (1681); *A Sad and True Relation of a great fire or two* (1662); *Truth brought to Light or Wonderful Strange and True Newes* (1662); *Bloody News from St. Albans* (1679).

The frequent occurrence of the catchword *newes* or the formula *true account/ report* is intended to announce the sensational information, at the same time assessing the veridicity of the subject-matter communicated. In some cases, the news-writer expresses an evaluation of the kind of story told through the use of adjectives such as *sad, fearful, wonderful* or *dreadful* which are part of a stock of evaluative lexicon used interchangeably both in broadsides and in pamphlets to present providential news.[7] The use of an emotional style in the heading adheres to the rhetorical convention, according to which, "facts are better represented and memorised if they involve or arouse strong emotions" (van Dijk 1988: 85). In this case, the author foregrounds the titillating aspect of the news in order to intrigue the audience from the outset. The news values of factuality and negativity which emerge respectively from the terms *account, relation, newes* and from the adjectives *sad, terrible, dreadful* are not the only ones to be considered relevant in the heading. The frequent combination of the word *newes* with the mentioning of the place in the formula *Newes from* documents the increasing importance assigned to the topicality of the event, intended not only in terms of its recency but also of its spatial proximity to the reader. A flood which has happened "next door", so to speak, acquires higher relevance for the reader as it could have happened to him too. The lexicon shared by the title headings of broadsides and pamphlets is one of those aspects of intertextuality which can be read as proof of the writer's ability/possibility to move from one genre to the other.

   The proto-lead which follows "summarises the central action and establishes the point of the story" (Bell 1991: 149). Both in occasional pamphlets and in broadsides the aim of the proto-lead is to orient the reader by supplying information about who-what-where-when. In order to enhance factuality, ballad authors and pamphleteers fill their proto-leads with: 1. precise and even quite long descriptions of the news event; 2. exact details about time and place; 3. evidence from close eyewitnesses; and 4. evidence from reliable sources such as authorities,

---

7.   These negative semantic clusters indicate that prodigies, earthquakes and celestial apparitions all arouse horror in an audience, which perceived them as manifestations of God's wrath (Daston 1998).

respectable people and professionals.[8] Below is a comparison of the proto-lead from the broadside *Newes from Hereford* (1661) and that from the pamphlet *The Full and True Relation of a Dreadful Storm and Tempest* (1680). Attention has been given to the detailed description of the main event and to the lexicon of newsworthiness adopted to increase sensationalism.

Table 1. A comparison of the proto-leads in the broadside *Newes from Hereford* (1661) and in the pamphlet *The Full and True Relation* (1680)

PROTO-LEADS	News Broadside *Newes from Hereford* (1661)	Occasional news pamphlet *The Full and True Relation of a Dreadful Storm or Tempest* (1680)
Lexicon of newsworthiness Details of time place and people Evidence from eye-witness testimony	OR, A **wonderful** and **terrible** Earthquake: With a **wonderful** Thunderclap, that Happened on *Tuesday* being the first of *October* 1661. Showing how a Church-steeple, and many gallant houses were thrown down to the ground, and people slain: with a **Terrible** Thunder-clap, and **violent** Storm of **great** Hailstone, **which were about the bigness of an Egg**, many Cattel being **utterly** destroy'd as they were feeding in the field. Also the **wonderful** Apparitions which were seen in the air to the **great** amazement of the Beholders, who beheld two perfect arms and hands; in the right hand being graspd a **great broad** sword, in the left a boul full of Blood, from whence they heard **a most strange** noise, to the **wonderful** astonishment of al present, the fright caused divers women to fall in Travail; amongst whom the Clerks wife one *Margaret Pellmore*, fell in labour, and brought forth 3 Children who had teeths and spoke as soon as ever they were born, as you shall hear in the following relation, the like not known in any age	Accompanied with Thunders, Lightnings, and Hailstones, some of them being **above Two pounds in weight**: As likewise a **terrible** Earthquake, continuing for above half an hour, giving **three furious** onsets, the which hapned on the 16th of *August* 1680, in the City of *Millain,* and the villages adjacent; so that in the space of Three hours and a half, it quite demolished **Twenty stately Houses**, and ruined about **one hundred and fifty more**, and **greatly** Endamaged two Churches, by blowing off their Steeples, and unloading them. As likewise An Account of Barns and Reeks fired by Lightning, Trees blown up by the Roots, and Villages adjacent destroyed with about **Sixty persons killed, and a Hundred wounded**, besides a number of Cattle that perished: the like not having been known to happen: The Damages sustained upon view of several worthy persons, being granted to be **One Million and a half**.

<hr>

8. The broadside *Newes from Hereford* (1661) shows a list of respectable eye-witnesses at the end of the second sheet: "A list of the names of the persons that witnesseth the truth of this, are as followeth. Fran. Smalman, Hen Cross, Churchwardens, Peter Philpot, Nich. Finch, Constables, Jales Tully, Geo. Cox Gent, John Groom, Robert Mauricee, Thomas Welford".

While in the broadside the newsworthiness of the event is mainly evoked through the usual stock of sensational adjectives which appeals to the emotions, rather than the use of facts; in the pamphlet the extraordinariness of the storm is basically conveyed through precise numbers whose implied exactness serves to reinforce the seriousness of the account. In broadsides and to a larger extent in pamphlets, numerical indications are an essential ingredient of their journalistic style. As we can see in the texts above, numbers can refer to: 1. the date and time of the events ("the first of October 1661", "on the 16th of August 1680"); 2. the weight, size and quantity of items ("3 children", "above Two pounds in weight", "three furious onsets"); and 3. people and buildings involved in the disaster ("Twenty stately Houses [...] one hundred and fifty more"; "Sixty persons killed and a Hundred wounded", "Damages [...] to be One Million and a half"). The last two types of figures, however, are often replaced or combined with metaphors appealing to common knowledge: "as big as an Egg" (*Newes from Hereford* 1661), "as big as a Man's Fist" (in the pamphlet *An Account of a strange and prodigious Storm,* 1680) or with generic quantifiers such as *many* and *several*, for example, "many gallant houses", "many Cattel", "diverse women", "several worthy persons". Numerical indications concerning the number of eyewitnesses are equally present in the two genres and are usually exaggerated in order to stress the reliability of the report, for example, "to the admiration of many thousand beholders" (*Strange Newes from the North* 1650; *The Most strange and wonderful apparition* 1645), "many hundreds of the beholders, many hundreds" (*Strange and Fearfull Newes from Plaisto* 1645; *A Wonder of Wonders* 1662). Apart from being proof of authenticity, the marked realism of the proto-lead was also exploited as a means of eliciting emotional responses in the reader. Gory details in fact engendered that frisson of horror and fear that convinced the audience of the powerful hand of God (Lake 1994).

Generally speaking, both in broadsides and in pamphlets, the events are structured in a chronological order as happens in personal narratives. Nonetheless, some proto-leads are constructed in a way which appears to anticipate the top-down structuring principle of twentieth-century journalism. The top-down principle presupposes that what is more important in the story, for example, the outcome of an accident or natural disaster, is told at the very beginning of the text, while the details of the event and its causes are given in later paragraphs (Jucker 2005: 13). In line with this text organisation in some proto-leads of occasional pamphlets, the writer concentrates most of the reader's attention on a list of damages caused by the natural disaster, whereas the circumstances of the event are given in the remainder of the text. This textual strategy is known as the fact-collecting approach and it is considered by Ungerer (2002) as one of the precursors of the top-down structure. The following extract from the pamphlet *A Full and True Account of the sad and dreadful Storm* (1689) provides an example (emphasis added):

Table 2. Top-down structuring of the news event in the proto-lead of the pamphlet *A Full and True Account of the sad and dreadful Storm* (1689)

A Full and True ACCOUNT of the sad and dreadful STORM That happened on *Sunday* Morning the 21th of *January* 1689 WITH A Relation how it happened, and continued, and **the Damage it has done by Land and Sea, by** **blowing down Houses, Chimneys, Trees, killing** **and wounding divers People, carrying away Hay-** **Reeks, Corn-Reeks, &c. in damaging Churches,** **casting away Ships, Boats, Lighters,** *&c. with other* *prodigious and fearfull Circumstances attending it;* *the like not known in any Age.*	⟶ OUTCOME ⟶ CIRCUMSTANCES

The outcome of the news event is put in a prominent position in order to impress the audience and increase its interest in the episode. The circumstances, on the other hand, are just mentioned in the last line.

The other textual strategy which paves the way for the outcome-cause structuring of the news item is the topical headline, which, as we have seen, orients the reader towards the main event of the news. Its function in seventeenth-century news presentation is more noteworthy still if we think that early modern newspapers lacked this basic category of modern journalism. In the *London Gazette,* the news item was reported with no mediation of headlines or leads, the only information provided being the attribution of the news (e.g. "Dublin, December 27").

The last component of the content page is the woodcut, which is an essential element of news broadsides and is also very frequent in occasional news pamphlets. The pervasive presence of illustrations in cheap print reveals to what extent visual communication continued to play a role in Protestant England and, conversely, "how post-Reformation religion continued to have a place in visual culture" (Watt 1991: 136). Contrary to Collinson's claim for a sort of "visual anorexia" or "iconophobia" in the English culture of the sixteenth and seventeenth centuries (1988), printers of news accompanied their texts with suitable images, often borrowing symbols from the late medieval sermon exempla and from stories linked to the life of the saints. Historians identify two types of woodcuts: general illustrations where the image is appropriate but not specific to the text, and direct illustrations where the image depicts a particular textual reference. In the first case, the printer chooses to re-use the same woodcut for different songs or pamphlets; in the latter, the printer commissions a new woodcut for each occasion (Watt 1991).

In the illustration of the broadside *Newes from Hereford* and of the pamphlet *Strange Newes from the North* (see Figure 1) we find a quite conventional representation of the city-nation – which reminds one of the corresponding biblical exempla of cities destroyed for their sins, *in primis* Jerusalem. We can also see heavenly arms descending from the clouds together with rods, swords, spears and fire tongues which symbolise God's vengeance on the nation for its covetousness. The similarity between the two images seems to suggest that these were part of a stock of woodcuts which could be attached to any news broadside or pamphlet dealing with natural calamities sent by God to punish his people. In both cases, the focus given to the theological interpretation of the event rather than to its factual representation is reflective of the priority assigned to the godly teaching. As Walsham claims, "it is intricably difficult to decide whether such texts [visual and written] are titillation under the pretence of religious admonition or homilies camouflaged as sensational news" (1999: 50).

5.   Structuring of the episode

In this second section of my paper, I wish to concentrate on the body of the news as it is reported in broadsides and pamphlets. As anticipated at the beginning, the interrelatedness between the two genres emerges as a result of their communal blending of realistic reportage and sermonizing editorial. The quite formulaic structuring of the news event envisages that the conventional homiletic reflection occurs in the opening or in the closing section of the text, while the journalistic reportage occupies the central part. This was particularly the case in broadsides where metrical and structural constraints left little room for editorial comments in the course of the telling. In occasional pamphlets, on the other hand, it was possible to find large sections of providential comments interspersed within the relation itself.[9]

As happens in the proto-lead, the journalistic report is characterised by a high degree of factuality both in broadsides and in pamphlets. Along with plausible numbers, precise names, locations and attributions to eyewitnesses, great impor-

---

9.   See the pamphlet *A Great and Wonderful Discovery* (1663) where the author reports the famous fire which destroyed Mr Delaun's house and burned alive his family. After introducing the main event, the writer mentions the curiosity of a female guest at Mr Delaun's house who refused to stay overnight and was thus spared from death. The case occasions providential comment where the author reflects on the power of God's mercy: "Yet great was the good hand and Providence of God towards a Gentlewoman.[...] But blessed be God for her Deliverance and the Lord grant she may for ever walk answerably, to the honour and praise of his great and glorious Name for so high and signal a mercy...".

tance is ascribed to quotations from people involved in the accident. Quotations are a sub-category of the factuality principle outlined by van Dijk (1988) and are quite common in seventeenth-century news discourse. Their pervasiveness is due to their potential as markers of truthfulness and authenticity. What is more, introducing participants as speakers has a strong emotional impact on the reader since their direct speech contributes to the human and dramatic dimension of the news event. News actors are represented as real actors and their words acquire an illocutionary force which, more than anything else, persuades the audience of the authenticity of the strange event as well as of its divine significance. What follows is a comparison between two extracts, one taken from the broadside *Newes from Hereford* (1661) and one from the pamphlet *A Strange and True Relation* (1661), both reporting the wonder which took place immediately after the earthquake at Hereford. The three children, who have been given birth to by the clerk's wife, suddenly utter prophetic words (emphasis added).

> (3) Broadside:
> And from the place came a most mighty cry,
> which said *wo wo to man that draweth breath*
> *And the Inhabitants of all the Earth.* [...]
>
> The first did say *no man can shun,*
> *Which is appointed and not yet begun:*
> Where will be found the second child it said
> *Sufficient men alive to bury the dead?*
>
> These words did then from the 3rd child proceed
> *Where will be corn enough to satisfy your need?*
> These were the words they said at that same dyd [?]
> And presently all these three children dyd.
> (*Newes from Hereford,* 1661)
>
> Pamphlet:
> [...] they heard a most strange and loud voice which said; *Woe, woe to thee and to the inhabitants thereof, for he cometh that is to come, and ye shall all see him* [...] The first said, *The Day is appointed which no man can shun.* The second demanded, *Where could be found sufficient alive to bury the Dead?* And the third said, *Where will there be Corn enough to satisfie the Hungry and the needy.*
> (*A Strange and True Relation,* 1661)

The orchestration of the three voices enhances the readers' emotional involvement in the miraculous happening thus convincing them of the necessity to repent before the prophecies come true.

Another example is provided by the broadside *A Sad and True Relation of a Great Fire or Two* (1662) and the news pamphlet *A Great and Wonderful Discovery* (1663) both reporting the same big fire that happened at Mr Delaun's house. Both texts increase the emotional effect of the event by reporting the direct speech of the people involved in the disaster.

(4)   Broadside:
      In the merchants lower Rooms she espied
      the Violent flames and then aloud she cryed
      Fire, Fire, and being in dread and fear,
      And then the Coffee man he did her hear

      And then the Coffee man immediately
      Looking out of the window heard a doleful cry,
      Lord have mercy on us, we are all undon,
      We know not how these miseries to spun.
      (*A Sad and True Relation of a great fire or two,* 1662)

      Pamphlet:
      A Woman [...] espied a great light in the Merchants lower Rooms [...] where-
      upon, though much amazed, she cryed out: *Fire, Fire* insomuch as the Coffee
      man looked out of his Window, and immediately heard the doleful cryes, *Lord*
      have mercy upon us we are all undone, which was all the words that they were
      heard speak (*A Great and Wonderful Discovery,* 1663)

The direct reporting of the dying people's speech is aimed at thrilling the reader, reminding him of the precariousness of his human condition and of his subjection to God's providence. In this sense, factuality and strong realism go hand in hand with the edifying purpose of the author.

Besides factuality, another crucial persuasive feature of news discourse is the construction of a strong relational structure of facts. This can be accomplished by "mentioning previous events as conditions or causes and describing the next events as possible or real consequences" or "by inserting facts into well-known situation models that make them relatively familiar even when they are new" (van Dijk 1988: 85). Both occasional news pamphlets and broadsides adopt a quite formulaic structuring of the story which guarantees people's familiarity with the news discourse and hence their acceptance of its sensational content. As happens in personal narratives, the news story follows a sequential organisation which includes cause-result sequences. Echoing the oral tradition of story-telling, this model helps the reader make sense of the event by applying the familiar script of chronological and logical narratives. By comparing broadsides and pamphlets narrating the same news event, we may see to what extent they adopt a similar structure:

history – main event – circumstance (this may also occur before the event) – consequence – evaluation (this may be anticipated in some pamphlets). In some cases the similarities between the two genres in terms of lexical choices, reported speech and relational structure of facts are so consistent as to suggest that the same author may have put his hand to both texts. Below is a comparison between the broadside *Newes from Hereford* and the pamphlet *A Strange and True Relation*.[10]

Table 3. A comparison of the structuring of the same episode in the broadside *Newes from Hereford* (1661) and in the pamphlet *A Strange and True Relation* (1661)

Ballad: *Newes from Hereford* (1661)	Pamphlet: *A Strange and True Relation* (1661)
History: too many wonders in this age but this is the strangest of all	History: "take notice of the several Disasters that hath befaln in and about London … yet non so wonderful … as this" Evaluation: "Lord manifests his will … in wonders and Signs"
Anticipation of the main event: Earthquake, Storm and Thunderclaps	Anticipation of the main event: Tempest and Earthquake
Event 1: Violent storm	Event 1: Violent storm
Circumstances: 2 o'clock in the afternoon "the earth did darken and did look unkind"	Circumstances: "the beginning was with a most terrible Wind".
Consequences: "it made the tyles from off o'th houses fly/…Church steeples were blown down/"	Consequences: "Tiles off the houses … blown down the Steeple of a Church … killed some persons"
Event 2: Thunderclap	Event 2: Claps of Thunder
Circumstance: "/at six or seven o'clock with might …/"	Circumstance: "about 6 and 7 of the clock in the Evening" Attribution: "several Gentlemen of quality … certifie that"
Consequences: "/it did destroy the Cattel in the field/"	Consequences: "they destroyed the Cattle in the Field"
Event 3: "/then followeth a terrible earthquake/"	Event 3: "Then followed a terrible and fearful Earthquake"
Consequences: ground and houses shake "it many famous buildings did deface"	
Reaction: "/people thought that the last day was come/"	Reaction: "inhabitants thought that the last Day has been come"
Circumstance of event 4: from brightness to complete darkness	Circumstance of event 4: great brightness and then thick black
Event 4: Apparition in the sky	Event 4: Apparition in the sky
Consequences: women fall into Travail; the children are bearers of prophecies	Consequences: women fall in travail; the children are bearers of prophecies
Evaluation: comments on the theological significance of the event	

---

10. Other examples may be mentioned to support the claim that the same author may have been employed to report the same event in the broadside and in the pamphlet form. The broadside

No matter if occurring in the middle of the text – as happens in a few pamphlets – or in the coda of the broadside, the evaluation (i.e. sermonising editorial) is an essential component of seventeenth-century news discourse as it supplies the lens through which the entire news is to be read and interpreted. From a certain point of view, it is even more important than the story itself as it is the homiletic commentary which gives significance to the event, making it relevant to the reader's life (see Würzbach 1990: 147). Both in broadsides and in pamphlets, the Protestant comment occurs in the opening and closing section of the text. The news-writer takes on the role of a preacher who exploits the attractive potential of the "strange but true news" as a vehicle for indoctrinating people through an interactive mode of discourse. In several cases this change of pragmatic role is signalled by a shift of pronouns: from the authorial *I/we* pronoun which explicitly refers to the writer's communicative function of news reporter and places the *you* as receiver of the providential news, to the consensual *we* pronoun, where the author claims solidarity with his audience as members of the Protestant community. From a rhetorical point of view, the pervasive use of the inclusive *we* functions as an effective means of persuasion. It, in fact, elicits the readers' emotional response to the moral teaching, enhances their agreement with the godly interpretation provided by the author and hopefully convinces them of the necessity of leading a righteous life. Let us compare some examples of pronoun shifts in news broadsides and pamphlets (emphasis added):

A Sad and True Relation of a Great Fire or Two and the pamphlet *A Great and Wonderful Discovery* show a similar structuring of the event, attribute the same words to the people involved in the disaster (see the previous analysis of direct speech), focus their attention on the same details (e.g. the woman who, thanks to God's will, had left Mr Delaun's house before the fire began) and provide the same providential reading of the events (e.g. God was so merciful as to raise instruments to help people put out the fire).

Table 4. The *I-We* pronoun shift in news broadsides and pamphlets

News Broadsides	Occasional News Pamphlets
Newes from Hereford (1661)	*A Strange and True Relation of … Earthquake*
Opening frame	(1661)
But this which here to you I shall unfold	Opening paragraph
It is the strangest thing that ere was told,	Before **I** mention any further concerning this
Yet not so strange but that it is as true,	strange and sudden Accident which hath so
Yea every word **I** dedicate to you	lately befaln at Hereford, and that this Real
[…]	and Authentique Truth may not seem doubt-
Closing frame	ful, **I** shall put the reader thereof in minde to
What man is able in *our* English Land	take notice and rememberth several Disasters
The meaning of these things to understand	that hath befaln; not long since in, and about
It doth has taken anger great from God	London, which **I** need not here to declare, yet
Now he will smite *us* with his heavy Rod	none so wonderful, or worthy of observation
	as this; but let it not be strange, for *we* know,
Except by prayer *we* speedly repent	and often read that the Lord doth sometimes
And of *our* wicked sins for to relent;	manifest his will unto the World in Wonders
The cup of blood appeared in the sky	and Signs … and that he sees and knows all *our*
And sharpen'd sword great wars doth signi-	ways, how slight so ever *we* make thereof: then
fie […]	how can *we* praise him sufficiently, when he
	hear of this strange Disaster that did so lately
The Wonder of Wonders (1670)	befall at Hereford, in that he was pleased to
Opening frame	keep the like from *us* here in London *we* being
Attend good Christians young & old	as sinful as any.
Observe what hear **I** shall unfold	
Strange example i'le rehearse	*A Full and True Account of the sad and dreadful*
The like was never put in verse […]	*Storm* (1689)
Strange wonders God to *us* doth send;	Opening paragraph
For to make *us our* lives amend,	none has ever proved so destructive as this
But some so unbelieving be,	*we* are about to describe, the dismal account
They'l not believe unless they see	of which, as *we* have been eyewitnesses; and
[…]	received from several places, takes as followeth
Closing frame	[…]
Then let *us* serve the Lord on high,	
And praise his name continually,	Closing paragraph
Let *us* keep still the right path way,	Then what remains but that *we* look upon this
Then *we* his blessings shall enjoy	Storm as an Admonition from Heaven, to give
	us timely warning to repent *us* of *our* Sins, and
	turn away from the Evil of *our* doing […]

If address pronouns and other orality features (exhortations, imperatives) are quite predictable in broadsides as their delivery is based on the speech performance of the ballad-monger, the inter-personal character of the opening and closing paragraphs of pamphlets is far more interesting as it represents one of the elements which distinguishes them from newspapers (Claridge 2000: 27). One example of the interactive mode is provided by the closing paragraph of the pamphlet *The*

Fatall Vesper (1623) which tells of the terrible collapse of the upper room in the Black-Friars during a sermon attended by more than three hundred people. Here the presenter takes on a position of moral superiority *vis à vis* his listeners and urges them to repent in time through a set of exhortative constructions: "For this cause, repent O England, repent O London, repent Protestants, repent Papists, for your transgressions and offences: repent, repent for by these wonderfull signes and tokens, it doth appear most clearly that the kingdom of heaven is at hand". Now, if we compare this example with the account of a similar accident reported in the *London Gazette,* we may see to what extent the more interactive-involved style of the occasional pamphlet differs from the fact-centred reportage of the newspaper where no sermonising editorial appears either in the opening or in the closing section of the article.

> (5)   Dublin, December 27
>   Yesterday happened here a very unfortunate accident, most of the Nobility and Gentry being at a Play, at the publick Play-house, the upper Galleries on a sudden fell all down [...]. There were many dangerously hurt, and Seven or Eight killed outright. Here is lately dead the Bishop of Dromore, and its thought that Doctor Essex Digby may succed him in that See.
>   (From Thursday 5 January to Monday 9 January 1670, Number 537)

The admonitory style of the pamphlet is clearly closer to the formulaic warnings that we commonly find in broadsides: "/Old England of thy sins in time repent/before the wrath of God to thee is sent/" (*Newes from Hereford* 1661); "/All you that fear the God on high/amend your lives and repent/" (*A Wonder of Wonders* 1662). Broadly speaking, in both genres the Protestant admonitions are quite stereotypical and banal, though in some pamphlets we may find a more elaborate kind of discourse which better fits the purposes of a text intended to be read rather than sung and memorised.[11] However, no matter how conventional the commentary might have been, it documented the central role played by Protestant preaching in the news discourse of seventeenth-century cheap print. Assuming the persona of puritanical indignation against national sins, hack writers of broadsides and

---

11. Consider the opening paragraph in the pamphlet *The Full and True Relation of a Dreadful Storm* (1680): "When angry Heaven designs to punish man for Disobedience, and to make him know he is but Durst, sundry means are used, and wise Omnipotence for-warns before he strikes, or gives his vengeance reins to overwhelm with ruine irrevocable the Sons of Men: for sure it is, Divine Justice is always tempered with Mercy, and many time some fall, to give the rest an opportunity for to repent, and so avoid the danger imminent, which otherwise would fall heavy on their heads [...] for as the holy Psalmist does declare, that lowd Thunder is his voice among the waters, so may it understood, that Tempests and Earthquakes are his warning-pieces, and as Heralds, give us notice of wrath designed to fall".

pamphlets responded to the demands of Puritan England by hijacking topical journalism as a vehicle for reaching otherwise unapproachable sectors of society (Walsham 1999: 50).

6.   Conclusion

Given the socio-cultural similarities between seventeenth-century news broadsides and occasional pamphlets, the aim of my paper has been to assess the several forms of intertextuality existing between the two genres and inspect the textual level at which they occur. Drawing a distinction between the summary section of the title page and the episode, this study has attempted to show how linguistic features commonly associated with one specific genre fluctuate between the two texts as a result of their common place of production, distribution and reception. Thus orality, dramatisation and woodcuts, which are typical ingredients of traditional broadsides, are also found in pamphlets, whereas factuality, which is consistent with the more formal and argumentative style of the prose genre enters the realm of news broadsides. Needless to say, this stylistic interplay between broadsides and pamphlets does not entail total identification as each genre preserves its discourse specificity in line with its different communicative pattern. This means that, as verse compositions commonly performed at street corners and market places, broadsides maintain their highly dramatic quality, combined with a metrical pattern and a formulaic structure which inevitably affect their narrative style. Pamphlets, on the other hand, were prose texts written to be read (either privately or collectively), with a consequently greater sophistication at argumentative, syntactic and lexical levels.

The comparison between the two news genres has also revealed to what extent broadsides and pamphlets anticipate text-organising principles of modern journalism. Indeed, the seventeenth-century topical headlines, proto-leads and woodcuts appearing on their content pages can be considered precursors of the corresponding headlines, leads and documentary pictures of modern newspaper articles. Similarly, the discourse and textual strategies adopted to convey the news and its ideological message can be seen in the persuasive language of modern journalism.

The discourse analysis uncovered the close connection existing between seventeenth-century cheap print and Protestantism. Given their exceptional popularity, in fact both broadsides and occasional pamphlets were turned into effective vehicles of religious indoctrination. Oscillating between impartial, fact-centred reportage and interpersonal Puritan commentary, their news discourse revealed a dialogical character which perfectly reflected the complex interplay existing at the time between the forces of the news market and those of the Church.

Sources

EEBO, *Early English Books Online* (1473–1700): http://eebo.chadwyck.com/home.
The Bodleian Allegro Catalogue of Broadside Ballads (from the 16th to the 20th century). http://www.bodley.ox.ac.uk/ballads/ballads.htm.

References

Bell, Allan. 1991. *The Language of News Media.* Oxford: Oxford University Press.
Burton, Robert. 1622. *The Anatomy of Melancholy,* Oxford.
Capp, Bernard. 1988. Popular Literature. In Barry Reay (ed.). *Popular Culture in Seventeenth-Century England.* London: Routledge, 198–243.
Claridge, Claudia. 2000. Pamphlets and early newspapers: Political interaction vs. news reporting. In Friedrich Ungerer (ed.). *English Media Texts – Past and Present. Language and Textual Structure.* Amsterdam: John Benjamins, 25–43.
Collinson, Patrick. 1988. *The Birthpangs of Protestant England.* New York: St.Martin's.
Daston, Lorraine, and Katherine Park. 1998. *Wonders and the Order of Nature 1150–1750.* New York: Zone Books.
Fox, Adam. 2000. *Oral and Literate Culture in England 1500–1700.* Oxford: Oxford University Press.
Jucker, Andreas H. 2005. Mass media communication from the seventeenth to the twenty first century. In Janne Skaffari, Matti Peikola, Ruth Carroll and Risto Hiltunen (eds.). *Opening Windows on Texts and Discourses of the Past* (Pragmatics & Beyond New Series 134). Amsterdam and Philadelphia: John Benjamins, 7–21.
Lake, Peter. 1994. Deeds against Nature: Cheap print, protestantism and murder in early seventeenth-century England. In Kevin Sharpe and Peter Lake (eds.). *Culture and Politics in Early Stuart England.* Houndmills: Macmillan, 257–283.
Levy, Fritz. 1999. The decorum of news. In Joad Raymond (ed.). *News, Newspapers and Society in Early Modern Britain.* London: Frank Cass, 12–38.
Raymond, Joad. 2003. *Pamphlets and Pamphleteering in Early Modern Britain.* Cambridge: Cambridge University Press.
Studer, Patrick. 2003. Textual structures in eighteenth-century newspapers. A corpus-based study of headlines. In Susan C. Herring (ed.). *Journal of Historical Pragmatics* 4.1. Special issue on media and language change, 19–43.
Ungerer, Friedrich. 2002. When news stories are no longer just stories: The emergence of the top-down structure in news reports in English newspapers. In Andreas Fischer, Gunnel Tottie, Hans Martin Lehmann (eds.). *Text Types and Corpora. Studies in Honour of Udo Fries.* Tübingen: Gunter Narr, 105–122.
van Dijk, Teun A. 1988. *News as Discourse.* Hillsdale, New Jersey: Lawrence Erlbaum Associates.

Walsham, Alexandra. 1999. *Providence in Early Modern England*. Oxford: Oxford University Press.

Watt, Tessa. 1991. *Cheap Print and Popular Piety*. Cambridge: Cambridge University Press.

Woolf, Daniel. 2005. News, history and the construction of the present in Early Modern England. In Brendon Dooley and Sabrina Baron (eds.). *The Politics of Information in Early Modern Europe*. London: Routledge, 80–118.

Würzbach, Natasha. 1990. *The Rise of the English Street Ballad*. Cambridge: Cambridge University Press.

Zaret, David. 2000. *Origins of Democratic Culture*. Princeton: Princeton University Press.

"From you, my Lord, professions are but words – they are so much bait for fools to catch at"

Impoliteness strategies in the 1797–1800
Act of Union pamphlet debate

Alessandra Levorato

1.   Aims and objectives

This paper builds on previous work on the pamphlet war that was waged around the prospect of a union between Ireland and Britain in the years that preceded its implementation in 1801, research that brought out interesting differences in the strategies adopted by the writers on the two opposing sides (Levorato 2006). This paper will focus on the role (im)politeness phenomena play in the argumentative strategies employed in these pamphlets, with particular reference to the communicative strategies that were used by one or the other side, supporters or detractors of the project, to attack their opponent's face and arouse social conflict, while at the same time enhance in-group social relationships.

The object of this study is the description and analysis of how impoliteness is used in anti- and unionist pamphlets. Drawing upon Culpeper (1996), Culpeper et al. (2003) and Bousfield (2008) I will look at the various possibilities rival writers employ for the linguistic realisation of disagreement in order to probe the role that important contextual factors, such as power and social distance, but also the writers' emotional attitudes to their audiences, play in the choice of particular strategies. In this way I hope I will be able not only to establish how impoliteness is actually realised in discourse but also assess its nature and role in persuasive communication.

The structure of the paper is as follows: I will first provide an outline of the context in which the political debate on the union took place; I will then outline the most recent research in the field, also attempting a clarification of how I use and understand the term impoliteness within this paper, and introducing the categories I will work with. In the analysis proper, I will investigate and discuss instances of impoliteness in the texts in order to understand how it is handled both aggressively and as a means of social self-defence.

2.   The data

The data for the present study was taken from the pamphlet section of The Act of Union Virtual Library Project, 254 pamphlets available online (www.actofunion. ac.uk) together with other material concerning the union; it consists of 21 pamphlets, with a total of about 100,000 words, that have been divided into two relatively equivalent corpora according to their position in the debate, either in favour of, or against, the Union (see Appendix for the pamphlets' title-pages, information concerning dates, and authorship). These pamphlets were all published in Dublin, mostly in the couple of years that preceded the Act. The first rumours that the British Government was contemplating the measure only began, in fact, in the autumn of 1798, after the publication of an anonymous pamphlet (*Arguments for and against an Union, between Great Britain and Ireland, considered)* that started what would become known as the "pamphlet war" (Mansergh 2001: 127–128).

The corpus represents a particularly intriguing subject for an investigation of impoliteness. First of all, the essentially persuasive function that characterises the genre makes pamphlets markedly reader-oriented, despite their monological nature. Moreover, there are two levels of communication to explore, both around and within the text, involving the pamphlet writers' prospective readers on the one hand, and other pamphlet writers, usually political opponents, on the other, whom writers directly or indirectly address in their texts. Finally, it should also be considered that in a public debate such as this, where participants attack one another to reach their strategic goals, what Kienpointner calls "strategic rudeness in public institutions" (Kienpointner 1997: 271), impoliteness may be perceived as a sign of power, and may therefore become a key element in the overall argumentative strategy.

3.   Some information on the context

3.1   The socio-historical and political background

Before the union with Great Britain took place, Ireland had been ruled for over four hundred years by an Irish Parliament, but there had been many reasons for discontent. The population's Catholic majority was denied both the right to vote (only granted in 1793) and the right to sit in Parliament; moreover, the executive branch of Government was appointed by the Crown and was answerable only to it. For all these reasons, much of the population did not fully trust the independence of the Parliament, and when Great Britain put the Union with Ireland on her political agenda, the British Prime Minister William Pitt must have thought that the Irish people would not oppose the extinction of their Parliament.

On the contrary, the setback that took place in January 1799 showed that the objective was not so near: a motion defending the right of the Irish people to an independent legislature was only defeated after an exhausting 21-hour debate, while an anti-unionist motion was approved within a few hours. The terms of the Union were clearly not convincing enough, and needed substantial changes both in content and tactics.

As the following table shows, in which a random sample selection of 65 pamphlets not included in this study is considered out of the 254 available, the year 1799 was characterised by the publication of a relatively higher number of pamphlets. This was certainly due to this temporary hold-up that the Union suffered in Parliament, which must have given new hope and new vigour to anti-unionist opposition, while on the other hand it must have persuaded the unionists that their pro-union campaign had been so far inadequate. Moreover, the already heated atmosphere was further inflamed by the British Government's brutal anti-insurrection campaign that followed the famous 1798 Wexford rebellion, whose leaders were arrested and tried for treachery.

Table 1. Temporal distribution of 65 pamphlets, randomly selected

	1751	1787	1798	1799	1800	Total number of pamphlets
Anti-union pamphlets	2	–	8	27	5	42
Pro-union pamphlets	1	2	1	12	7	23
Total number of pamphlets per year	3	2	9	39	12	65

Meanwhile, Pitt's attitude to the concessions needed in order to win the hearts and minds of the Irish people to the unionist cause changed dramatically. The May-nooth agreement, with which the British Government and the Bishops agreed on a state payment for the clergy, is only one example of the many tactics adopted to obtain a majority for the Union in the Irish Parliament (Geoghegan 2001: 4–43). Whatever could be used (titles, bishoprics, deaneries, peerages, pensions etc.) was promised, and, by the winter of 1799–1800, Pitt had the majority he needed (see Keogh and Wheelan 2001 for a fuller account of causes and consequences of the 1800 Act of Union).

3.2   The participants

Most anti-unionist writers had United Irishmen connections. The association, founded in 1791 to free Ireland from British control, and outlawed in 1793, after which date members continued their work in clandestinity, was in fact the forma-tive political experience for many of them. The Irish Bar also significantly contrib-uted to the debate, writing numerous pamphlets. As far as the prospect of a union was concerned, in their pamphlets writers pointed out fears of economic ruin, of an increase in absentee landlords, and of the decline of Irish cities (Dublin in par-ticular). But most of all they insisted on what they called the tragedy of Ireland's political death, the extinction of Irish national existence, and, with it, of the rights of the Irish people. Many of these pamphlets also tried to delegitimise the Union arguing that the Irish Parliament was corrupt or legally unable to enact it, and that the measure would therefore be unconstitutional. This implied that a popular re-fusal, in other words violent resistance, would not only be justifiable but also legal. Anti-unionist pamphleteers were clearly aiming at stirring up a public storm of such violence as to force either Parliament or Government, or both, to abandon the Act (Mansergh 2001: 134–35).

Pro-union pamphlet writers usually enjoyed a high social position; they in-cluded the undersecretary at Dublin Castle, clergymen, a colonial secretary, the chairman in London, and other renowned politicians. These writers, most of whom were employed by the Castle, the seat of the English Government and ad-ministration for all of Ireland, rebutted anti-union arguments with promises of greater security, prosperity, and even greater happiness for all Irish people. Obvi-ously, they rejected all charges of corruption, and insisted that the Parliament was indeed competent to enact legislation and, therefore, any resistance to the Act would be illegal (Mansergh 2001: 134–35).

As to their addressees, anti-union writers usually address their *fellow country-men*, and take their anti-unionist stand for granted, which allows them greater freedom in the use of a more passionate and aggressive language. Only two of the pamphlets I have examined for the purpose of this paper are apparently addressed to an individual, but in both cases the whole country is really called in as witness to the interaction. Moreover, unlike unionist pamphlets, almost all the texts also interact with rival pamphlet writers, whether in second or third person, so that there is generally wider scope for the use of impolite strategies.

Unionists, on the other hand, usually write to win over hesitant Protestants apparently not yet fully convinced of the convenience of a union between the two countries. Their texts usually point out the advantages of a union for the Protestants, but despite the fact that the writers could count on a favourable, if yet timid, attitude of their audience to the issue, the tone is everywhere quite cautious and temperate. This is likely to be due to the ambiguous situation in which unionists found themselves: the support of the Catholics was crucial to the success of a union, but an open commitment to them was impossible, as the majority of those who were potentially in favour of a union was so for reasons of protecting themselves from the Catholics. A circumspect tone, designed to offend neither party, was then clearly necessary. As Mansergh remarks (2001:136), the British Government could not afford to endanger its position in the middle of the French Revolutionary War, either by bringing about more Irish restlessness and dissatisfaction, or alienating the sympathies of the political classes that had always been loyal.

Concluding this brief presentation of the main contextual elements, it should be remarked that the position taken, either against or in favour of the union, the composition of the two opposing groups and the identity of their respective addressees may anticipate preferences in terms of argumentative strategies, where the more marked choices are likely to come from the more marked position, the opposition to the union. But before we proceed with the analysis of the texts, I will briefly outline the most recent impoliteness research in order to contextualise the present study.

4.   Outline of impoliteness research

Politeness research has usually viewed aggravating language as just an exception to normally polite behaviour, so that impoliteness has only recently been considered a notion in its own right. Bousfield describes it as

> the broad opposite of politeness, in that, rather than seeking to mitigate face-threatening acts (FTAs), impoliteness constitutes the communication of intentionally gratuitous and conflictive verbal face-threatening acts (FTAs) which are purposefully delivered: (i.) unmitigated, in contexts where mitigation is required,

and/or, (ii.) with deliberate *aggression*, that is, with the face threat exacerbated, 'boosted', or maximised in some way to heighten the face damage inflicted. (2008: 72, italics in original)

This is how I use and understand the term in this paper.

According to Bousfield (2008: 82–93) there have been three innovative approaches to impoliteness, Lachenicht's (1980), Austin's (1990), and Culpeper's (1996). Of the three, Austin's work is the most receiver oriented, as it describes how utterances can be understood and interpreted as abusive, quite neglecting the role of the speaker. By contrast, both Lachenicht and Culpeper concentrate on the role of the speaker. Lachenicht (1980: 607) considers the use of impolite language as an intentional attack on the interlocutor's need to be approved of or to act freely, and he considers four super-strategies to account for aggravating language: off record, bald on record, positive aggravation, and negative aggravation. Bousfield (2008: 89–90) identifies two major weaknesses in Lachenicht's approach. First is the fact that he applies politeness variables to aggravation strategies in a mechanical way, claiming, for example, that off record strategies are typically used to aggravate powerful addressees, positive aggravation for people with whom we have a closer relation, and negative aggravation for socially distant people; second is the fact that the model is not based upon real life data, and so its author's claims remain theoretical. On the other hand, Bousfield points out that Lachenicht's work describes a wide range of linguistic strategies that can be used to damage the addressee's face, and he also contemplates the possibility for strategies to be mixed, unlike Brown and Levinson (1987).

Culpeper's (1996: 349–350) approach to impoliteness is similar to Lachenicht's. He also defines impoliteness as the use of an intentional aggravating linguistic behaviour to damage one's interlocutor and produce disharmony. The threat can be to the addressee's positive face (her/his wish to be approved of) or to her/his negative face (her/his need to act free of any imposition), a concept that evokes Lachenicht's positive and negative aggravation. Unlike Lachenicht, however, besides extending Brown and Levinson's model, Culpeper also develops a parallel system of five impoliteness super-strategies which include: 1. bald on record impoliteness strategies, devised to damage the face of the interlocutor; 2. positive impoliteness strategies meant to aggravate the addressee's positive face needs; 3. negative impoliteness strategies, conceived as damaging the addressee's negative face wants; 4. sarcasm and 5. withholding politeness where the context would rather require it. These strategies can be combined and/or repeated to boost the overall impolite effect. According to Bousfield (2008: 91) the chief merit of Culpeper's work lies in the fact that it has been tested with real life data across different types of discourse, providing the model with a greater analysing power.

Moreover, the linguistic output strategies Culpeper indicates for both positive and negative face damage are not meant as a closed set, and so the model can adapt to changes in linguistic usage. However, as Bousfield argues, such open-endedness can also prove a weakness, as there does not seem to be any clear way of curbing the number of strategies within the model.

Culpeper (2005) indicates an interesting opportunity for the development of his approach in the adoption of a more complex model of face, such as the one developed by Spencer-Oatey (2002), a combination that, when fully pursued, might offer deeper insights into the analysis of face. Spencer-Oatey's (2007) recent contribution on face draws upon current theories of identity. She distinguishes between face and identity, claiming that face should be analysed as an interactional phenomenon, since it involves the evaluation of others. She criticises Brown and Levinson's general distinction between positive and negative face, considering it inadequate to account for the complexities of face claims. She also argues that Brown and Levinson's (1987) model is focused on individual face sensitivities, and needs to be complemented by wider relational, collective perspectives. My data actually calls for such a perspective, as it is not so much the individual face of the writer which is often at stake, but rather the face of the Irish people on one side, and of England on the other.

Although Culpeper's work on impoliteness (Culpeper 1996; Culpeper et al. 2003) has the merit of having filled the gap existing in politeness research, Bousfield (2008: 93–95) points out a weakness in his super-strategies, arguing that a clear-cut dichotomy between positive and negative impoliteness does not exist in real life, as often both aspects of the addressee's face are attacked by the same utterance. This can be seen in the following example where the Irish interlocutor's positive face is threatened by the impolite belief the speaker's words imply (people who remain silent or indifferent are criminal), while her/his negative face is also threatened by the imposition (s/he has to speak out otherwise s/he is a criminal):

(1) At a period like the present, when the very existence of Ireland as a Nation, is about to be annihilated, it is criminal in Irishmen to remain silent or indifferent. (*English Union, is Ireland's ruin! Or an address to the Irish Nation*, 1799: i)

In order to overcome such weaknesses, Bousfield proposes a simplified version of Culpeper's model of super-strategies, that merely distinguishes between on record and off record impoliteness (2008: 95).

On record impoliteness refers to the intentional application of strategies devised to "*explicitly* (a) attack the face of an interactant, (b) construct the face of an interactant in a non-harmonious or outright conflictive way, (c) deny the expected face wants, needs, or rights of the interactant", or any combination of these. Off record impoliteness, on the other hand, concerns strategies "where the threat or damage to an interactant's face is conveyed indirectly by way of an implicature [...] and can be cancelled". This also involves Culpeper's super-strategies "sarcasm", the use of strategies "which, on the surface, appear to be appropriate but which are meant to be taken as meaning the opposite in terms of face-management" (Bousfield 2008:95), and "withholding of politeness" in contexts where this would be expected, as failing to communicate politeness may be interpreted as "the absence of a polite attitude" (Brown and Levinson 1987:5). Culpeper's linguistic impoliteness output strategies are still applicable within this model (Bousfield 2008:101), and so my analysis of the texts will make use of these strategies to investigate how impoliteness is communicated.

5.   The realisation of impoliteness in anti/unionist discourse

Goffman (1967:14) identifies three types of action that may constitute a threat to face (intentional, incidental and accidental threats) depending on whether the speaker acts with the intention of causing insult or not; but it is only when the offensive intention is manifest and it is clearly understood by the receiver that we have impoliteness. Incidental or accidental threats can be accounted for using the existing politeness framework and are therefore not included in the present study, as the speaker's intention in these cases is not to cause face damage (Bousfield 2008:69). It should be admitted, however, that it is sometimes difficult to establish whether the writer's intention was to offend or not. In extract (2), for example, taken from the pamphlet that started the paper war, the anonymous writer (the Englishman Edward Cooke, undersecretary at the Civil Department in Dublin Castle) takes a deceptively impartial stance to the Union and tries to convince the Irish audience (also using inclusive "we") of the many advantages deriving from the project. Although the arguments that he uses in support are certainly more likely to offend than to convince, there is nothing in the text that suggests the intentionality of the offence; however the reaction of the people, the dozens of angry pamphlets written in reply, of which extract (3) is an example, establish it as impoliteness beyond any doubt :

> (2)   Let us compare then the situations of Great Britain and Ireland. The former enjoys the best practical Constitution and Government which any nation has ever experienced; the people are in general the most civilized, the most obedient to Law, the most honest in dealing, the most decent in morals, the most regular in Religion of any people in Europe [...]. Now, in many of these particulars, we acknowledge and lament the inferiority of Ireland – our civil and religious discontents, jealousies and disturbances; the conspiracies, the

insurrections, the rebellions which have disgraced us, proclaim our defects in civilization and policy [...]. If any person has a son uneducated, unimproved, and injured by bad habits, and bad company; in order to remedy these imperfections, would it not be his first endeavour to establish him in the best societies, and introduce him into the most virtuous, the most polished, and the most learned company; and if he could once reconcile him to such companies, and teach him to relish their conversation, would he not be certain of his son's improvement, and of his finally turning out to his credit and satisfaction? (*Arguments for and against an Union, between Great Britain and Ireland, considered*, 1798: 10–12)

(3)   Do you hope to conciliate us, by telling us that we are a savage, immoral, irrational, ill-mannered race, with almost every other degrading and contemptuous insinuation. – I well know, such are the sentiments which the low and vulgar of your country entertain of the people of Ireland, but in a long intercourse with that country, I declare I never had the misfortune of meeting a single gentleman so weak and illiberal as to avow those prejudices. (*An Union neither necessary nor expedient for Ireland: being an answer to the author of "Arguments for and against an Union, between Great Britain and Ireland, considered"*, 1798: 6–7)

Although not explicitly conflictive, in fact, the writer offends his hearers' dignity and pride, and by thus constructing their face "in a non-harmonious way" (Bousfield 2008: 95) and denying their face wants and needs, he transforms his possibly unintended offensiveness into on-record impoliteness.

The pamphlets contain a great variety of examples of impoliteness, too many, in fact, to be dealt with in such a short space as this paper allows. I will therefore just touch on the most obvious features that characterise the two sides, bearing in mind that clear-dividing lines between categories don't always exist, and that, as Bousfield (2008: 100) convincingly shows, individual impoliteness strategies rarely occur on their own.

6.   Analysis: On record strategies

6.1   Rhetorical and response seeking challenges

The writer-reader interaction in these pamphlets illustrates various strategies which lend themselves to an analysis in terms of impoliteness. Questions are used to challenge the addressee (for example asking a challenging question, questioning her/his stance or beliefs, or even her/his assumed power (Bousfield 2008: 132), and as such they represent potential threats to the addressee's face. They are in fact one of the most common and most effective linguistic devices employed in the corpus for both the realisation and the communication of impoliteness.

Culpeper et al. (2003:1559) consider impolitely challenging the addressee a threat to her/his negative face; in fact, as Bousfield (2008:132) argues, it can concern both aspects of face because of the two ways in which face-threatening challenges work, as either rhetorical or response seeking challenges, although the difference is not always unproblematic.

The rhetorical aspect of challenges can damage the addressee's negative face, as s/he is forced to answer in a highly controlled way; however, it can also be positively face damaging because it can be used to imply impolite beliefs, and bring the addressee to make a self-damaging assertion (Bousfield 2008:241), as in the following example where, by providing the expected answer ("nobody"), the interlocutor has to admit the illegitimacy of what he is doing, namely depriving Ireland of her independence:

(4)   Ireland has never given a king to England – her independence has been acknowl-
       edged, even after conquest; and who now, can have a right to dispose of it?
       (*Observations on "Arguments for and against an Union between Great Britain
       and Ireland"*, 1799:7)

As to response-seeking challenges, Bousfield (2008:243) distinguishes between challenges that really offer the addressee the opportunity to justify the action/s that caused the speaker's impolite challenge, and those which he calls "verbal traps", insincere requests for information that force the interlocutor to make a self-damaging assertion, and may also trigger further impoliteness. These are often used in the corpus to cast doubt on the validity or even sincerity of the writer's opponent's beliefs, a strategy that occurs more frequently in the anti-union corpus than in the unionist one. In this way, the writer expresses strong views opposed to the addressee, simultaneously aggravating his positive and his negative face, as in the following example:

(5)   As to the benefit of the corn trade, and the other advantages you promise her
       [Dublin] from the canals both in England and Ireland, how are those matters
       connected with a Union? Is the Union necessary as a means of procuring
       to Dublin the corn trade with England? And cannot the canals in England
       and Ireland be brought to perfection without it? (*An Union neither neces-
       sary nor expedient for Ireland: being an answer to the author of "Arguments
       for and against an Union, between Great Britain and Ireland, considered"*,
       1798:40–41)

The qualitative analysis I carried out shows that anti-union writers make use of questioning strategies more frequently than their rivals (56.95%:43.04%), but it also reveals a difference in the types of questions employed in the pamphlets belonging to the two sides (Table 2).

Table 2. Distribution of different types of questions in the corpus in percentage (feature/ total number of the same type of questions in the subcorpus, raw figures in parenthesis)

	Wh-questions	Yes/no questions	Alternative questions	Negated yes/no questions	Negated wh-questions
Anti-union corpus	56.32% (98)	58.38% (87)	100% (6)	51.78% (29)	33.33% (1)
Pro-union corpus	43.67% (76)	41.61% (62)	–	48.21% (27)	66.66% (2)
TOTAL number of questions in corpus	44.84% (174)	38.40% (149)	1.54% (6)	14.43% (56)	0.77% (3)

Since this difference may imply different impoliteness potentials and different degrees of control over the addressee's answer, I will now look at the different types of questions in greater detail.

6.1.1 *Wh-questions*

Wh-questions in the corpus are usually rhetorical, as the speaker does not really expect an answer from the reader. In their positive form they correspond to strong negative statements, while the less common negative wh-question is comparable to a strong assertion (Quirk et al. 1985:82). The impolite potential of this type of question derives from the fact that they are used as rhetorical challenges that admit only one answer, while at the same time they also express strong views against the interlocutor's position. Consider the following examples:

(6) What proof can be adduced that Ireland will be happier by an Union with England? (*Observations on "Arguments for and against an Union between Great Britain and Ireland"*, 1799:6)

(7) What man in his senses would embark a capital in a kingdom, where he had not the security of a day's enjoyment of it, where the industry of a laborious and successful life might be sacrificed in a moment, to the wantonness of the rioter or the ravages of the robber? You are yourselves the causes of your shame, and it rests upon you to remove it. (*A letter to the people of Ireland they all can understand and ought to read*, 1799:24)

In extract (6), the writer is rebutting the arguments that the author of the rival pamphlet has brought in support of the union. By activating in the reader a negative answer as the only possible one, he damages the interactant's negative face, but also questions the validity of his whole argument, a criticism that is equivalent to an attack to his positive face. In extract (7), on the other hand, the unionist writer is trying to convince the readership of the many advantages of a union; by means of the rhetorical challenge he aggravates both aspects of his addressees' face, as the challenge forces them to provide a self-damaging answer that implies a strong criticism of their possible anti-unionist view. Ireland is associated with negative aspects (rioters and robbers), while the readers are openly criticised for being responsible for the situation.

Moreover, some of the questions might appear as incidental face threats, just voicing the writer's own personal grief and anger, but the use of personalised pronouns transforms them into threats intentionally made to damage the interlocutor's face, as is the case with extract (8):

(8)   Why then Englishmen take away from us that Parliament which has favoured you in all your wishes, and supported you in all your designs? How shall we term such unkind treatment? Ingratitude at least, you yourselves will allow it to be, but I will tell you, it is something more than Ingratitude, I say, it is treachery, it is robbery, it is rapacity, it is tyranny on your side, towards a brave, frank, generous and free-spirited people.
      (*English Union, is Ireland's ruin! Or an address to the Irish Nation*, 1799: 12)

The face damage relies on the fact that the unilateral discourse does not offer the interlocutors the possibility to reject the accusation (so their freedom of action is encroached); moreover, the rhetorical challenge is equivalent to a form of enhanced criticism, as the addressees are not only criticised for their past actions, but also implicitly accused of having provoked the writer's exasperation (Bousfield 2008: 134). This particular extract also highlights another aspect of the impolite potential of this type of question, so frequently employed by writers of both sides, which derives from the fact that they can be used to present something as given information: the knowledge assumed in the proposition, whether correct or not, is presupposed, and the writer is able to position the readers as sharing this knowledge.

6.1.2 *Yes/no questions*
Yes/no questions are also frequently used in the corpus to present certain versions of events as uncontroversial, and thereby position the reader as sharing the writer's view. The writer provides her/his own versions of events and the addressee can only either confirm or deny what has been said. In this way, not only can

writers predict the answer they are going to hear, they can also orient the questions accordingly. A positive rhetorical yes/no question is equivalent to a strong negative assertion, which is sometimes reinforced by the answer provided by the writer, maximising disagreement. In extract (9), for example, the writer is refuting the arguments that the author of the pamphlet *Arguments for and against an Union, between Great Britain and Ireland, considered* has brought in support of his unionist thesis. The repeated use of questions enhances the aggravating effect of the writer's criticism, also questioning the addressee's assumed authority:

(9)   We are told an Union will bring us an increase of commerce, agriculture, wealth and harmony. But the proof is what we have a right to examine. Will commerce increase by a decrease of consumption? Will agriculture increase by the more frequent absence of landlords? Will wealth increase by more specie being drained from the kingdom? Will harmony increase by the constant comparisons of English wealth, of English elegancies, and conveniences? These will be more easily proved to be some of the effects of an Union, than the benefits that are presupposed. *(Observations on "Arguments for and against an Union between Great Britain and Ireland",* 1799: 12)

Yes/no questions in the corpus are usually conducive, in other words "the speaker is predisposed to the kind of answer he has wanted or expected" (Quirk et al. 1985: 83), which greatly accounts for the impolite potential of this type of question. By leading the reader to provide a certain answer, in fact, the speaker can also set it up to be self-face damaging, as in the following examples from the anti-unionist (10) and the unionist (11) corpus:

(10)   To my Catholic countrymen I would say, respect the voice of those of your clergy who confine themselves to the sacred functions of their office; who, imitating the example of the founder of their religion, meddled not with the business of this world, nor engaged in its political warfare. Does [sic] your Lordship's priestly and Episcopal supporters imitate such an example, by wasting away their time in endeavouring to frighten the innocent peasantry of Ireland into a submission to the most annihilating, ignominious, and debasing measure that ever was agitated in a civilized nation – the public prints will give you the best answer. (*A letter to a Noble Lord, containing a full declaration of the Catholic sentiment on the important question of Union,* 1800: 6)

(11)   A very few lines must shew the great Body of Catholics, what sort of a friend they have got in Mr Catholic, or rather Mr. Hypocrite – off with the disguise, for your tricks can no longer go down even with the most pliant dupes that attended the late meeting at the Royal Exchange! – What! are the Catholics to remain content under the brand that they are, at this moment, marked with,

and never hope for better times? – Yet, you and your Anti-union Evening Post scribblers do advise it. (*A short address to the pretended Catholic Addresser of a Noble Lord, by a citizen, but not a French one*, 1800: 1)

By contrast, as Quirk et al. (1985: 83) claim, yes/no questions with a negative orientation are biased towards a positive answer, and are always conducive. The implication for impoliteness is that if the addressee answers according to the writer's expectations, then s/he will not be able to avoid a self-damaging admission. Consider the following examples:

(12)   Has not Ireland had her season of calamity? Have not her calamities arisen within herself shall we add – from her own misconduct? (*Union or not?* 1799: 8)

(13)   In short, the *degrading sentiments* you profess to feel towards Ireland, and the *complete subjection* to which England may reduce her in case of non-compliance, seems throughout to be the whole foundation of your argument. Is not the following the true substance of your address? – Mean, beggarly, vicious, and contemptible nation, come forward to this treaty with your elevated, wealthy, august, and powerful neighbour. Rely upon it, you shall enjoy equal advantage in the arrangement of the terms, for *she knows your worthlessness*, and *her own merit*. (*An Union neither necessary nor expedient for Ireland: being an answer to the author of "Arguments for and against an Union, between Great Britain and Ireland, considered"*, 1798: 8–9)

Sarcasm is also often employed by anti-union writers to enhance face threats in yes/no questions. In the following extract, the writer is once more rejecting the unionist argumentation developed in the pamphlet *Arguments for and against an Union, between Great Britain and Ireland, considered*. The strong assertion to which the negated yes/no question corresponds questions the validity of the opponent's line of reasoning, while sarcasm is used to belittle his authority:

(14)   And the Catholics are amused with a prospect of (what he humorously terms) total Emancipation and the possibility of gaining political power, through the channel of Protestant Ascendancy, at a time when the monopoly of that power shall have been so considerably narrow'd, as nearly to exclude the whole Protestant body itself: and are not these cogent reasons for an Union? He next takes a geographical survey of the island, and informs the citizens of the metropolis, that Dublin will be the residence of a Viceroy, the seat of the revenue, and the head-quarters of the army; as if this was not the case already [...]. Are not these weighty arguments in favour of an Union? (*Pitt's Union*, 1799: 6)

Alternative yes/no questions occur rarely in the corpus, and only in anti-unionist texts. As happens with the other types of questions, they are highly conducive and admit only one answer. This strategy is always used impolitely by anti-unionist writers to entail impolite beliefs concerning the opponents' behaviour or beliefs, as in the extracts below:

(15)   I beseech you to consider, fairly and seriously, for what purpose the British troops are here; consider it only with a reference to this measure: and to this measure alone do I consider it as referring. What is to be the result? Are they meant to protect the freedom of debate, or to destroy it? If you reject an Union, are they to support the rejection, or to contradict it? I ask you, whether it is your wish to have them here; and if it is, I will tell you that you are not the Parliament of the country but of the Minister, and that you will soon cease to be a Parliament. (*An address to the people of Ireland, shewing them why they ought to submit to an Union*, 1799: 9).

(16)   Has the Parliament any fixed limit or has it not? From whence is the answer to come, the People or the Parliament? The creator or the creature? Locke is of opinion the people shall be judge, "for who, (says he) shall be judge whether his trustee or deputy acts well, and according to the trust reposed in him, but he, who deputes him" […]. (*The conspiracy of Pitt and Co. detected in a letter to the Parliament of Ireland*, 1799: 4)

In extract (15) the writer is addressing the "legislators of the country" and challenging the impartiality of their position; the conducivity of the alternative questions maximises the criticism, that results in the final threat to their positive face ("I will tell you that you are not the Parliament of the country but of the Minister") which is equivalent to an accusation of being disloyal to the country. In extract (16), the alternative questions enhance criticism of the Irish Parliament, highlighting its abuses and consequently also questioning its power and authority.

6.2   Negative impoliteness strategies

6.2.1 *Condescend, scorn, ridicule*
The corpus contains a wide range of utterances which are mainly directed at damaging aspects of face concerning freedom of action. However, while anti-union writers display a variety of examples of negatively-oriented impoliteness, pro-unionist writers usually appear more cautious and selective. Challenges occur less frequently, and, of the eleven pamphlets I have examined for the purposes of this paper, there is only one where the writer appears to condescend to, or even ridicule, his rivals. This is by the Orangeman Harding Gifford, who refers to a rival

writer's ideas on the subject of a union as the "extatic oaths of the bedlamite barrister, who dares to array his Creator as at party in political debate" and to his worries about Irish independence as "rant" ("then follows usually a good deal of rant about independence and imperial dignity", "pretty nearly as good argument", he says, "as the ravings of a maniac for his straw coronet and wooden sceptre"). These expressions can be strongly impolite, as every utterance simultaneously combines more than one strategy: they are abusive and humiliating, as the rival writer is explicitly compared to a "maniac", and his worries about Irish independence compared in importance to the "straw coronet and wooden sceptre" of a madman. The offender is contemptuous, and the interlocutor's authority is consequently challenged, as the unionist writer openly seeks and maximises his disagreement.

Anti-unionists, on the other hand, often scorn or belittle their rivals. The following extracts provide typical examples of this strategy:

(17)   When I look at the names of so many Irishmen renouncing their Country, in the public prints; and with prone obsequiousness, filling up the lists presented to them by the civil or military agents of corruption, I shudder at the prostitution of internal principle and conviction. (*Protest from one of the people of Ireland, against an Union with Great Britain*, 1800: 8)

(18)   To him who would stop for a moment and cast his eye over the scenes which have been acted and are now acting in this devoted country […] what has he to see? He will there behold some of his Catholic countrymen licking the hand so lately raised against them […]. Must he not blush at the prostitution of his fellowmen, and heave a sigh of sorrow at the depravity of human nature? […]. Thank God, the actors in the scene are not very numerous, nor are they the most respectable or esteemed characters of the Catholics of Ireland; their influence in politics has long dwindled into insignificance […]. (*A letter to a Noble Lord, containing a full declaration of the Catholic sentiment on the important question of Union*, 1800: 5)

The impoliteness of these extracts is enhanced by the strongly emotive language adopted by the writers; it can be considered negatively oriented because it impinges on the opponent's freedom to support a different position, but also positively oriented for the impolite beliefs the writers' words imply. Both extracts use the term "prostitution" which is highly suggestive, further reinforced by verbs such as "shudder" and "blush", both evoking a sense of shame; the negated yes/no question ("Must he not blush…"), moreover, positions the reader as sharing the writers' damning view of the unionist choice some of the Catholics have made.

6.2.2 *Threaten/frighten*

Threatening is not common in either corpus; however, the stylistic difference in the few examples we find in the two corpora is worth commenting on. The only explicit example of a threat we find in the unionist corpus is, in fact, indirect ("They are seriously warned not to be the tools of party but to listen to reason") so that it does not sound aggressive, despite the presence of the verb "warn". In anti-union texts, on the other hand, the threat is often personalised and its effect boosted by means of other devices, as in extracts (19) and (20), where either religious echoes ("Woe to..."), the use of highly emotive lexis or structural repetitions ("be not", "take care", "know well", "think not" etc.) amplify the threatening effect.

(19)   Woe to the man and to the million who are willing or are able to calculate the profit or the loss resulting from the sale of their Country! The man must have the heart of a huxter, and the million must be destined to wander, like Jews, over the earth, without the honour or happiness of a home. (*Protest from one of the people of Ireland, against an Union with Great Britain*, 1800: 13)

(20)   Be not too precipitate Mr. Pitt [...] take care then how you proceed, you may do an act, which you cannot recall, and which may be destructive of the life of both kingdoms – I tell you such a measure may shake the throne of your gracious master, know well then the sentiments of the Irish before you proceed any farther. Think not you have the voice of this Nation by purchasing the voice and interests of your Borough-mongers. Never persuade yourself so far as to imagine that you will be able to purchase Irish independence. [...] Ministers before the present day, have been denominated Traitors to their King and Country, for pursuing, or allowing to be pursued measures, which, in their consequences might be ruinous to both; they have been impeached, and have forfeited their lives too, for such criminal conduct; presume not then to bring forward a question which may lead you up to the block, and in its consequences may shake the empire [...]. (*English Union, is Ireland's ruin! Or an address to the Irish Nation*, 1799: 14–15)

In both extracts the threat concerns both aspects of face, as the writer threatens her/his interlocutor's freedom of action, intimating that her/his behaviour will eventually prove harmful (Culpeper 1996: 358), but he also implies a strong criticism of her/his past actions and possible future decisions, which enhances the damage to face.

6.2.3 *Explicitly associate the other with a negative aspect*

Culpeper (1996: 358) classifies this strategy as a threat to the interlocutor's negative face, but, as was the case with the other negative strategies I have just discussed, it can also be interpreted as an intentional threat to the addressee's need for approval

(Bousfield 2008:116), which clearly confirms how problematic the distinction between positive and negative impoliteness is. Consider the following example:

(21)   The grand Artificer, sends clouds of locusts, hurricanes and earthquakes to visit the earth with plague, pestilence and famine, for what wise purposes the limited senses of Man cannot conceive; wolves, tigers, serpents, hyenas, crocodiles, he has created: with what intent Man cannot comprehend. He has produced – a Nero, a Caligula, an Alva, a Robespierre, a Pitt; – we know not why – but this we know – all are useful – for God makes nought in vain. (*The conspiracy of Pitt and Co. detected in a letter to the Parliament of Ireland*, 1799:22)

In the extract, the writer associates Pitt with disturbing historical protagonists, and to the worst plagues on earth, implying that his actions have been as destructive. In this particular case, the damage to the interlocutor's positive face seems even greater than the threat to his negative face, enhanced by the sarcastic comment the writer makes at the end ("all are useful for God makes nought in vain").

6.3   Positive impoliteness strategies

6.3.1   *Snub*

Both pro- and anti-union writers make wide use of positive impoliteness strategies, especially offensive forms of address, words or phrases used to maximise disagreement or dissociate from one's opponent/s. One of the most frequent strategies employed, at least as far as the anti-unionist corpus is concerned, is snubbing, which openly attacks the interlocutor's wish to be approved of through the strong disapproval it conveys. However, as was the case with the negative impoliteness strategies discussed so far, the threat concerns both aspects of face, as it also denies the interlocutor the right to communicate with the speaker, as in the following extracts, where the writers are commenting on rival pamphlets written in support of the union:

(22)   Conceiving contemptuous silence to be the best answer to his insolence, and his own pamphlet to be the best reply to his ignorance, I do not purpose to waste your time, or tire your patience by more comments on this Author […]. (*Pitt's Union*, 1799:12–13)

(23)   As to the mercantile effects of the measure, were I competent to the discussion of the little question, I should disdain to meddle with it. (*Protest from one of the people of Ireland, against an Union with Great Britain*, 1800:13)

Snubbing does not occur as frequently in the unionist corpus where, rather, writers try to challenge their rivals' credibility, undermining their arguments as a consequence. The following extract provides a typical example:

(24)   I must again say, that when reading Mr. Weld's Pamphlet, I am more and more astonished, when I see a Man in his line, advance assertions with regard to the past and present situation of Scotland, a country not so distant, or unknown to the inhabitants of this, as to allow the possibility of what he states with regard to it, being in the least credited. Surely it is no good account of his cause, when he has recourse to misrepresentation and false colouring; he seems not to trust to the soundness of his argument, but endeavours to dazzle the reader, and like a skilful veteran of the law, to throw what light he pleases upon the subject. (*A few thoughts on an Union with some observations upon Mr. Weld's pamphlet of "No Union!", addressed to the yeomanry of Dublin*, 1799: 8–9)

6.3.2 *Derogatory denominations and epithets*

Although taboo words are not used by any of the writers, derogatory denominations occur in both corpora, conveying strong views opposed to the addressee. They can be considered threats to her/his positive face, because they usually imply impolite beliefs, casting doubt on the validity of their rivals' ideas and honesty, ("this Proteus", "Mr Hypocrite", "political dreamers", "speculating demagogues", "maniac"), or even on the morality of their supporters' behaviour ("United Irish conspirators", "factious and desperate adventurers with nothing to lose", "unprincipled and desperate republicans of no religion", "malevolent abettors") as often happens in pro-union pamphlets. They indicate an exceedingly negative attitude of the writer towards the addressee, or the political opponent. This strategy is often combined with other strategies.

In anti-union pamphlets derogatory denominations are often employed to aggravate William Pitt's face, attacking his political capacity and honesty ("Belial, apostate Pitt who never spoke but to deceive", "domineering Minister", "for fifteen years you have held the helm of Britain, […] you have ruled her ill – you have been to England a bad Minister – to Ireland a destroying spirit"). Offensive denominations are sometimes also used to address those who are expected to defend Ireland's independence but betray this expectation, like some of the Catholic priests who are defined as "so many prostituted elements in the hands of the public enemy". This is particularly significant if we consider that in seventeenth- and eighteenth-century argumentation there was more formal respect for one's adversary than one might expect.

6.3.3 *Seek disagreement / avoid agreement*

Impoliteness in these texts also includes other literal uses of negative and/or abusive words by means of which the writer maximises her/his disagreement with, and disapproval of, the addressee's actions. As far as this strategy is concerned, anti-union writers again make greater use of it than their rivals and also appear more aggressive in their word choices. For example, they speak of the unionists' "wretched, ignominious names", and describe them as "despicable and dishonourable, entitled to pity", while the British are described as "an enemy who would give no quarter", and having an "indiscriminate and insatiable fury". This strategy is often combined with others, as in the following extract where the writer engages in both disagreement and disassociation, while also associating England with such negative characters as Manzoni's "crafty bravo". Moreover, in order to enhance impoliteness still further, sarcasm ("*magnanimous* England") is also employed:

(25) I conjure you by every tie that binds you to your native land, to remonstrate – to arouse and resist an union with England; is this the time for *magnanimous* England, like the crafty bravo, to give the death blow to what was called *the Independence of Ireland*! Is it generous, or is it just in that power to seize the unsuspecting moment of rendering you a contemptible province to aggrandize her insatiable ambition, intoxicated with her naval successes, and madly persevering in a destructive war, when, had she the generosity, as she has the power, she might effect an honourable peace? (*No Union! Bing [sic] an appeal to Irishmen*, 1798: 12–13)

The Union is presented as the "most annihilating, ignominious, debasing measure that ever was agitated in a civilized country", as "folly, treachery, danger", "the grave of your hopes", "destructive, ruinous", and "disgusted, ungenerous, unworthy treatment"; rival writers are also often abused, and common ground denied, as in the following extract:

(26) My reasons for believing him to be the Author, are founded upon the ignorance of the writer, appearing through every line of the work, and the insolence of the language, in which the sentiments are delivered. (*Pitt's Union*, 1799: 3)

Although unionist writers may seem less aggressive in their threats to face, they also often impolitely attack their political opponents, insisting on Ireland's presumed inferiority; they define her as "the weaker vessel", and blame "the rude and indolent habits" of her people, as opposed to the more civilised way of life of the English who are repeatedly defined as her "natural superior", as the real cause for Ireland's problems. Extracts (27) and (28) are typical examples:

(27)   When, therefore, one of the States, desirous to form a Union, is inferior in point of civilization, agriculture, commerce, manufactures, morals, manners, establishments, constitution; and the other state is eminent and superior to all the world in these advantages; it is evident, that an union, in such a case, must be most beneficial to the former; for there is every probability, that the Union will communicate, by degrees, all its advantages and excellencies; and the inferior Society will be thus placed in a state of continual emulation, and improvement. (*Arguments for and against an Union, between Great Britain and Ireland, considered*, 1798: 10)

(28)   A crisis is past; – we are floating upon the bosom of another; – we clearly see, we are deeply impressed with the political necessity of our entire incorporation; – we propose certain terms of union; we think them just, we think them liberal; – if there should in your judgement appear parts incomplete, we are open to conviction, and willing to reconsider and improve; – our union is for life, and it is our duty and our interest to give you a just participation in our power, in our trade, in our establishments, and in our capital; – you, too, must make some sacrifice – like a virgin that resigns her maiden honours for the legitimate embrace and necessary protection of her natural superior. You shall enter the firm upon the most honourable footing; you are confessedly deficient in point of capital; you cannot therefore expect an equal share, – we offer you an equitable proportion – while you trade on your own bottom you lie open to combination and ruin; our incorporation will give your industry its full spring, by producing interior tranquillity – and never lose sight of this great political truth, that OUR UNION WILL BE THE BEST SECURITY TO YOUR PROPERTY. (*An exposition on the principal terms of Union, and its probable effects on Ireland*, 1800: 17)

The less emotive lexical choices are certainly not enough to mitigate the writer's threat to face.

6.3.4 *Impolite beliefs*

It should by now be clear, the extent to which writers mix and combine strategies in this corpus in order to be maximally offensive and reach their persuasive goal. This often makes it extremely difficult to distinguish between categories. Abusive language can also take the form of open accusations, by means of which writers express impolite beliefs as to their rivals' social roles. The content of the accusations varies, again depending on the side of the writer. Unionist writers often accuse their rivals of lying, discrediting their ability (or will) to tell the truth, as in examples (29)–(31):

(29) If this gentleman is not himself ignorant, what then does his writings mean? why are they fraught with so much Misinformation, Misconstruction, and Violence? Surely to mislead the ignorant, and rouse a spirit of revolt, against everything that reason, humanity, or religion can suggest. (*A few thoughts on an Union with some observations upon Mr. Weld's pamphlet of "No Union!", addressed to the yeomanry of Dublin*, 1799:7)

(30) I'm sure the gentleman found no such kind of argument in support of an Union in the anonymous pamphlet, and I don't know why he makes use of such a one against it, it can be only for the purpose of leading the mind astray by a kind of ridicule, which is by no means praiseworthy. (*An answer to some of the many arguments made use of against a pamphlet, entitled "Arguments for and against an Union"*, 1799:19)

(31) The best refutation I can offer, to your false and scandalous libel, is to tell you who and what those Orangemen, whom you revile, are, which you may possibly not thoroughly know, though I suspect there is much of pretended ignorance, affected terror, and wilful perversion, among those of your sect in regard to the Orange institution. (*A Letter to Theobald McKenna, Esq., the Catholic Advocate; in reply to the calumnies against the Orange Institution; contained in his pamphlet purporting to be a memoire on some questions respecting the projected union*, 1799:6)

Anti-unionist pamphlets, on the other hand, are full of heavy accusations against Great Britain in particular, whose sense is well embodied in the following simile, where England's vested interest in a union is exposed and severely criticised, while the honesty of her proposal is also bitterly challenged:

(32) As to the justice we are to meet, it will be like that which is shown to a child by the guardian who wrests his all from him while he tells him; I will make you happy; and gives the child a whistle, or a cake. The boy may feel that he is injured, but he must *then* submit! (*An address to the people of Ireland, shewing them why they ought to submit to an Union*, 1799:11)

England's ability to rule impartially is almost everywhere attacked; she is accused of "base impolitic conduct", and of pursuing her own interests at Ireland's expense, but also of "robbing" and "oppressing", of "wickedness" and "machinations", or even of "throwing out concessions to deceive the unwary". Terms like "rapacity", "plunder", "treachery" occur in the writers' opposition to "an Union perfidiously undertaken by those who can smile and murder while they smile". Impolite beliefs are openly declared, rather than just implied.

6.3.5 *Disassociate from the other*

Straightforward, unmitigated disagreement also occurs in the pamphlets of both sides. Unionist writers, however, keep a moderate tone on the whole ("Britain wishes not, as Mr W. rashly and ungenerously asserts, to humble you as a rival", "as is erroneously asserted by Mr W.", "writers have fallen into error", "Mr. R. argues in my mind very erroneously", "The arguments are not maintainable"). By contrast, anti-unionists appear more determined, insistent and also often more openly abusive than their rivals, even adopting emotive words or changes in character types to emphasise the contrast ("I do express my abhorrence", "with my whole soul and strength do I utter it: NO", "I heard with disgust").

(33)   Should they, valuing themselves on their power, within their own province, presume to usurp an authority, with which they never were invested – I will, and do maintain that their laws are entitled to no obedience; and I for one declare myself discharged from any obligation, other than the law of the sword, and the right of the strongest may impose upon me. (*The conspiracy of Pitt and Co. detected in a letter to the Parliament of Ireland*, 1799:3)

(34)   I do, therefore, with my whole heart, and understanding, PROTEST against an Union of Ireland and Great Britain thus desiring to grow greater by the absorption of my native country […] I do say, In the first place, that there is not upon this earth a rightful Power competent to such a measure […] I protest against this measure, in the second place, because it despoils the people of their COUNTRY. (*Protest from one of the people of Ireland, against an Union with Great Britain*, 1800:5,7)

Disassociation is part of a strong and bitter criticism of the opponent's language and behaviour, which may sometimes also have important political implications, such as the threat of a possible rebellion, as in extract (31) above.

7.   Off record strategies

There is clearly little scope in this corpus for indirect threats to face but, before I conclude my analysis, I want to briefly discuss the use of sarcasm, as it characterises a great part of the anti-unionist production, although it is very rarely employed in the unionist corpus. Culpeper defines sarcasm as the performance of "politeness strategies that are obviously insincere, and thus remain surface realization" (1996:356), conveying therefore impoliteness. Bousfield (2008:120) considers it an off record tactic, because the criticism is never directly expressed. As far as anti-unionist writers are concerned, biting sarcasm against rival writers or Britain herself can be found in almost every pamphlet. Extracts (35) and (36) below are just two examples:

> (35) And the Catholics are amused with a prospect of (what he humourously terms) total Emancipation, and the possibility of gaining political power, through the channel of Protestant Ascendancy, at a time when the monopoly of that power shall have been so considerably narrow'd, as nearly to exclude the whole Protestant body itself: and are not these cogent reasons for an Union? [...] Perhaps the province of Connaught has been considered as wholly unworthy of the sublime contemplation of an Englishman, as more purily Irish than any other part of the island. (*Pitt's Union*, 1799:6)

> (36) In my mind I could never liken the Union with England to anything but the marriage of a young good-natured poor Irish gentleman, to an old, emaciated, painted English bawd, by whom the poor fellow was inveigled with a promise of a large fortune but *unfortunately* after the indissoluble knot is tied poor Paddy finds himself disappointed with a bag of bones and a load of debt. (*Pitt's Union*, 1799:10)

In extract (35) the writer uses sarcasm to challenge the opponent's position, belittling his authority. Extract (36), on the other hand, a clear example of the writer's intention to be maximally offensive, employs the simile to damage the English interlocutor's positive face, the "old, emaciated, painted English bawd" is certainly an unattractive picture, while by italicising the adverb "unfortunately" the writer sarcastically implies that England is malignantly aware of the deception she is responsible for.

8.   Conclusion

In attempting a definition of impoliteness, Culpeper claims that it is not simply a question of failed politeness, but rather "obviously offensive acts that cannot be completely mitigated by any surface realisation of politeness" (Culpeper 1996:350). The analysis has shown that impoliteness in its various forms is a common feature in these texts, both in the opinions arguing against, and those in favour of, a union. However, on the basis of the data I have examined, it seems to be a far more widespread and eye-catching phenomenon among anti-union than among pro-union writers, which may indicate some sort of a socio-cultural dividing line between the two sides, that I will now try to explain in terms of social distance, emotional attitude and power.

   First of all, it should not be forgotten that anti-unionist writers were a sort of "freedom fighter" calling their fellow countrymen to battle, so they were always careful to make their audience feel as close as possible to them ("my fellow citizens", "my fellow-countrymen", "my beloved countrymen"); after all, their hopes to succeed depended on their ability to raise a public storm against the union. Unionists, on the other hand, needed to defend a more difficult position, where an open commitment to either Catholics, whose support was crucial to the success of a union, or Protestants, traditionally loyal to the British Government and who wanted a union to secure themselves against the Catholics, was impossible. The social distance between readers and writers did not leave scope for passionate personal addresses. Secondly, the hatred for the British Government's brutal anti-insurrection campaign to counteract the widespread rebellions in the country certainly inflamed the debate, momentarily tilting the popular emotional balance in favour of anti-unionists. Finally, it should be kept in mind that the opposition must have felt stronger as a consequence of the unexpected setback in the run for the Union that occurred in January 1799. The force of unmitigated disagreement became the visible sign of this greater power, and therefore a crucial element in the argumentative strategy adopted by the writers to rouse popular resistance. On the other hand, the unionists must have felt that more circumspection and tact, but also more involvement, were rather needed on their part; moreover, their primary objective was not a large-scale popular support of the measure, as all they needed was to build a majority in the Irish Parliament to guarantee the success of the measure.

Concluding, then, although the passage of the Union has usually been explained in terms of what happened in Parliament and Government, the anti-union movement's continuous attempts to bring the discussion among the common people, of which the use they make of impoliteness strategies represents one of the most visible aspects, shows the importance that public opinion must have had in the debate, and confirms the need to engage with the socio-political context in order to fully exploit the potential of a complex discipline such as historical news discourse.

References

Austin, Paddy. 1990. Politeness revisited: The dark side. In Allan Bell and Janet Holmes (eds.). *New Zealand Ways of Speaking English.* Philadelphia: Multilingual Matters, 277–93.

Bousfield, Derek. 2008. *Impoliteness in Interaction.* (Pragmatics & Beyond New Series 167). Amsterdam and Philadelphia: John Benjamins.

Brown, Penelope, and Stephen C. Levinson. 1987. *Politeness: Some Universals in Language Usage.* Cambridge: Cambridge University Press.

Culpeper, Jonathan. 1996. Towards an anatomy of impoliteness. *Journal of Pragmatics* 25.3, 349–367.

Culpeper, Jonathan, Derek Bousfield, and Anne Wichmann. 2003. Impoliteness revisited: With special reference to dynamic and prosodic aspects. *Journal of Pragmatics* 35, 1545–1579.

Culpeper, Jonathan. 2005. Impoliteness and entertainment in the television quiz show: *The Weakest Link. Journal of Politeness Research* 1.1, 35–72.

Geoghegan, Patrick. 2001. The making of the union. In Dáire Keogh and Kevin Wheelan (eds.). *Acts of Union: The Causes, Contexts, and Consequences of the Act of Union.* Dublin: Four Courts Press.

Goffman, Erving. 1967. *Interaction Ritual.* Chicago: Aldine Publishing.

Keogh, Dáire, and Kevin Wheelan (eds.). 2001. *Acts of Union: The Causes, Contexts, and Consequences of the Act of Union.* Dublin: Four Courts Press.

Kienpointner, Manfred. 1997. Varieties of rudeness: Types and functions of impolite utterances. *Functions of Language* 4, 251–87.

Lachenicht, Lance G. 1980. Aggravating language: A study of abusive and insulting language. *International Journal of Human Communication* 13.4, 607–688.

Levorato, Alessandra. 2006. Wisdom, moderation and propaganda in the Act of Union debate of 1801. In Nicholas Brownlees (ed.). *News Discourse in Early Modern Britain.* Bern: Peter Lang, 273–295.

Mansergh, Daniel. 2001. The Union and the importance of public opinion. In Dáire Keogh and Kevin Wheelan (eds.). *Acts of Union: The Causes, Contexts, and Consequences of the Act of Union.* Dublin: Four Courts Press.

Quirk, Randolph, Sidney Greenbaum, Geoffrey Leech and Ian Svartvik. 1985. *A Comprehensive Grammar of the English Language.* London: Longman.

Spencer-Oatey, Helen. 2002. Managing rapport in talk: Using rapport sensitive incidents to explore the motivational concerns underlying the management of relations. *Journal of Pragmatics* 34, 529–545.

Spencer-Oatey, Helen. 2007. Theories of identity and the analysis of face. *Journal of Pragmatics* 39, 639–656.

Appendix

Anti-union pamphlets:

No Union! Bing [sic] an appeal to Irishmen. By Matthew Weld, Esq. Barrister at law. Printed 1798.

An Union neither necessary nor expedient for Ireland: being an answer to the author of "Arguments for and against an Union, between Great Britain and Ireland, considered". By Charles Ball, Esq. Printed 1798.

Pitt's Union. Author: W. J. MacNeven. Printed 1799.

An address to the people of Ireland, on the projected Union. By John Collis, Barrister at law. Printed 1799.

An address to the people of Ireland, shewing them why they ought to submit to an Union. Printed 1799.

English Union, is Ireland's ruin! Or an address to the Irish Nation. By Hibernicus. Printed 1799.

Observations on "Arguments for and against an Union between Great Britain and Ireland". Printed 1799.

An address to the Roman Catholics of Ireland on the conduct they should pursue at the present crisis; on the subject of an Union. Printed 1799.

The conspiracy of Pitt and Co. detected in a letter to the Parliament of Ireland. By one of the people. Printed 1799.

Protest from one of the people of Ireland, against an Union with Great Britain. Printed 1800.

A letter to a Noble Lord, containing a full declaration of the Catholic sentiment on the important question of Union. By an Irish Catholic. Printed 1800.

Pro-union pamphlets:

Atticus, A letter to the people of Ireland. (undated)

Arguments for and against an Union, between Great Britain and Ireland, considered. Printed 1798.

The probable consequences of a Union impartially considered. By a Barrister. Printed 1799.

A Letter to Theobald McKenna, Esq., the Catholic Advocate; in reply to the calumnies against the Orange Institution; contained in his pamphlet purporting to be a memoire on some questions respecting the projected union, &c. &c. &c. with observations on the new and further claims of the Catholics, as affecting the Constitution and Protestant Establishment. By an Orangeman. Printed 1799.

An answer to some of the many arguments made use of against a pamphlet, entitled "Arguments for and against an Union". By an attorney. Printed 1799.

A few thoughts on an Union with some observations upon Mr. Weld's pamphlet of "No Union!", addressed to the yeomanry of Dublin. By a wellwisher of Ireland. Printed 1799.

A letter to the people of Ireland they all can understand and ought to read. Printed 1799.

Union or not? Printed 1799.

An exposition of the principal terms of Union, and its probable effects on Ireland. Printed 1800.

A short address to the pretended Catholic Addresser of a Noble Lord, by a citizen, but not a French one. Printed 1800.

Scientific news discourse

"Joyful News out of the Newfound World"

Medical and scientific news reports in Early Modern England[1]

Irma Taavitsainen

1.   Introduction

The discovery of the American continents by Spanish and Portuguese navigators was without doubt one of the most influential events in world history. News of the broadening of the world took the form of reports on voyages, descriptions and observations of new plants and animals, as well as accounts of the indigenous peoples and their customs. Fact and fiction often mingle in these reports and link them to earlier traditions of travel literature with elements of fantasy. But, more importantly, as the distribution of information took place through eye-witness accounts, real-world features started to be reported. In the literature, the beginning of scientific news has been dated to the Royal Society period, and correspondence between research community members was a new feature (see Valle 1999 and 2006, Gotti 2006), but seeds for such developments can be found earlier and relevant material is extant from the previous century. Both foreign and domestic news are relevant for the present research task. The first news reports on the new continents date from the first half of the sixteenth century and increase towards the end of the century. They can be classified under foreign news, and there is a clear line of development in these texts, as I hope to demonstrate. Domestic news was distributed by pamphlets and newsletters in the written form, but oral practices of news distribution were important in Early Modern England. The reciprocity between the substance of the oral and the literate realms was an essential feature of culture at this time (Fox 2000: 39).

1.   Research for this paper was supported by the Academy of Finland project number 113787. I am grateful to the audience of the conference for comments and Andreas H. Jucker for constructive criticism of an earlier version of this paper.

2.   Aim and method of the paper

My aim in this paper is to investigate the forerunners of medical and scientific news reports. I shall focus on the time of the earliest news reports, the sixteenth century. In an earlier article, I used an eclectic method combining ethnography, discourse analysis and linguistic stylistics with corpus methodology to survey the professional identity of "merchant" with a historical perspective (Taavitsainen 2006). Before this study, another study on speech act verbs of verbal aggression had led to the finding that the context of the verb *insult* provided an ethnographic view of what was considered insulting in nineteenth-century England (Taavitsainen and Jucker 2007).[2] In these studies the respective search words, *merchant* and *insult*, revealed interesting features of societal developments. Encouraged by these explorations, I decided to adopt the same approach with the search word *news* in this article to define what was called *news* in the corpus of *Early Modern English Medical Texts* (see below). The leads were then followed in searches in *Early English Books Online* (EEBO) for other similar texts. I applied the KWIC concordance function of WordSmith 4 to detect the occurrences of the word (Key Word In Context; for the method, see e.g. Baker 2006). Examples of both domestic and foreign news were found. I shall first survey the findings and then focus on the most interesting news reports and study them in more detail. As a point of departure for my news analysis, I took some pertinent features of modern news reports. The statement that a point of view is always present either implicitly or explicitly is important, and much news analysis focuses on making the implicit features transparent. I shall take the same line and pay attention to stance and how the ideological underpinnings of the period are reflected in these texts. On the one hand, news from the new continents continues the earlier traditions of travel writing and describing the edges of the world in special ways. On the other hand, a new era had begun when eye-witness accounts shook the grounds of ancient knowledge and new features in reporting observations of nature emerge. Modern news reporting has developed a deviant structure far removed from everyday narratives, but in the early news the patterns follow everyday storytelling conventions and a resemblance to natural narratives can be established (see below).

---

2.   Ethnography is concerned primarily with the description and analysis of culture, and it sets out to define meanings and contexts as sociocultural phenomena in order to uncover people's views and authentic study contexts (Agar 2003).

3.   What do we mean by news reports?

The concept of "news" has gained specialised meanings. In linguistic studies of modern news discourse, a specialised definition is taken as the point of departure (van Dijk 1988a: 4). This restricted definition ties news to the media of reporting, to newspapers and broadcasts on radio, television or the internet (*Collins Cobuild; OED*), but news existed before the times of modern media as well, transmitted orally, or by pamphlets, early printed books and early journals. The broadest definition of *news* as "new information" is mentioned in several dictionaries. Item 2 in OED under *news* gives the following definition: "The report or account of recent (esp. important or interesting) events or occurrences, brought or coming to one as new information; new occurrences as a subject of report or talk; tidings". The first occurrences of this meaning are from the fifteenth century: the collocation "soe gracious and joyous newes" is from the year 1417 and a phrase that somebody "ratifieth the newes" from 1489. A related meaning "new things; novelties" occurs in the late medieval period, e.g the phrase "daiys of newis" is found in the Wycliffite Bible. Other dictionary entries with the same definition are found in the *Longman Dictionary of English Language and Culture*: "Facts that are reported about a recent event or recent events; new information" and in *Collins Cobuild*: "Information about a recent event or a recently changed situation". An inclusive view would encompass dissemination of information and the diffusion of knowledge in society at large. This view is relevant to my assessment as my focus is on medical and scientific news (cf. Taavitsainen 2005a).

4.   The structure of news reports

Modern news reports have their own special features that deviate from narratives in everyday interaction, stories told by people in face-to-face situations, news reported in private letters, and tales told in novels and in children's books. The new structure is mentioned as a characteristic development of the twentieth century (Ungerer 2000: 181). In modern news narratives the typical structure is top down, the inverted pyramid, with headline, lead and body. The most important facts are given first, the heading serves as a summary with the first paragraph as its extension, and further divisions specify thematic structural components.[3] The model has been criticised for being difficult, or impossible, to apply to a sizeable number

---

3.   According to van Dijk (1988a), they include the main event, consequences, circumstances, previous event, history, verbal reaction, evaluation and expectation. Some of them are similar to the components of natural narratives (discussed later in the paper).

of news stories (Ungerer 2000: 177). At earlier times news narratives were more like everyday narratives, and whether they deviate at all is an issue to be assessed here. News structure in modern mass media provides a "frame through which the social world is routinely constructed", and a viewpoint is always present either explicitly or implicitly (van Dijk 1988a: 8). Stance is an important element in news discourse as the same events can be reported in different ways from various viewpoints: cultural, historical, social, political and ideological differences between countries, regions and newspapers produce differences in news discourse about a given world event (van Dijk 1988b: 32).

A relevant point of reference for early news reports is provided by natural narratives of oral storytelling. Late medieval and early modern written narratives display an episodic structure of the same kind that operates in conversational storytelling even today (Fludernik 1996, 2007). The Labovian model[4] presents prototypical oral storytelling structure and gives an analytical frame that can be projected against early news narratives in the written form. The key points are an abstract stating what the story is about; orientation giving the coordinates who, when, and where; actions and complicating actions; evaluation of why the story is interesting; result or resolution and coda bridging the interaction back to the present situation (Labov and Waletzky 1967; Toolan 1988: 148). Late medieval and early modern narratives of various genres like romance, saints' lives, and narrative in early letters, follow the patterns of natural narratives (Fludernik 1996, 2007), and the same features are present in early medical case reports (Taavitsainen forthcoming). The stories follow the iconic order by preserving the temporal sequence of the original course of events. The other main regularity is that the stories state explicitly what the point is and why it is worth telling. Narrative is one of the basic text types among description, instruction, exposition and argumentation, defined according to their text-internal features in text linguistics. All these text types have their prototypical linguistic manifestations (Werlich 1983). Narrative versus non-narrative concerns were the second most important dimension of variation and change in Biber's seminal study (1988). Inventories of linguistic features of help in the identification of the narrative text type, for example past tense forms in the middle of a description serve as an alert to the narrative mode, and often text types alternate and sometimes they are mixed.

---

4.   Regularities in oral story telling were established by the sociolinguistic interview method in a groundbreaking article in 1967. The empirical study by Labov and Waletzky (1967) revealed fundamental regularities in narrative structures of oral stories of personal experience – the ordinary narratives of ordinary speakers.

5.   *News* in the corpus of *Early Modern English Medical Texts*

To draw an outline of the developments and locate possible news reports I traced
the occurrences of the word *news/newes* in our register-specific corpora 1375–
1700 containing a wide range of medical texts from different traditions and genres
of vernacular writing.[5] The first corpus, *Middle English Medical Texts 1375–1500*
(MEMT) did not give any hits. The narratives here are mostly case studies (see
Taavitsainen forthcoming). There were several occurrences of *news* in *Early Modern English Medical Texts 1500–1700* (EMEMT).[6] A KWIC concordance of the
Philosophical Transactions section of the corpus reveals that *news* occurs six times
and refers to tidings or new information about important and irreversible events:
news of death and a sad accident, but it is also found in context with accounts of
experiments. According to the literature, the category of *news* in the first scientific
journal included brief reports and short observations, and many of these items
follow a well-organised structure (Gotti 2006: 50–51). The topics of news are often
curiosities, unusual manifestations, or marvellous or monstrous forms of nature
(see below). Ten other occurrences of the word *news* are found in EMEMT. In an
argumentative text *news* is used in the sense of bad tidings: "For ill newes or matter to weepe for" (2childre.rtf [125]: 53323). Six times a person is described as "a
caryer or teller of newes" in a physiognomical text from 1556 giving prognostications for children (1556_Hill_Phisiognomie). The word collocates with negative
adjectives of character.[7] Obviously the role of a newsmonger was not held in high
esteem. Another prognosticatory text according to the School of Salerne contains
the word in a description of the sanguine character: "Likes pleasant tales, and
newes, plaies cards and dice" (2salerne.rtf [127]: 25). The quotations reveal an
interesting connection with the genre of prognostications. Precursors of news reports can be found in medieval community predictions as "reverse" antecedents
in the sense that they refer to the future instead of the past or present.[8] Sometimes
such predictions included "unnatural murders, rapes and piracies", accounted for

---

5.   The corpus consists of three parts and reflects the widening range of texts in medical writing over several centuries.

6.   The size of this pilot version of EMEMT was 1.7 million words.

7.   The collocated adjectives are: *enuious or hatefull; sumwhat prodigall or wastfull; a lyare, full
of wordes, gluttonouse feader, vnclenlye or nastye, of a grosse wytte; soone credytyng one, and
more symple then wyse; vayne or a lyar, dysdaynfull, secret, a betraier, a bearer or teller of newes,
fearefull, wycked, vngratious.*

8.   In the following example the starting point is thunder, and it contains a description of the
state of affairs at the time of the pestilence:

in sixteenth-century ballads and later on in newspapers; the resemblance is so great that an author of the seventeenth century gave a definition of the newspaper as "a retrospective almanac" (Capp 1979: 24). The most interesting hits from the present point of view occur in two sixteenth-century texts. They contain early news reports. One of the texts deals with the outbreak of pestilence and belongs to the category of domestic news on dismal topics, while the other deals with the brighter side of life, the opening up of new possibilities on the new continents, with riches to be gained and new, effective medicines to be found. I shall focus on these two lines of news reporting: domestic and foreign news.

6.   An early domestic news report

A news report on the domestic state of affairs is given in William Bullein's *A Dialogue against the Feuer Pestilence* (1564). William Bullein (c. 1515–1576) was a medical doctor and wrote several medical books for both professional and heterogeneous audiences. Newsworthy topics dealt with outbreaks of the plague, diseases, and famine, all of which affected people's lives profoundly. The description resembles medieval community predictions. The structure of Bullein's work is episodic and the passage of the news report serves as the opening scene, painting the landscape with broad brush strokes. Civis and Uxor meet Mendicant on the road and they start to converse about the way of the world. The text is in dialogue form, and the conversation reveals how news spread by word of mouth in "the constant buzz of people talking to each other: asking for news, swapping stories, exchanging news" (Fox 2000: 336). The news is told as an eye-witness report about what is going on and describes the conditions at the time of the pestilence in a vivid way. In modern news stories, eye-witnesses and direct quotes are an important feature to enhance the credibility of the contents, and the same devices are employed here.

> Ciuis. What newes as you come by the waie, Countrie man?
> *Mendicus.* Nene but aude maners, faire saiynges, fause haltes, and ne deuotion, God amende the market! Miccle tule for the purse, decieuyng of eche other. In the countrie strife, debate, runnyng for euery trifle to the Lawiers, hauyng nethyng but the nutshelles, the Lawiers eate the carnelles. Ause muche reisyng of rentes and gressomyng of men, causyng greate dearth, muche pouertie. God helpe, God helpe, the warlde is sare chaunged; extortioners, couetous men, and

---

> And hit [th]onder in that tyme [th]e mone shall com al dyrke and grete pestilence in that rigeone. And erbis shall wante vertue and myche folke seke. Wormes shall multiply and betokenyth grete famyll in the este contre and grete disses in many citeis and commenys that yer (BL MS. Sloane 5: 173v; c. 1450; my transcription).

hypocrites doe much preuaile. God cutte them shorter, for thei doe make a blacke warlde, euen hell vpon yearth. I thinke the greate feende or his deam will wearie them all. Nene other newes I ken, but that I did se mucle prouidence made in the countrie for you in the Citie, which doe feare the Pestilence. I met with wagones, Cartes, & Horses full loden with yong barnes, for fear of the blacke Pestilence, with their boxes of Medicens and sweete perfumes. O God, how fast did thei run by hundredes, and were afraied of eche other for feare of smityng.

(Bullein's *Feuer Pestilence*, p. 8)

An ideological message is explicit. The passage shows how religion penetrated all areas of life, including medicine: illness was considered punishment for the sins of mankind, the Fall had brought disease and death into the world, and the plague especially was seen as a punishment for the community's sinful behaviour (Wear 2000:30). The attitude is strongly present in this passage. The report is a first-person narrative, giving a voice to the inner feelings and emotions of the narrator, caused by the grave circumstances describing the situation as hell on earth. The emotional stance of despair can be pinpointed to the pious invocations and exclamations *God amende, O God*, and repetitions with an expressive function *God helpe, God helpe*. They serve to bring the interpersonal and interactional dynamics to the fore (see Culpeper and Kytö 2006:83). Lists like *extortioners, couetous men, and hypocrites*, and emotive language use in general with several exclamatory sentences in a short passage and Biblical overtones with appeals to God give the whole scene an affective stance. Similar passages of news delivery are common in early plays and depict an aspect of culture in the early modern world, where the written and spoken modes were more reciprocal and intertwined, and hence very different from their modern counterparts; for example, newsletters and broadsheets were read aloud, and what was heard spread through the grapevine, from urban centres into the surrounding countryside (Fox 2000:41). The mendicant in the above passage illustrates news broadcasters of the period, who relied on observation and hearsay.

7.   Foreign news

The mode of written news delivery is illustrated by news stories in early printed books. The voyages of discovery changed the world: America was discovered, Africa, India and the Far East became better known, and new sea routes made distances shorter. The economic gain from gold, silver, new commodities, exotic drugs and new medicines was great (Wear 2000:68–70). Knowledge of the new world and its riches spread through early printed books. The KWIC concordance revealed two occurrences of *newes* in Monardes' *Ioyfvll Newes Out Of The*

Newfound World (see below). To place the booklet more firmly in its sociohistorical context among news in early modern England, I searched EEBO for *news*.[9] In all, EEBO contains over 125,000 early prints (books, pamphlets and almanacs) in full digital facsimile. The titles can be searched electronically with lexical items. The search word *news/newes* gave 81 hits in 62 different items in the sixteenth century. Most of these writings dealt with foreign news, armies and warfare, and politics, but news about natural catastrophes was also given. Religious affairs were prominent both intertwined with politics, such as in news from Rome, but also in moral and devotional works. For an overview of the dissemination of information about the new world, I searched for news from the widening world which now included *America*.[10] EEBO gave 32 hits in 21 different items. Prints are mostly translations from Spanish, French, Latin or Portuguese, but the delay in rendering the works in English was not great, which proves the importance of the topic and people's enthusiasm to learn about the new drugs.

7.1   *Of the newe la~des and of ye people* (1520?)

The earliest printed book in English on the topic is an anonymous account of the new lands from the year 1520. I chose this book for closer scrutiny because of its early date.[11]

> Of the newe la~des and of ye people founde by the messengers of the kynge of porty~gale named Emanuel. Of the. x. dyuers nacyons crystened. Of pope Iohn~ and his landes, and of the costely keyes and wonders molodyes that in that lande is. Antwerp: Emprenteth by me Iohn of Doesborowe, 1520?

The text starts in the narrative mode in the first-person plural, with a detailed account of the journey. This passage provides the orientation setting the tone of the whole account. The facts sound accurate and reliable.

> Here aforetymes in the yere of our Lorde god MCCCC.xcvi. & so be we with shyppes of Lusseboene sayled oute of Portyngale thorough the co~maundeme~t of the kynge Emanuel Johane we had our vyage/for by fortune ylandes ouer the great see with great charge and dau~ger so haue we at the laste fou~de oon lord-

---

9. EEBO proved indispensable in compiling EMEMT, and it can easily be applied to research tasks like the present one.

10. I tested several other searches as well, but this word combination proved to be the best.

11. I studied the copy in the Huntington Library, San Marino, California. EEBO has images from the British Library copy.

shyp where we sayled well .ix. C. mylee by the cooste of Jelandes there we at ye laste went a lande but that la~de is not nowe knowe~ for there haue no masters wryten therof nor it knowethe and it is named Armenica. (f. A2r)

Likewise, the end of the book assures the reader that the contents are true. The last sentence relates to the medieval tradition of finishing written documents with threats and curses. They serve as warnings not to misuse or misinterpret the text and are usually addressed to the reader (see Arnovick 1999:77–78). In this case the threat is targeted at the author "god and sey~t thomas sholde punysshe vs" for not telling the truth, and the function of the threat is to enhance the veracity of the contents. The author is bold enough to risk his dignity and good reputation if his words are found to be untrue:

> And it is not well possyble to wryite all maner of goodness they whiche y=t =be in oure lande. And ye shall vnderstande that we writte nothynge to you but that trewe is. For if we sholde wryte lyes to you/ god and sey~t thomas sholde pu-nysshe vs/ for we sholde lese all our dignyte and oure worshyp. (f. E3v)

The text itself provides a surprise. The body of the text contains a description of strange people and their customs in accordance with the medieval tradition of presenting the unknown and distant as marvellous and monstrous. Tales that the travellers brought back from the New World spread with letters, broadsheets and early books. They included descriptions of wild, naked cannibalistic and incestuous natives, far removed from civilised Europeans and divine law (Simek 1992:82).[12] The passage below reveals a sharp contrast between "us" and "them", good Christian people and wild savages with customs that break the taboos of the civilised world. The unknown is described as "the other", and the book consists of separate descriptions of strange animals, plants and customs without a coherent plan. The people and their way of life are described as strange and sinful.

> [T]here we sawe meny wo~ders of beestes and fowles y=t= we haue neuer seen byfore/ the people of this lande haue no kynge nor lorde nor thyer god But all thinges is comune/ this people goeth all naked But the men and women haue on theyr heed necke/ Armes/ Knees/ and fete all with feders bou~den for there bew-tynes & fayrenes. These folke lyuen lyke bestes without any resonablenes and the wymen be also as common. And the men hath conuersacyon with the wymen / who that they ben or who they first mete/ is she his syster his moder/ his daughter / or any other ky~red. And the wymen be very hoote and dysposed to lecherdnes. And they ete also on another The man etethe his wife his chylderne/ as we also haue seen… (ff. A2r-v)

---

12. References to German sources are given in a note of Simek's book (1992), but English material is not discussed in Simek (1992).

The above passage deals with America, but other marginal and distant parts of the world are covered as well. Descriptions of wonders and riches of the strange continents follow in accordance with the tradition of late medieval travel stories:

> Here fynde men gynger, peper/ comeyn and all manere of spyces/ & costely stones for lytell money. There be also many maner of frute fygges of good sauy-our. vij ynches longe and .iij. ynches brode. There be bulfeldes and coyes but the coyes slepe they not/ there growth good wyne/ muche honeye/ ryse/ costely corne whyte as wete mele/... (ff. A5v-A6r)
> ...In Arlinia is great brode fygge Trees with great fygges well .vij. ynches longe and .iij. ynches brode and the Fygge tre is so brode of brau~che and leues that .xl. men may be hydde vnder the forsayd brauches and leues for the hete of the sonne/ and there for to reste all to gather at theyr one pleasure. (f. B1v)

The echoes of earlier travel literature and the wonders of the East are clear. *Mandeville's Travels*, for example, contains very similar passages:

> In that contre ben longe apples of gode sauour, whereof ben mo than an c. in a cluster and als manye in another, And thei han grete longe leves and large, of ii. forte long or more... (*Mandeville's Travels*, p. 191)

The resemblance is striking. Marvels and monsters abound, including accounts of mythical animals like the unicorn and centaurs; cyclopes, pigmies, dwarfs, phoe-nix birds, the well of youth, and other fictional motifs are also dealt with:

> In our lande be olypha~tes/ dromedaries/ wylde oxes the wyche haue .vij. hornes. also Beeres and Lyons of dyuers colours/ as ye redd/ grene/ blacke/ & whitte. Item and also be wylde asses the which haue longe eeres/ and haue twoo smale hornes. &c. Ite~ In our lande is also a grete deserte or forest ther i~ dweleth people bothe men & wymmen the whyche haue nomore than one eye afore. and behinde they haue .iij. or.iiij. eyen. (ff. C6r-v)

Although the text is cast as an eye-witness story, observation plays no role in it. Rather than a precursor of the new, it is an aftermath of the old. But the tradition is strong and continues later in the eighteenth century with Swift's social satires, and even today's fantasy literature and science fiction contain elements from this tradition.

7.2   *A new iuterlude [sic] ... of dyuers straunge landys and of dyuers straunge effects [and] causis* (1520?)

The number of texts about the new world increases in the latter half of the cen-tury, but most of the books deal with voyages and cosmography. An interesting dialogue is provided by John Rastell (d. 1536). The text is written in rhymed couplets, the most popular means of disseminating knowledge in the late medieval and early modern period in practical verse, found, for example, in the popular scientific encyclopedia of *Sidrak and Bokkus*. The book must have been targeted at a heterogeneous audience, as rhymes provided an aid to memory in the largely oral culture. The main topic is cosmology. The text relies on the traditional theory of the elements as constitutive parts of the universe, but at the same time new ways of thinking are introduced. The passage below tries to convince the readers that the earth is not flat but round:

> The yerth of it selfe is ponderous and heuy
> Colde and dry of his owne nature *proper*
> Some parte lyeth dry continually
> And parte therof coueryd ouer with water
> Some with the salt see some with freshe ryuer
> Whiche yerth and the water togyder with all
> So Joynyd make a rounde fygyre sperycall (f. A4v)

Familiar imagery is employed to make the argument more readily understandable: the air surrounds the earth "as the white aboute the yolke of an egg doth lye". In spite of its promising title, the book does not contain descriptions of the new world. The end of the booklet contains entertaining songs for recreation, which is another feature typical of writings aimed at a broad and heterogeneous audience (see Taavitsainen 2005b). Such booklets provide a link between the oral and the written modes of news transmission and would deserve further scrutiny from this perspective.

7.3   *Ioyfull nevves out of the newe founde worlde...* (1580)

Ioyfull nevvs out of the newe founde worlde represents a very different phase in news reports from the new continents. The book is important in medical history for several reasons. Nicolás Monardes (c. 1512–1588) was a physician from Seville. His works *Dos Libros* came out in 1565, 1571, 1574, and were translated into English by John Frampton, who had been a merchant in Spanish-English trade. The book deals with the therapeutic virtues of American plants and reveals new remedies for diseases. The speech act of promise is typical in early book titles and prefaces to enhance the efficacy of the text. The title is informative as it also describes the contents and reflects the new optimism of the period: the traditional expression of the limits on knowledge *ne plus ultra* 'no further' was replaced by *plus ultra* 'further yet' (Shapin 1996: 20). This text belongs to a new phase of foreign news in the written mode.

> *Ioyfull nevves out of the newe founde worlde wherein is declared the rare and sin-*
> *guler vertues of diuerse and sundrie hearbes, trees, oyles, plantes, and stones, with*
> *their aplications, aswell for phisicke as chirurgerie, the saied beyng well applied*
> *bryngeth suche present remedie for all deseases, as maie seme altogether incredible:*
> *notwithstandyng by practize founde out, to bee true: also the portrature of the saied*
> *hearbes, very aptly discribed: Englished by Ihon Frampton marchaunt.* Imprinted
> at London: In Poules Churche-yarde, by Willyam Norton, 1577 [i.e. 1580?]

The treatise begins with facts and details about the voyage. A similar factual beginning is found in the 1520 text but there it soon gives way to the conventional "other", whereas the factual style of reporting continues in this later account. Precise details are given and the newness and newsworthiness of the topic is emphasised.

> IN the yere of our Lord God, a thousa~d, foure hundreth ninetie two, our Span-
> iards were gouerned by sir Christopher Colo~, being naturally born in the
> cou~trie of Genoua, to discouer the Occide~tal Indias, that are called at this day,
> the newe world, and they discouered the first land thereof, the xi. day of October,
> of the said yere ... there haue beene founde out, things that neuer in these partes,
> nor in any other partes of the worlde haue beene seene, nor vnto this day knowen:
> and other thinges which nowe are brought vnto vs in great abundance... (f. 1r)

Precious stones and metals are enumerated, but soon the text turns to medicinal issues, and the great profit the new medicines and remedies bring to people is stressed. Health is worth more than worldly goods.

> ...And besides these great riches, our Occidentall Indias doe send vnto vs many
> Trees, Plants, Hearbes, Rootes, Iuices, Gummes, Fruites, Licoures & Stones that
> are of great medicinall vertues, in the which there be founde, and haue been
> found in them, very great effectes that doe exceede much in value and price all
> the aforesayde thinges, by so muche as the corporall health is more excellent, and
> necessary then the temporall goodes: the which thinges all the world doth lacke,
> the want whereof is not a litle hurtefull, according to the greate profite which wee
> doe see, by the vse of them to follow, not onely in our Spayne, but also in all the
> world. (f. 1r)

The major part of the contents deals with new plants, for example, tobacco is discussed (see Ratia 2006). In addition to the descriptions, short narratives are included. The following passage contains news on a new healing method for the new disease of French pox (see Wear 2000: 69, 80). The passage below contains a story about the discovery of a healing method, the last sentence repeating the common conception of the time "from whence it came, thence should come the

remedy". This belief still lives on in folk medicine. The pattern of natural narratives is present with the constituent sequences clearly discernable in the simple
storyline: the beginning states briefly what the story is about, and details of orientations are given with the formulaic introduction of a tale: "There was an In-
dian…". The storyline proceeds in a straightforward manner, with a brief account
of the spreading of the news of the remedy. Evaluative phrases praise the cure as
the "best, & the most chiefe remedy", but elaborations and reservations "if they
be wel handled" and "as it ought to be" and "except" also occur. This part can be
analysed as the result. The coda is provided at the very end, as the final formulaic
saying with an appeal to God serves to bridge back to the geographical location
that is the topic of the book.

> Of the Guaiacan and of the holie Wood.
> THe Guaiacan, that is called the wood of the Indias **was discouered** forthwith,
> **whe~ the first Indias were fou~d**, which was the Island of Sancto Domingo,
> where is great quantity thereof. **There was an Indian that gaue knowledge there-
> of to his Maister, in this maner**. Ther was a Spaniard that did suffer great paines
> of the Poxe, which he had taken by the company of an Indian woman, but his
> seruant being one of the Phisitions of that countrie, gaue vnto him the mater
> of Guaiaca~, wherewith not onely his grieuous paynes were taken away that he
> did suffer, but he was healed verie well of the euill: with the which many other
> Spaniardes, that were infected with the same euill were healed also, **the which
> was communicated immediatly, with them that came from thence, hither to
> Seuill, and from thence it was di_[^orig. blurred^]lged throughout all Spaine,
> and from thence through all the world,** for that the infection was sowen abroade
> throughout all partes thereof: and surely for this euill it is **the best, & the most
> chiefe remedy** of as many as hitherto haue been found, and **with most assur-
> aunce, and most certeintie, it healeth and cureth** the sayde disease, if they be
> wel handled: and this water giuen as it ought to be, **it is certaine that it healeth it
> most perfectly,** without turning to fall againe, except the sicke man doe returne
> to tumble in the same bosome, where he tooke the first infection. Our Lord God
> would from whence the euill of the Poxe came, from thence shoulde come the
> remedy for them.

This news report is very different from the description of 1520 and breaks away
from medieval traditions of the monstrous. The contrast of "us" and "them" is
not maintained but an ideology of expansion and potential for increased wealth
is very strongly present. In all, the end of the sixteenth century is very different
from its beginning.

8.   Conclusions

Early modern medical news reports can be found well before the time of the Royal Society, which has previously been taken as the earliest point of departure for scientific news. Some of the characteristics of modern news seem to apply to the early examples, for instance, a strong ideological bias is present in the reports under scrutiny in this article. In the early domestic news, the outbreak of pesti-lence is described with religious overtones in affective language with appeals to God. The conviction that disease, especially the plague, was a punishment for the sins of the community is the underlying ideological tenet. The earliest news from America, circa 1520, describes the continent according to the medieval conven-tions of travel literature, depicting the edges of the world as strange, marvellous and monstrous. The statement about news always having a viewpoint and stance is very true in this case as well. The contrast of "us", good Christian people, and "them", wild savages, applies here. There is a time lag before observation of real-ity replaces the traditional travel writing conventions. The old ways of thinking and describing distant regions continue in the first half of the sixteenth century, with new modes of reporting emerging only in the latter half of that century. The book bringing joyful news from the new world (1580) contains some narrative passages that can perhaps be considered early news reports in the new mode with the structure of natural narratives. In order to make more far-reaching conclu-sions, the study would require a wider range of material, but the general line of development presented here is in accordance with changing thought-styles, with observation gaining more weight after the mid-sixteenth century.

Sources

Anon. *Of the newe la[n]des and of ye people founde by the messengers of the kynge of porty[n]gale named Emanuel. Of the. x. dyuers nacyons crystened. Of pope Iohn and his landes, and of the costely keyes and wonders molodyes that in that lande is.* Antwerp: Iohn of Doesborowe, 1520? STC (2nd ed.) / 7677.

Bullein, William. 1888/1931. *William Bullein's Dialogue Against the Feuer Pestilence* (Ed. 1578). Early English Text Society E.S. 52. M. W. Bullein and A. H. Bullein (eds), Part I. London: Oxford University Press.

Mandeville's Travels. M.C. Seymour (ed.). Oxford: Clarendon Press, 1967.

Monardes, Nicolás. *Ioyfull nevves out of the newe founde worlde wherein is declared the rare and singuler vertues of diuerse and sundrie hearbes, trees, oyles, plantes, and stones, with their aplications, aswell for phisicke as chirurgerie, the saied beyng well applied bryngeth suche present remedie for all deseases, as maie seme altogether incredible: notwithstandyng by prac-tize founde out, to bee true: also the portrature of the saied hearbes, very aptly discribed:*

Englished by Ihon Frampton marchaunt. Imprinted at London: In Poules Churche-yarde, by Willyam Norton, 1577 / 1580? STC (2nd ed.) / 18006.5.

Rastell, John, *A new iuterlude [sic] and a mery of the nature of the .iiii. element declarynge many proper poynt of phylosophy naturall, and of dyuers straunge landys and of dyuers straunge effects [and] causis,...* London: J. Rastell, 1520? STC (2nd ed.) / 20722.

Bibliography

Agar, Michael. 2003. Ethnography. In Jan-Ola Östman and Jef Verschueren (eds.). *Handbook of Pragmatics.* Electronic version. Amsterdam and Philadelphia: John Benjamins.

Arnovick, Leslie K. 1999. *Diachronic Pragmatics.* Amsterdam and Philadelphia: John Benjamins.

Baker, Paul. 2006. *Using Corpora in Discourse Analysis.* London and New York: Continuum.

Biber, Douglas. 1988. *Variation Across Speech and Writing.* Cambridge: Cambridge University Press.

Capp, Bernard. 1979. *Astrology and the Popular Press. English Almanacs 1500–1800.* London and Boston: Faber and Faber.

Collins Cobuild Dictionary of English Language. 1988. London and Glasgow: Collins.

Culpeper, Jonathan, and Merja Kytö. 2006. "*Good, good* indeed, the best that ere I heard": Exploring lexical repetitions in the Corpus of English Dialogues 1560–1760. In Irma Taavitsainen, Juhani Härma and Jarmo Korhonen (eds.). *Dialogic Language Use.* Mémoires de la Société Néophilologique de Helsinki LXVI. Helsinki: Modern Language Society, 69–85.

Early English Books Online (EEBO). http://eebo.chadwyck.com/home/

Early Modern English Medical Texts 1500–1700 (EMEMT). Forthcoming. Compiled by Irma Taavitsainen, Päivi Pahta, Turo Hiltunen, Ville Marttila, Martti Mäkinen, Maura Ratia, Carla Suhr and Jukka Tyrkkö.

Fludernik, Monika. 1996. *Towards a 'Natural' Narratology.* London: Routledge.

Fludernik, Monika. 2007. Letter as narrative: Narrative patterns and episode structure in early letters, 1400 to 1650. In Susan Fitzmaurice and Irma Taavitsainen (eds.). *Methods in Historical Pragmatics.* Berlin and New York: Mouton de Gruyter, 241–266.

Fox, Adam. 2000. *Oral and Literate Culture in England 1500–1700.* Oxford: Clarendon Press.

Gotti, Maurizio. 2006. Disseminating early modern science: Specialized news discourse in the *Philosophical Transactions.* In Nicholas Brownlees (ed.). *News Discourse in Early Modern Britain Selected Papers of CHINED 2004.* Bern: Peter Lang, 41–70.

Labov, William, and Joshua Waletzky. 1967. Narrative analysis: Oral versions of personal experience. In J. Helm (ed.). *Essays on the Verbal and Visual Arts.* Seattle: University of Washington Press, 3–38.

Longman Dictionary of English Language and Culture. 1992/2005. Pearson Longman.

Middle English Medical Texts 1375–1500 (MEMT). Compiled by Irma Taavitsainen, Päivi Pahta and Martti Mäkinen. CD-ROM. Amsterdam and Philadelphia: John Benjamins.

Oxford English Dictionary Online. http://www.oed.com/

Ratia, Maura. 2006. "Con" and "pro": Early modern texts in dialogue. In Irma Taavitsainen, Juhani Härma and Jarmo Korhonen (eds.). *Dialogic Language Use.* Mémoires de la Société Néophilologique de Helsinki LXVI. Helsinki: Modern Language Society, 87–106.

Shapin, Steven. 1996. *The Scientific Revolution*. Chicago and London: The University of Chicago Press.

Simek, Rudolf. 1992. *Heaven and Earth in the Middle Ages*. Translated by Angela Hall. Cambridge: The Boydell Press.

Taavitsainen, Irma. 2005a. Genres and the appropriation of science: *Loci communes* in English literature in late medieval and early modern periods. In Janne Skaffari, Matti Peikola, Ruth Carroll, Risto Hiltunen and Brita Wårvik (eds.). *Opening Windows on Texts and Discourses of the Past*. Amsterdam and Philadelphia: John Benjamins, 179–196.

Taavitsainen, Irma. 2005b. Genres of secular instruction: A linguistic history of useful entertainment. *Miscelánea: A Journal of English and American Studies* 29, 75–94.

Taavitsainen, Irma. 2006. Merchant in historical corpora. In Gabriella Del Lungo, Marina Dossena, and Belinda Crawford (eds.). *Variation in Business and Economics Discourse: Diachronic and Genre Perspectives*. Rome: Officina Edizioni, 21–44.

Taavitsainen, Irma. Forthcoming. *Narratives in Late Medieval and Early Modern Scientific Writing*.

Taavitsainen, Irma, and Andreas H. Jucker. 2007. Speech acts and speech act verbs in the history of English. In Susan Fitzmaurice and Irma Taavitsainen (eds). *Methods in Historical Pragmatics*. Berlin and New York: Mouton de Gruyter, 107–138.

Toolan, Michael. 2001 [1988]. *Narrative: A Critical Linguistic Introduction*. London: Routledge.

Ungerer, Friedrich. 2000. News stories and news events – a changing relationship. In Friedrich Ungerer (ed.). *English Media Texts – Past and Present: Language and Textual Structure*. Amsterdam and Philadelphia: John Benjamins, 177–195.

van Dijk, Teun. 1988a. *News as Discourse*. Hillsdale, New Jersey: Lawrence Erlbaum Associates.

van Dijk, Teun. 1988b. *News Analysis: Case Studies in International and National News in the Press*. Hillsdale, New Jersey: Lawrence Erlbaum Associates.

Valle, Ellen. 1999. *A Collective Intelligence. The Life Sciences in the Royal Society as a Scientific Discourse Community, 1665–1965*. (Anglicana Turkuensia 17). University of Turku.

Valle, Ellen. 2006. Reporting the doings of the curious: Authors and editors in the *Philosophical Transactions* of the Royal Society of London. In Nicholas Brownlees (ed.). *News Discourse in Early Modern Britain. Selected Papers of CHINED 2004*. Bern: Peter Lang, 71–90.

Wear, Andrew. 2000. *Knowledge and Practice in English Medicine, 1550–1680*. Cambridge: Cambridge University Press.

Werlich, Egon. 1983 [1975]. *A Text Grammar of English*. Heidelberg: Quelle and Meyer.

News filtering processes
in the *Philosophical Transactions*

Lilo Moessner

1. Introduction

News discourse has four important aspects: the producer(s) of news, its recipient(s), its contents, and the channel(s) through which it is communicated. This study will focus on scientific news and on the *Philosophical Transactions* as one of the available channels of news discourse in the seventeenth century. It will be shown that for the first volumes of the *Philosophical Transactions* the question of news producer/disseminator is rather delicate, because most articles are not signed, and Henry Oldenburg, as the first editor of the *Philosophical Transactions*, played a crucial role in the decisions as to which news was to be published in the journal and how it was presented. These decisions will be interpreted as quantitative and qualitative filters. Different types of news filtering processes will be revealed through a detailed analysis of volumes 5 to 10 of the *Philosophical Transactions*. The resulting picture of a changing shape of the *Philosophical Transactions* will be complemented by an analysis of the first year of volume 1. It will be shown that, with the exception of the year 1674, during the first ten years of the *Philosophical Transactions* scientific news discourse started to move away from a news-mediator-controlled to a news-producer-controlled process of communication.

2. Channels of scientific news discourse in the seventeenth century

The growth of the scientific community and its spread across several continents made it impossible for scientists in the seventeenth century to rely only on oral communication for the exchange of information on new discoveries or the invention of more sophisticated instruments. Among the established forms of written communication were printed books, pamphlets and newsletters, fair catalogues, almanacs and calendars, corantos and newspapers (Kronick 1962: Chapter 4). Books had the disadvantage that their production was time-consuming and expensive, they were published in small numbers and therefore often difficult to come by. The other forms shared the feature of periodicity, but were not specialized in scientific news.

The most convenient communication channel for scientists was therefore the private letter, especially after the introduction of regular postal services and improvements in roads and transport (Gotti 2006a: 42f., 2006b; Kronick 1962: 50–59). These letters served several purposes. The letter-writers asked fellow scientists for information about topics of common interest, they established professional contacts by means of these letters, they advertised research principles, they described results of their own experiments, they commented on news previously received, and they provided advice or instruction. The letters were also often regarded as drafts of subsequent longer publications. Several persons, whose circle of correspondents was especially wide and ranged over a large geographical area, developed into clearinghouses of scientific news. Among them were Père Marin Mersenne (1588–1648) in France, and Theodore Haak (1605–1690), Samuel Hartlib (1600–1662), Henry Oldenburg (1618/19[?]–1677), and John Collins (1624–1683) in England (Stimson 1939). Haak, Hartlib, and Oldenburg were German by birth, and they had emigrated for political reasons or because they were hoping for a more promising professional career in England. The scientific community profited from their knowledge of foreign languages: in their offices letters could not only be copied and redistributed, but they could also be translated into the languages of the addressees. In the present context, Haak and Oldenburg are of special relevance, the former because he initiated the meetings which led to the formation of the Royal Society,[1] the latter because he became the first editor of the *Philosophical Transactions*.

3.   Henry Oldenburg: The first editor of the *Philosophical Transactions*

After receiving his degree of Master of Theology, Oldenburg left his home town of Bremen to become a student at the University of Utrecht. He then travelled extensively across Europe for some years as a tutor to sons of English gentlemen, among them Robert Boyle's nephew Richard Jones (Hall 1965: 277f.). In 1653, he was sent to London by his home town to negotiate with Cromwell about the consequences of the Navigation Act for the City of Bremen. As a consequence of this diplomatic mission he became acquainted with many of the leading English

---

1.   "Mr. Theodore Haak, a native of the Palatinate of Germany, who first gave occasion to, and suggested these meetings" (Birch 1756, vol.1: 2).

intellectuals. In 1656, he joined the group of learned men who were to initiate the foundation of the Royal Society on November 28, 1660, and he was among the 40 persons who were proposed as its founding members (Birch 1756, vol.1: 4). According to Hall (2002: 58), Oldenburg's election took place at the end of December 1660.[2] Early in 1661, he was appointed to several committees of the Society. He was particularly well qualified as a member of the "Committee for considering of proper questions to be inquired of in the remotest parts of the world". Although the Society now met regularly once a week, it was not before July 15, 1662, that it was incorporated under the title "Royal Society", and together with John Wilkins, Henry Oldenburg was appointed its secretary. The Royal Charter granted the Society the right to license books for publication and to correspond with persons abroad without hindrance. From this time on, Oldenburg wrote his letters in his capacity as the secretary of the Royal Society, and letters sent to Oldenburg were intended as information as much for the Royal Society as for Oldenburg himself. Since the Society did not pay him any salary for his extended services, Oldenburg had to find an income somewhere else. He was employed by Boyle as a private secretary and as a translator and editor of his books, and he earned some money from these occupations. As early as 1663, there are references in his letters (Hall 2002: 80) that he was thinking of setting up an information service to which potential clients could subscribe, and that he may have, in fact, done so. The need for a periodical publication of news seems to have been felt on the continent as well. In a letter to Boyle of November 1664, Oldenburg notes that he was informed of a plan to publish a journal of political and scientific news in France and that he was asked to contribute to it (Hall and Hall, vol. 2: 319f.; Hall 2002: 83). What he alludes to in his letter is the *Journal des Sçavans*, the first issue of which appeared early in January 1665. Only two months later, at the meeting of the Council of the Royal Society, it was ordered:

> That the Philosophical Transactions, to be composed by Mr. Oldenburg, be printed the first Monday of every month, if he have sufficient matter for it; and that that tract be licensed by the council of the society, being first reviewed by some of the members of the same; and that the president be desired now to license the first papers thereof [...] (Birch 1756, vol. 2: 18)

The full title of the journal was *Philosophical Transactions: Giving some Accompt of the Present Undertakings, Studies, and Labours of the Ingenious in Many Considerable Parts of the World*. Although the monthly issues of the *Philosophical Transactions* had to be licensed by the Council of the Royal Society, as it was laid

---

2. Birch (1756, vol.1: 8), by contrast, mentions his name among those who "were proposed candidates for election".

down in the Royal Charter, the journal was Oldenburg's personal enterprise. He negotiated his financial contribution as well as the selling price for each copy with the printers. Oldenburg chose and edited the news items, and he wrote most of the book reviews.[3] The readers of the journal, however, associated it more with the Royal Society than with its publisher. This is why Oldenburg added a note at the end of number 12 of May 1666, in which he explicitly stated that he "upon his Private Account [...] hath begun and continues both the composure and the publication" of the *Philosophical Transactions*. His eminent influence on the shape of, especially, the first volumes of the *Philosophical Transactions* is aptly summed up by Bazerman (1988: 131): "All was filtered through his voice". The different filtering processes that the news went through, before it reached its recipients will be analysed in the following section.

4.   Oldenburg's news filters

There is general agreement in the publications on the *Philosophical Transactions* that the first volumes of the journal mainly contained Oldenburg's version of the news he had received through his vast correspondence network and that only very gradually did the amount of authored articles increase (Atkinson 1999: 21; Bazerman 1988: 129–133; Kronick 1962: 75f.; Gotti 2006a: 46f., 2006b: 24; Hall 2002: 85; Iliffe 1995: 173). Valle (1999, 2006) presents this change in quantitative terms. She uses the concept of text framing, which is based on the amount of intervention by the editor. The main categories of this model are "editorial framing" and "authorial framing". The former contains texts in which "the controlling, directly speaking voice is that of the editor", comprising "book reviews and reports of published articles and unpublished letters, whether received at first or at second hand", whereas in texts of the category "authorial framing" "the directly speaking voice is that of the original author(s), regardless of the chain of transmission" (Valle 2006: 76f.). Analysing 100 articles of volumes 1 to 4, covering the years 1665 to 1669, she finds that the share of editorial texts decreased from 69 percent to 45 percent, whereas authorial texts increased from 18 percent in 1666 to 42 percent in 1669. The remainder of between six and 31 percent could not be attributed to either of these categories. Since "editorial framing" can be interpreted as the application of a filter, this model will also be applied to the following analysis of volumes 5 to 10 of the *Philosophical Transactions*.

---

3.   Hall (2002: 85) points out that for mathematical books Oldenburg had help from Wallis.

4.1   The quantitative filter

Birch's *History of the Royal Society* (1756) is the most comprehensive record of Oldenburg's activities in the Royal Society. After he was elected secretary, he was responsible for the minutes of the meetings. Hall (2002: 71) notes their increased quantity and quality after Oldenburg had taken over the position from his predecessor Croone. From the many entries in Birch's collected minutes we can therefore infer that, at the meetings of the Royal Society, Oldenburg faithfully reported the communications which he had received. Yet nowhere do we find mention that he was asked to insert a particular piece of news into the *Philosophical Transactions*. It was completely at his discretion which communications he considered relevant and important enough to impart to his readers. Complete exclusion of a piece of news from publication is the most radical type of filter, which Oldenburg certainly used. A more moderate version of this quantitative filter is realised when only part of the news is withheld from the readers.

Measuring the more extreme form of Oldenburg's quantitative filter is very difficult, if not impossible. Checking the minutes over a period which corresponds to that covered by one volume of the *Philosophical Transactions* and comparing the letters mentioned in the former with those printed in the latter proves a futile experiment. It is neither the case that all of the letters in the former are part of the latter – this would indicate a quantitative filter – nor is it the case that all letters printed in the *Philosophical Transactions* can be traced in the minutes. It must therefore be assumed that Oldenburg received more letters than he reported in the meetings.

Unfortunately Oldenburg's correspondence does not yield a clearer picture either. Checking the period of March 1675 to February 1676, I counted letters from nearly 50 different correspondents. The corresponding volume 10 of the *Philosophical Transactions* contains letters, or extracts of letters, of only 16 correspondents. The topics of some letters (e.g. Spinoza's theological arguments) or their functions (e.g. Crawford's reports about books delivered to various persons) explain their omission. The absence of others is not so easy to account for. The calculation of tangents must have been a topic Oldenburg thought worthy of inclusion in the *Philosophical Transactions*. In volume 7, No.90, he published a letter by Renatus Slusius on this topic, and in volume 8, No.95, another one by the same correspondent. Therefore it is very surprising that the letter by Ehrenfried Walter von Tschirnhaus (letter 2698 in the correspondence), which explicitly refers to the one by Slusius in volume 7, did not find its way into the *Philosophical*

Transactions. Here, as in many other cases, Oldenburg's arbitrary quantitative filter was at work.[4]

Extracts of letters also illustrate the use of a quantitative filter, but since they are embedded in contexts provided by Oldenburg they will be interpreted as instances of a qualitative filter.

4.2   The qualitative filter

The qualitative filter appears in more different forms than the quantitative filter, but it is easier to detect and to measure. The following analysis will show its share in the articles of volumes 5 to 10 of the *Philosophical Transactions*.

Editorial texts, i.e. texts in which a qualitative filter was applied, occur in the form of book reviews, translations, or news reports. All book reviews will be treated as editorial texts, although the possibility cannot be excluded that Oldenburg had some help from other members of the Royal Society for the reviews of mathematical books. Translations will be divided into two groups: those articles which are explicitly marked as translations, and others which can be identified as translations because of certain expressions in the titles or the texts themselves.

Authorial texts, i.e. texts which reach their recipients without a filter, are divided into three groups. There are Latin texts taken over in their original form and uncommented by the editor, English texts whose authors are identifiable by name, and texts which are clearly recognizable as authorial, although their authors remain unknown.

All volumes have basically the same structure. They cover twelve months starting with March and ending with February of the following year. They contain between nine and twelve numbers of the journal, the first number of each volume starts with a preface by the editor, and the last number is followed by an index. The length of the numbers ranges between 16 and 40 pages.

4.2.1 *Volume 5 (1670)*
All numbers of this volume end with a set of between two and five book reviews. Although they are not signed, it can be assumed that they were written by Oldenburg himself. This is all the more probable because there are passages in his correspondence where he is either asked by a scientist to send a special book, or where he acknowledges receipt of a book. Oldenburg was one of the few persons likely to possess a special book: "[T]he Publisher [...] very much doubteth, whether any

---

4.   On the other hand, many of the letters sent to Oldenburg are only preserved because they were published in the *Philosophical Transactions*.

Copies of this intimation, Printed at Pisa this very year, besides that one, which lately came to his hands, be to be found in England" (No.65: 2095). Oldenburg's authorship of reviews can also be inferred from statements like the following: "This small Tract being but very lately sent out of Denmark to the Publisher, he thought fit to give forthwith the following Accompt of it" (No.64: 2081). The number of book reviews amounts to 40.

Oldenburg's mother tongue was German. He achieved "a complete mastery of Latin together with some Greek and Hebrew", and later on "fluency in Dutch, French, Italian and English" (Hall 2002: 4, 8). These linguistic skills qualified him as a translator of most of the letters which reached him from foreign scientific communities. Nine articles are explicitly marked as translations, their titles end with the remark "English'd as follows" or "English'd by the Publisher". The source language of five of the translations is French, another three texts are translations from Italian. The source languages can be inferred from the names or characterisations of the authors, for example, "An Extract of an Italian Letter Written from Venice by Signor Jacomo Grandi [...] English'd by the Publisher" (No.58: 1188) or by the fact that the original text was published previously in another journal, for example, "An Experiment Concerning the Progress of Artificial Conglaciation, and the remarkable Accidents, therein observed by the Florentin Philosophers; and publish't in their Saggi di Naturali Esperienze" (No.66: 2020). The source language of the remaining translation is probably Latin. Its author is Johannes Hevelius, and he mostly wrote in Latin. This is evident from his other contributions to the *Philosophical Transactions* (e.g. No.66: 2023) and from the beginning of the letter which Oldenburg translated into English:

> Would to God, that those Excellent Books that are publish't in English, were, for the benefit of the whole Learned World, made Latin; All Learned men would be exceedingly obliged to you for it. I am perswaded, Sir, you will do your part in taking care, that so useful and necessary a work may not be left undone. (No.64: 2059)

Although not overtly marked as translations, four more texts also qualify as such. These are extracts from letters by French correspondents of Oldenburg's, and they are presented as first person narratives.

Linguistic features (for example: "The former writeth in a Letter of his [...]. That he observ'd [...]" No.65: 2093; "there came to hand a Letter from that Inquisitive Gentleman, Mr. Martin Lister", No.65: 2104) or the provenance of a news item (France, The Netherlands, Germany) help to identify Oldenburg as the author of eight more texts.

At the other end of the editorial versus authorial scale, we find three Latin texts and 22 others whose authors are clearly identifiable. Among them are famous scientists like Robert Boyle and John Wallis, but also less well-known scholars. Two texts stand out from the others. One combines contributions on the same topic by two authors, Dr. Ezerel Tonge and Francis Willoughby, the other is a letter from John Evelyn, a Fellow of the Royal Society, to its president Lord Viscount Brouncker, and it contains a translation of a Spanish description of a special kind of plough. Although its title is followed by the usual addition "English't out of Spanish", Oldenburg cannot have translated this text because he did not speak Spanish.

The remaining five texts are of mixed authorship. Oldenburg has a hand in each of them, but his contribution is restricted to some lines of introduction or comment. Since the authors of the main parts of these texts are clearly identifiable and Oldenburg plays only a minor role in them, they are counted as authorial texts.

The volume contains 91 articles, 61 (67 percent) belong to the category "editorial texts", 30 (33 percent) to the category "authorial texts".

4.2.2 *Volume 6 (1671)*

The editorial texts of this volume comprise 49 book reviews: nine overt translations of French and Italian source texts, two translations from French, and eight texts which can be identified as Oldenburg's. One of the latter is especially interesting, because we learn from it that a Latin translation of the *Philosophical Transactions* was published at Frankfurt. Oldenburg must have read it very carefully, because he comments on some of the many errors in this translation ("pauca ex per-multis in versione dicta commissis erroribus & vitiis enormibus", No.75: 2269). Since he assumes that this translation will be mainly read by foreign readers, he writes his comments in Latin.

The group of 41 authorial texts consists of seven Latin texts, 29 articles by identifiable authors and four more whose authors cannot be identified. The latter were sent to Oldenburg by "an Inquisitive person" (No.69: 2096) or "in a Letter written from Cairo" (No.71: 2151). The author of one of these articles obviously preferred to remain anonymous because of his harsh critique of some theses proposed by Hobbes. In the first paragraph, he calls Hobbes's arguments "Cavilling", and his contribution ends with the statement: "What in it [= Hobbes's paper] concerns Mathematicks [...] is so weak and trivial [...] that I shall trust it with those to whom he makes his appeal, without thinking it to need any Reply" (No.75: 2241–2250). The last text which is attributed to the category "authorial texts" consists of a Latin text by Wallis, which is followed by a very short comment by Oldenburg.

Volume 6 contains 109 articles, 68 (62 percent) belong to the category "editorial texts", 41 (38 percent) to the category "authorial texts".

4.2.3 *Volume 7 (1672)*

This volume contains 50 editorial texts. Among them are 34 book reviews and seven articles which are marked as translations from Latin, Italian or French. There are three more translations from French which are only indirectly identifiable as translations: the source language of a letter written by Christian Huygens to the publisher of the *Journal des Sçavans* was certainly French, and the same holds for observations made at the Royal Observatory in Paris. The last group of editorial texts consists of six contributions made by Oldenburg in his capacity as publisher of the *Philosophical Transactions* (appeals to subscribe to certain books, an announcement of the publication of a particular book, a notice to the reader that the next issue of the *Philosophical Transactions* will be published later than expected) or as secretary of the Royal Society, giving notice of news which he decided not to transmit in its original form.

The group of authorial texts consists of 21 articles by identifiable authors, ten Latin texts, and one article of whose author we are only informed that he was "from Somersetshire" (No.90: 5138). Among the articles which were attributed to the category "authorial texts" with identifiable authors, are three which also contain passages by Oldenburg, but their titles suggest that they were intended as original contributions by Newton (two letters) and by the physician Walter Needham (one letter).

Volume 7 contains 82 articles. The 50 editorial texts represent a share of 61 percent, the 32 authorial texts amount to 39 percent.

4.2.4 *Volume 8 (1673)*

All forms of editorial texts are represented in this volume. As usual, most of them are book reviews. Their overall number amounts to 23.

Five articles are explicitly marked as translations. The source language of three of them is French, one article was translated from Dutch, and the source language of another is given as "High-Dutch" (No.94: 6040). The *OED* offers two glosses for this language; it can either be a synonym of Dutch or of German.[5] Since the author of the text is described as "a German Physitian residing at Frankfort on the Mayne", one can assume that he wrote in German.

The communications which Oldenburg received from French authors were usually in their native language, and volume 8 contains three texts which were translated from this language, even if this is not explicitly stated.

---

5. "*High Dutch*, of or pertaining to the South Germans who inhabit the more elevated parts of Germany, High German" (*OED*, s. v. Dutch); "High Dutch (S. Afr.) [tr. Afrikaans Hooghollands], Netherlands (literary) Dutch as distinguished from Cape Dutch or Afrikaans" (*OED*, s. v. Dutch).

The form of presentation and remarks in the texts ("he begins with blaming those, that divide Salts into Fixt and Volatil" No.92:5185) and/or details in the titles ("An Account of some of the Natural things, with which the Intelligent and Inquisitive Signor Paulo Boccone, of Sicily, hath lately presented the Royal Society, and enriched their Repository" No.99:6158) give Oldenburg away as the author of nine more texts. In one of them, Oldenburg lists a set of topics to be investigated, and this was one of his tasks as the secretary of the Royal Society.

Three more texts are also subsumed under the category "editorial texts" because Oldenburg's translations form the main part of these articles.

Nine of the authorial texts are articles in Latin, two of them with short comments by Oldenburg.

Among the 18 articles which have identifiable authors and count therefore as authorial texts, three have a special structure. These are letters in which another text is included. The letter-writers are the astronomer John Flamsteed, the natural scientist Robert Boyle, and the physician Martin Lister. Flamsteed includes in his letter a Latin text of his own, Boyle an English translation of a Dutch text, and Lister includes letters which he received from the "Learn'd Gentleman Mr. Jessop" (No.100:6179).

Although their authors cannot be identified because they are described only as "an Intelligent person now residing in Jamaica" (No.93:6007), "a Gentleman of Scotland" (No.98:6139) or "one of the principal Chirurgions of His Majesties Fleet" (No.97:6115), five more articles clearly belong to the category "authorial texts".

One article is particularly difficult to assign to one or the other category. It consists of a set of five reports about experiments; the first is signed "Walter Needham", the second "Richard Wiseman", and the others are not signed at all. By the linguistic form of the last, Oldenburg can be identified as its author, and it is probable that he is also the author of the remaining two reports.

For the 76 articles of volume 8, three categories have to be distinguished. The category "editorial texts" is represented by 32 articles (42 percent), 43 articles (57 percent) belong to the category "authorial texts", and one article (one percent) is indeterminate.

4.2.5 *Volume 9 (1674)*

The editorial texts comprise 33 book reviews, three overt translations from Italian, Dutch, and Latin, and eleven translations, whose status as translations must be inferred from details in the titles or in the texts themselves.

The author of five of these is Antonie van Leeuwenhoek, a Dutch microscopist (1632–1723), who did not speak any foreign language. The authors of another two articles are described as a "Learned and Inquisitive Physitian in Holland" (No.106:131) and "an Experienced person residing at Amsterdam" (No.101:3).

These hints establish Dutch as their source language. Another article must have been translated from French because it was sent by Christian Huygens, who usually wrote in French. It is highly probable that the letters from Johannes Hevelius and Christophorus Sandius are translations from Latin. Latin is probably also the source language of a letter from "a person of great veracity in Germany" (No.105: 100), because it would be very unusual for this person to write in English.

The category of "editorial texts" is completed by seven articles which can be attributed to Oldenburg.

The list of 22 authorial texts comprises twelve articles by identifiable authors and four Latin texts. The authors of the remaining six texts are not identifiable by name; their titles specify them as, for example, "a Fellow of the R. Society" (No.103: 41).

With 54 (71 percent) out of 76 articles, the share of the category "editorial texts" is exceptionally high; only 22 articles (29 percent) belong to the category "authorial texts".

4.2.6 *Volume 10 (1675)*

The biggest group among the editorial texts are the book reviews. The 25 books reviewed in this volume belong to different scientific fields, such as architecture, zoology, chemistry, botany, medicine, biology, mechanics, geography. As none is about mathematics, Oldenburg can safely be established as their author. A particularly clear case is the review which opens with the following statement: "Touching the Contents of this Book, as far as they relate to the Instruments therein described, I need say nothing here: I shall only touch upon some passages in the Post-script of it, in which I find one of these our Tracts concerned" (No.118: 440). The book under review is *A Description of Helioscopes and some other Instruments* by Robert Hooke, where Hooke in a postscript indeed complained about Oldenburg's decision to include an article by Christian Huygens in the *Philosophical Transactions*, in which Huygens claimed that he had constructed a special type of watch before Hooke, and Oldenburg had left this claim uncommented. In the remaining part of the book review Oldenburg rejects Hooke's accusation.

Two articles are explicitly marked as translations, and another nine can be identified as such. Two source languages are involved, namely French and Dutch.

In four articles, Oldenburg summarizes news items which he had received from France and Italy. He stresses his function as an intermediary in remarks like the following: "This Account hath been printed about two years since, in French; but very few Copies of it being come abroad [...] it will be no wonder, that all this while we have been silent of it. Having at length met with an Extract thereof, and been often desired to impart it to the Curious; we shall no longer resist those desires, but faithfully communicate in this Tract what we have received upon this Argument from a good hand" (No.112: 261).

Among the 31 authorial texts are 16 where the authors are identifiable by name. Three of them are complete letters with both an initial and a final greeting formula and signed by their authors, John Ray, John Beal, and John Flamsteed. The names of two authors are only given as initials: A. I. and J. L. The latter can be identified as John Locke, because the letter is mentioned in Birch's *History* (1756, vol.3: 220), and it is contained as letter No.2667 in Oldenburg's correspondence (Hall and Hall, vol.11: 322).

The authors of six articles are only vaguely described as "an Intelligent Gentleman" (No.113: 293), or "a good Hand" (No.118: 417), etc.

The last group of authorial texts consists of nine articles in Latin. They had reached Oldenburg from different parts of Europe.

One article is as much an editorial as an authorial text. It has the title "Of the Incalescence of Quicksilver with Gold, generously imparted by B. R." (No.112: 515). In a few introductory lines Oldenburg explains that he had persuaded the author to let him publish his article as a kind of preprint. He must have been very proud of this privilege because he adds: "Now, to gratifie the Curious amongst Strangers, as well as those of our own Nation, the Publisher was not unwilling to give this discourse In Latin, as the Author hath been pleased to impart it in English". The article is printed in two columns, the English text on the left, Oldenburg's Latin translation on the right.

The 72 articles of volume 10 can thus be divided into 40 (56 percent) editorial and 31 (43 percent) authorial texts, one (one percent) belongs to neither of these categories.

5.   Discussion of results

The results of the analysis of volumes 5 to 10 basically support the claim of earlier studies that "[t]he authorial voice gradually begins to take over control of the actual text" (Valle 2006: 88). Tables 1 and 2 summarize this development.

Table 1. Distribution of text categories in volumes 5–10 of the *Philosophical Transactions* (absolute)

	Vol. 5	Vol. 6	Vol. 7	Vol. 8	Vol. 9	Vol. 10
Book reviews	40	49	34	23	33	25
Overt translation	9	9	7	5	3	2
Translation	4	2	3	3	11	9
Oldenburg's texts	8	8	6	12	7	4
Total editorial	**61**	**68**	**50**	**43**	**54**	**40**
Latin texts	3	7	10	9	4	9
Identifiable authors	27	29	21	18	12	16
Unidentifiable	0	5	1	5	6	6
Total authorial	**30**	**41**	**32**	**32**	**22**	**31**
Others	0	0	0	1	0	1
Grand total	**91**	**109**	**82**	**76**	**76**	**72**

Table 2. Distribution of text categories in volumes 5–10 of the *Philosophical Transactions* (percentage)

	Vol. 5	Vol. 6	Vol. 7	Vol. 8	Vol. 9	Vol. 10
Book reviews	44	45	41	30	43	35
Overt translation	10	8	9	7	4	3
Translation	4	2	4	4	14	13
Oldenburg's texts	9	7	7	16	9	6
Total editorial	**67**	**62**	**61**	**57**	**71**	**56**
Latin texts	3	6	12	12	5	13
Identifiable authors	30	27	26	24	16	22
Unidentifiable	0	5	1	7	8	8
Total authorial	**33**	**38**	**39**	**42**	**29**	**43**
Others	0	0	0	1	0	1
Grand total	**100%**	**100%**	**100%**	**100%**	**100%**	**100%**

With the exception of volume 9, there is a steady decrease in the relative share of editorial texts and a corresponding increase in authorial texts. The difference from one year to the next ranges from one to five percent. This clear picture is disturbed if one compares the figures for volume 5 with those for volume 4 in Valle's quantitative analysis (2006:77). Her analysis yielded 46 percent editorial texts. Compared to 67 percent for volume 5, this would mean an increase by 21 percent. The explanation of this unexpected result lies in the set of data analysed by Valle. In her doctoral dissertation, on which her 2006 article is based, she explains that she considered only those articles in the *Philosophical Transactions* which belong to the life sciences (Valle 1999: 104, 147).[6] A more realistic picture of Oldenburg's role as editor of the *Philosophical Transactions* over the first ten years of the life of this journal can only be gained if at least the first year of volume 1 is additionally analysed.

Volume 1 differs from the other volumes in that it covers two years, namely the period from March 1665 to February 1667. Here, only the first part from March 1665 to February 1666 will be considered. It opens with a dedicatory address to the Royal Society, which is followed by Numbers 1 to 9. Probably because of the restriction that every number should have at least 16 pages, the *Philosophical Transactions* did not appear between August and October 1665. Most numbers of volume 1 do not go beyond the minimum size, in fact, the December issue consists of only 12 pages. As in the other volumes, the March number starts with Oldenburg's preface.

Oldenburg's later practice of explicitly stating that a text was translated from another language is adopted only once, namely in the article with the title "Of the way, used in the Mogol's Dominions, to make Saltpetre" (No.6: 103). From his introduction we can infer that the source language of this description is French:

> This is delivered in the same Book of Monsieur Thevenot, and the manner of it having been inqired after, by several curious Persons, to compare it with that which is used in Europe, 'tis presum'd, they will not be displeased to find it inserted here in English, which is as followeth.

The linguistic form of first person narratives and the names or places of residence can be used to identify ten more texts as translations. The source language of four of them is French ("written from Paris" No.2: 18; "practised in France" No.6: 99; "Monsieur Auzout's Speculations" No.7: 120; "Monsieur Auzout returns this consideration" No.7: 123), that of another four is Latin (descriptions of mineral springs in Germany), one article even combines a translation of a French and a Latin letter, and one was probably translated from Dutch because its author is described as: "A very curious Person, studying Physick at Leyden" (No.8: 138). These eleven articles clearly belong to the category "editiorial text".

Oldenburg himself is identifiable as the author of 50 articles. Three of them are a mixture of Oldenburg's original contribution and a translation of a letter (one from Hevelius, who usually wrote in Latin, one from a German Jesuit, and one from an "Inquisitive Parisian" No.8: 131). Although the numbers of the first year do not contain proper book reviews, several of the articles which were clearly written by Oldenburg very closely resemble later book reviews. Their titles often have the form: "An Account of ...", and they are introduced by phrases like: "The Ingenious and knowing Author of this Treatise ...". The first example of this kind

---

6.   Her analysis of volume 4 is based on 20 articles (cf. Valle 1999: 457f.).

is Oldenburg's review of Robert Hooke's *Micrographia* at the end of No.2. From March 1666 onwards, the last part of every issue has the title: "An Account of some Books".

The category "authorial texts" is represented by only twelve articles. The authors of ten of them are identifiable by name, the authors of the other two are not mentioned.

Four articles cannot be attributed to either category because they consist, in equal parts, of communications by Oldenburg and by other authors.

With 77 articles, the first year of volume 1 is comparable in size to the other volumes. The 61 editorial texts represent a share of 79 percent, twelve texts (16 percent) belong to the category "authorial texts". The distribution of the text categories in absolute numbers and as percentage values is given in Table 3.

Table 3. Distribution of text categories in volume 1 (1665) of the *Philosophical Transactions*

Volume 1	Absolute	Percentage
Book reviews	0	0
Overt translation	1	1
Translation	10	13
Oldenburg's texts	50	65
Total editorial	**61**	**79**
Latin texts	0	0
Identifiabe authors	10	13
Unidentifiable	2	3
Total authorial	**12**	**16**
Others	4	5
Grand total	**77**	**100%**

From a comparison of these figures with those in Tables 1 and 2 it can be inferred that the decrease in editorial texts between 1665 and 1670 is only slightly bigger (twelve percent) than that between 1670 and 1675 (eleven percent). Oldenburg's news reports contribute most to the overall decline in numbers of editorial texts: their share falls from 65 percent in 1665 to six percent in 1675. The average yearly decrease in editorial texts lies between one and two percent (1.3 percent).

The category "authorial texts" shows a different development. Here the increase in the first five-year period is nearly twice as big (17 percent) as in the second five-year period (ten percent). Yet at 1.7 percent, the average yearly increase is not much higher than the average yearly decrease in editorial texts.

Reasons for the deviation from both trends in volume 9 could not be found, but it is improbable that they indicate a change in Oldenburg's editorial policy.

If the developments identified in the first ten years of the *Philosophical Transactions* had continued at about the same pace, it would have taken another two to three years before the shares of the two text categories would have been balanced and the *Philosophical Transactions* would have been well on their way towards being the type of scientific journal we are used to today. Unfortunately, Oldenburg died in September 1677, and the last issue edited by him came out in June 1677. The scientific community had to wait until 1683 before the *Philosophical Transactions* were revived, although no longer under the continued editorship of the same person. In 1752, finally, what had begun as a private enterprise by Henry Oldenburg became the official organ of the Royal Society.

6.   Conclusion

It was to be expected that with the foundation of the *Philosophical Transactions* as a new channel, through which scientific news could be transported, the character of early scientific news discourse would change. The nature and extent of this change was revealed through an analysis of the first ten years of the publication of this journal.

As long as scientific news discourse mainly relied on private correspondence, it was the individual scientists who decided if, and to whom, the observations they made, the results they achieved, or the projects they were engaged in were communicated. The risk of lost or miscarried letters excepted, they were in complete control of the science dissemination process. This direct exchange of ideas had the advantage that manipulation by a mediator was excluded. It had the disadvantage that it was slow and meant an extra work load for those scientists who wanted to share their ideas with many fellow researchers.

Scientific news discourse worked differently through the newly established *Philosophical Transactions*. They appeared regularly every month, thus providing "hot news". They were read all over England and abroad, thus guaranteeing that a piece of news published there reached a wide circle of interested readers. These advantages were counterbalanced by the great influence Henry Oldenburg exercised over the choice of news to be included in his journal and on the way news was presented. It was no longer the individual scientists who controlled the scientific news discourse, but the editor-publisher of the *Philosophical Transactions*. Yet Oldenburg's attitude towards his almighty position changed during the first ten years of publishing. In a gradual but steady process he started to hand over control of the scientific news discourse to the scientists again. This process stopped midway, with Oldenburg's death. The publication of the *Philosophical Transactions* was interrupted for several years, then taken up again under various editors, before the journal changed its function completely when it became the official organ of the Royal Society in 1752. How this development changed the nature of scientific news discourse is another promising field of study.

Primary source

The Royal Society of London. *Philosophical Transactions*. Volume 1, 5–10. Reprinted 1963. New York: Johnson Reprint Corporation/Kraus Reprint Corporation.

References

Atkinson, Dwight. 1999. *Scientific Discourse in Sociohistorical Context. The Philosophical Transactions of the Royal Society of London, 1675–1975*. Mahwah: Laurence Erlbaum Associates.
Bazerman, Charles. 1988. *Shaping Written Knowledge*. Madison: University of Wisconsin Press.
Birch, Thomas. 1756 [1968]. *The History of the Royal Society of London for the Improving of Natural Knowledge*, 4 vols. London: Millar [facsimile reprint Hildesheim: Olms].
Gotti, Maurizio. 2006a. Disseminating early modern science: Specialized news discourse in the *Philosophical Transactions*. In Nicholas Brownlees (ed.). *News Discourse in Early Modern Britain. Selected Papers of CHINED 2004*. Bern: Peter Lang, 41–70.
Gotti, Maurizio. 2006b. Communal correspondence in Early Modern English: The *Philosophical Transactions* network. In Marina Dossena and Susan M. Fitzmaurice (eds.). *Business and Official Correspondence: Historical Investigations*. Bern: Peter Lang, 17–46.
Hall, Marie Boas. 1965. Oldenburg and the art of scientific communication. *The British Journal for the History of Science* 2.8, 277–290.
Hall, Marie Boas. 2002. *Henry Oldenburg. Shaping the Royal Society*. Oxford: Oxford University Press.
Hall, A. Rupert, and Marie Boas Hall. 1965–1986. *The Correspondence of Henry Oldenburg*, 13 vols. Madison, Milwaukee and London: The University of Wisconsin Press (vols. 1–9, 1965–1973), London: Mansell (vols. 10–11, 1975–1977), London and Philadelphia: Taylor and Francis (vols. 12–13, 1986).
Iliffe, Robert. 1995. Author-mongering. The 'editor' between producer and consumer. In Anne Bermingham (ed.). *The Consumption of Culture, 1600–1800*. London: Routledge, 166–192.
Kronick, David A. 1962. *A History of Scientific and Technical Periodicals*. New York: The Scarecrow Press.
Stimson, D. 1939. Hartlib, Haak and Oldenburg: Intelligencers. *International Review Devoted to the History of Science and Civilization* 31, 310–326.
Valle, Ellen. 2006. Reporting the doings of the curious: Authors and editors in the *Philosophical Transactions* of the Royal Society of London. In Nicholas Brownlees (ed.). *News Discourse in Early Modern Britain. Selected Papers of CHINED 2004*. Bern: Peter Lang, 71–90.
Valle, Ellen. 1999. *A Collective Intelligence: The Life Sciences in the Royal Society as a Scientific Discourse Community, 1665–1965*. Turku: University of Turku.

Index

A

A Dialogue against the Feuer Pestilence   194, 195

A few thoughts on an Union with some observations upon Mr. Weld's pamphlet of "No Union!" addressed to the yeomanry of Dublin   177, 180

A Full and True Account of the sad and dreadful Storm   146, 147, 153

A Great and Wonderful Discovery   148, 150, 152

A letter to a Noble Lord, containing a full declaration of the Catholic sentiment on the important question of Union   171, 174

A letter to the people of Ireland they all can understand and ought to read   169

A Letter to Theobald McKenna, Esq., the Catholic Advocate; in reply to the calumnies against the Orange Institution; contained in his pamphlet purporting to be a memoire on some questions respecting the projected union   180

A Member of the Aristocracy   36, 37, 44, 49

A Most Wonderful and Sad Judgement of God upon one Dorothy Mattle   139

A new iuterlude [sic] and a mery of the nature of the .iiii. element declarynge many proper poynt of phylosophy naturall, and of dyuers straunge landys and of dyuers straunge effects [and] causis   198

A Sad and True Relation of a Great Fire or Two   150, 152

A short address to the pretended Catholic Addresser of a Noble Lord, by a citizen, but not a French one   172

A Strange and True Relation   140, 149, 151, 153

academic writing   94, 122, 128

Addison, Catherine   99

advertisement   4, 15, 16, 18, 19, 29, 79, 80, 103

also see want ad

Agar, Michael   190

aggravation   164

An Account of a strange and prodigious Storm   146

An address to the people of Ireland, shewing them why they ought to submit to an Union   173, 180

An answer to some of the many arguments made use of against a pamphlet, entitled "Arguments for and against an Union"   180

An exposition on the principal terms of Union, and its probable effects on Ireland   179

An Union neither necessary or expedient for Ireland: being an answer to the author of "Arguments for and against an Union, between Great Britain and Ireland, considered"   167, 168, 172

Anderson, Laura   67

animadversion   67

announcement   4, 16, 29

Applebee's Original Weekly Journal   103

Arguments for and against an Union, between Great Britain and Ireland, considered   160, 167, 171, 172, 179

Arnovick, Leslie K.   197

Athenian Mercury   102

Atkinson, Dwight   208

auf dem Keller, Caren   3, 74

Austin, Paddy   164

B

Baker, Paul   190

Bartley, James   60

Bazerman, Charles   208

BBC style guide   109

Bell, Allan   2, 13, 131, 142, 144

Bell's Life in London   129

Biber, Douglas   94, 112, 120, 192

Bible   83, 111, 191

Bible translation   73

Bingley's Journal   109

Birch, Thomas   207, 209, 216

Blair, Hugh   92

Blake, Norman   61

BNC *see* British National Corpus

Bodleian Allegro Catalogue of Broadside Ballads, The   138
Bonham-Carter, Victor   92
Bös, Birte   6, 116, 118, 123
Bousfield, Derek   159, 163–168, 170, 176, 181
Bowen, Lloyd   62
British National Corpus (BNC)   121
broadside   6, 137–155
broadside ballad   6, 139
Brown, Penelope   164–166
Brownlees, Nicholas   3–5, 67
Buck, Anne   45
Bullein, William   194, 195
Burger, Harald   92
Burton, Robert   137

C
Capp, Bernard   194
Cecconi, Elisabetta   6
Certaine Informations   65
Champion, The   110
Claridge, Claudia   5, 99, 100, 153
Clark, Billy   120
Cockney   36
Collins, Peter   121, 122
Collinson, Patrick   147
collocation   5, 31, 34, 46, 74, 78, 83–88, 191
comparative   94
comparison   5, 91–112
Corpus of *Early Modern English Medical Texts* see
    Early Modern English Medical Texts (1500–1700)
Corpus of English Religious Prose   74
correspondence 209
    ~ network   208
Costa, Rachel M.   120
court report   28
Craftsman, The   93, 105, 107, 109
crime report   4, 13–29
Crystal, David   73, 88
Culpeper, Jonathan   159, 164–166, 168, 175, 181, 195
Current Intelligence, The   78

D
Daily Courant   96
Daily Express, The   115, 120, 121, 123, 126–129
Daily Mail, The   115, 116, 120, 121, 123, 125, 126, 130
Daily Mirror, The   115, 119, 121, 123, 126, 130
Daily Post, The   17, 80, 100, 105
Daily Sketch, The   123, 126, 128
Daston, Lorraine   144
Davies, Eirlys   120

Davy, Derek   73, 88
De Clerck, Bernard   120, 130
Defoe, Daniel   93
Dickens, Charles   48, 49
Domestick Intelligence, The   104
Dos Libros   199
Downie, J. A.   93
Dürscheid, Christa   2

E
Early English Books Online (EEBO)   138, 190, 196
Early Modern English Medical Texts (1500–1700)
    (EMEMT)   7, 190, 193
editorial   94
    ~ framing   208
EEBO *see Early English Books Online*
EMEMT *see Early Modern English Medical Texts*
    (1500–1700)
English Civil War   4
English Union, is Ireland's ruin! Or an address to the
    Irish Nation   165, 170, 175
entertainment   66, 68, 92, 107, 109
ethnography   190
evaluation   99, 100, 101, 103, 107, 108
Evening Mail   96, 101, 105, 106, 109
explanation   99, 104–106, 111

F
face   165, 168
    ~ threat   164, 168
    ~ threatening act (FTA)   163
Fairclough, Norman   115
Feather, John   93
filtering process   205, 208
Finegan, Edward   112
Fishelov, David   91
Flesch, Rudolf   115, 131
F-LOB Corpus see *Freiburg Lancaster-Oslo/Bergen*
    Corpus
Fludernik, Monika   192
Flying Post, The   84, 100, 101
foreign news *see* news
Fox, Adam   137, 189, 194, 195
Frampton, John   199
Freiburg Lancaster-Oslo/Bergen Corpus
    (F-LOB)   5, 93, 94, 96–98, 100, 101, 107
French Revolutionary War   163
Fries, Udo   3, 74, 97

G
Gay, John   93

General Advertiser   108
General Evening Post   108
Generosity Maxim   127
genre   5, 13, 73, 74, 77, 78, 85-88, 94, 96-98, 119, 131,
    132, 138-140, 143, 144, 146, 148, 151, 154, 155, 160,
    192, 193
Geoghegan, Patrick   162
Goffman, Erving   166
Gotti, Maurizio   3, 8, 189, 193, 206, 208
Grabes, Herbert   3
Griffiths, Dennis   3
Guardian, The   115

H
Haak, Theodore   206
Hall, A. Rupert   207
Hall, Marie Boas   207–209, 211
hard news *see* news
Harris, Richard Jackson   99
headline   5, 7, 15, 65, 70, 115, 119, 124, 128, 141–144,
    147, 155, 191
Hecht, Jean J.   35, 36, 39, 53
Hill, Bridget   50, 53
Hobbes, Thomas   110
home news *see* news
Hopper, Paul J.   120
Huddleston, Rodney   93, 120–122
Hüllen, Werner   3

I
ICE–AUS *see International Corpus of English*
ideology   102, 138, 141, 155, 190, 192, 195, 201, 202
Iliffe, Robert   208
illocutionary force   6
Impartial Protestant Mercury, The   110
imperative   6, 115–132
impoliteness   159–183
    ~ strategy   7
    ~ super-strategy   164
    negative ~ strategy   173
    off-record ~   165, 181, 182
    on-record ~   165, 167–181
    positive ~ strategy   176
information   68, 92, 93, 98, 99, 104, 105, 108, 112
informative function   65
infotainment   4, 57–71
intensification   99, 100
International Corpus of English (ICE)–AUS   121
intertextuality   144, 155
Ioyfull nevves out of the newe founde worlde   199

J
Journal des Sçavans   207, 213
Jucker, Andreas H.   2, 25, 66, 146, 190

K
Keogh, Dáire   162
keyword   74–88
    ~ analysis   5, 74–77, 88
Kienpointner, Manfred   160
Kohnen, Thomas   5, 74, 121, 130
König, Ekkehard   120
Kronick, David A.   206, 208
KWIC concordance   190, 193, 195
Kytö, Merja   195

L
Labov, William   192
Lachenicht, Lance G.   164
Lake, Peter   146
Lampeter Corpus   98
Leech, Geoffrey   115, 121, 127
Lehmann, Hans Martin   74
let-construction   120, 122–125, 129–131
letters   206, 209, 211
Leviathan   110
Levinson, Stephen C.   164–166
Levorato, Alessandra   7, 159
literacy   110
Lloyd's Weekly Newspaper   119, 122, 125, 126, 129
Locke, John   216
London Chronicle, The   79, 80, 102
London Daily Advertiser   103
London Daily Post, The   17
London Evening Post, The   80–82, 118, 119
London Gazette, The   14, 16, 17, 19, 80–82, 87, 93,
    104, 105, 107, 142, 147, 154
London Post   109
London Review of Books   31
lonely hearts   31
Lord, Peter   62

M
Manchester Guardian   126, 130
Mandeville's Travels   198
Mansergh, Daniel   160, 162, 163
Mardh, Ingrid   65
McGrath, Alister   73
McIntosh, Carey   92, 112
medical news report *see* news
Melchers, Gunnel   61

Meldrum, Tim   45, 53
MEMT see Middle English Medical Texts (1375–1500)
Mercurius Aulicus   66, 67, 70
Mercurius Britanicus   70
Mercurius Cambro-Britannus, the British Mercury, or the Welch Diurnall see Welch Mercury
Mercurius Reformatus   100
metaphor   92, 108
Middle English Medical Texts (1375–1500) (MEMT)   193
Moessner, Lilo   7, 8
Monardes, Nicolás   199
Moon, Rosamund   109
Morning Chronicle, The   95, 111
Morning Herald, The   4, 31–54, 108
Morning Post   102, 117, 125, 126
Mosier, Noah Jacob   99

N
New News-Book, A   85
Newes from Hereford   140–142, 145, 146, 148, 149, 151, 153, 154
news   191
    foreign ~   14, 20
    hard ~   4, 13, 14, 29, 65
    home ~   14, 15, 20
    medical ~ report   189–202
    ~ broadside   6
    ~ discourse   80
    ~ narrative   191
    ~ structure   192
    ~ values   5
    news   193
    scientific ~ report   189–202
    ship ~   14, 15
    soft ~   13, 14, 29
    spot ~   13
newspaper commentary   25, 29
No Union! Bing [sic] an appeal to Irishmen   178
Norrick, Neal   99, 109

O
Observations on "Arguments for and against an Union between Great Britain and Ireland"   168, 169, 171
OED see Oxford English Dictionary
Of the newe la[n]des and of ye people founde by the messengers of the kynge of porty[n]gale named Emanuel.   196
Old Bailey Online   40, 46, 51

Oldenburg, Henry   3, 8, 205–220
Onions, C. T.   31
oral performance   6
oral storytelling   192
Ortony, Andrew   93
Oxford English Dictionary (OED)   1, 4, 26, 27
Oxford Gazette   14

P
Pacquet of Advice from France, The   96
Pahta, Päivi   3, 61
Partridge, Astley C.   73
Perfect Diurnall of Some Passages in Parliament, A   57, 59
personalization   115, 117
    ~ of mass media communication   6
persuasion   92, 98, 107, 141, 155, 159
Philosophical Transactions   3, 8, 193, 205–220
Pitt's Union   172, 176, 182
politeness   159–183
Pope, Alexander   38
Post Boy, The   105
Post Man, The   87, 111
prayer   73, 76–88
prayer corpus   74–77, 84–86
Protest from one of the people of Ireland, against an Union with Great Britain   174–176, 181
Protestant Intelligence, The   104
proto-headline   65, 70
Public Advertiser, The   79, 101, 102
Pullum, Geoffrey K.   93, 120–122

Q
quality paper   13, 29
Quirk, Randolph   93, 120, 169, 171, 172

R
Rastell, John   199
Ratia, Maura   200
Raymond, Joad   3, 57, 139
register   5, 73, 74, 88, 91, 93, 94, 112, 193
religious discourse   74, 77, 79, 80, 88
religious language   73–88
reportage   94
reporting clause   66
rhetoric   57, 58, 64, 67, 71, 92-94, 96, 108, 110, 112, 122, 138, 140, 152, 167–171
RNC see Rostock Newspaper Corpus
Rostock Newspaper Corpus (RNC)   6, 116–131
Royal Society   8, 207–209, 214, 218, 220, 221
Royle, Trevor   60

Ruef, Beni   74
Russell, Conrad   60

S
sarcasm   181
Schneider, Kristina   13, 29, 92, 112, 117
Schneider, Peter   74, 97
scientific news report *see* news
Scotish Dove   66
Scott, Mike   74
Searle, John R.   121
Seppänen, Aimo   120
Shapin, Steven   200
ship news *see* news
Shuman, Amy   67
Sidrak and Bokkus   199
Siebert, Fredrick Seaton   93
Siemund, Peter   120
Simek, Rudolf   197
simile   92–94, 96, 106, 109
soft news *see* news
Sommerville, John   3, 93
Spencer-Oatey, Helen   165
spot news *see* news
Steele, Richard   93
Strange and Fearfull Newes from Plaisto   146
Strange Newes from the North   141–143, 146, 148
Studer, Patrick   3, 143
Sun, The   115, 120, 123, 126–128
superlative   94
Swales, John M.   120, 122, 128, 129
Swift, Jonathan   93

T
Taavitsainen, Irma   3, 7, 61, 190–192, 199
Tact Maxim   127
text class   13–15, 20, 29, 103
text type   91
The Act of Union Virtual Library Project   160
The conspiracy of Pitt and Co. detected in a letter to the Parliament of Ireland   173, 176, 181
The Fattal Vesper   154
The Full and True Relation of a Dreadful Storm   145, 154
The Great and Grievous Punishment   139
The Most strange and wonderful apparition   146
Thomas, Alan   62
thought-style   202
Times, The   115, 121, 125, 129

Toolan, Michael   192
Traugott, Elizabeth Closs   120
True Informer, The   59

U
Ungerer, Friedrich   146, 191, 192
Union or not?   172

V
Valle, Ellen   3, 8, 189, 208, 216–218
van Dijk, Teun A.   138, 140–142, 144, 149, 150, 191, 192

W
Waletzky, Joshua   192
Walsham, Alexandra   140, 148, 155
want ad   4, 31–54
Watt, Tessa   140, 147
Wear, Andrew   195, 200
Weekly Remarks, The   108
Welch Mercury, The   4, 57–71
Welch-Mans Complements, The   59, 61
Welsh English   58, 60–62, 65, 68, 71
Werlich, Egon   192
Westminster Journal   80, 83, 109
Wheelan, Kevin   162
Wh-questions   169
Wikberg, Kay   94
Wodehouse, P. G.   39
Wonder of Wonders   146, 153, 154
woodcut   140–143, 147, 148, 155
Woolf, Daniel   137
WordSmith   74, 84, 190
World   130
Wright, Laura   4, 62
Würzbach, Natasha   152

X
Xekalakis, Elefteria   13

Y
yes/no question   170–173

Z
Zaret, David   137
ZEN *see* Zurich English Newspaper Corpus
Zurich English Newspaper Corpus (ZEN)   3–5, 13, 15, 16, 25, 26, 29, 40, 46, 51, 73–78, 80, 83–86, 88, 91, 93, 94, 96–98, 101, 103, 104

Pragmatics & Beyond New Series

A complete list of titles in this series can be found on *www.benjamins.com*

190 FINCH, Jason, Martin GILL, Anthony JOHNSON, Iris LINDAHL-RAITTILA, Inna LINDGREN, Tuija VIRTANEN and Brita WÅRVIK (eds.): Humane Readings. Essays on literary mediation and communication in honour of Roger D. Sell. *Expected September 2009*

189 PEIKOLA, Matti, Janne SKAFFARI and Sanna-Kaisa TANSKANEN (eds.): Instructional Writing in English. Studies in honour of Risto Hiltunen. xiii, 239 pp. + index. *Expected July 2009*

188 GILTROW, Janet and Dieter STEIN (eds.): Genres in the Internet. Issues in the theory of genre. *Expected Forthcoming*

187 JUCKER, Andreas H. (ed.): Early Modern English News Discourse. Newspapers, pamphlets and scientific news discourse. 2009. vii, 227 pp.

186 CALLIES, Marcus: Information Highlighting in Advanced Learner English. The syntax–pragmatics interface in second language acquisition. 2009. xviii, 293 pp.

185 MAZZON, Gabriella: Interactive Dialogue Sequences in Middle English Drama. 2009. ix, 228 pp.

184 STENSTRÖM, Anna-Brita and Annette Myre JØRGENSEN (eds.): Youngspeak in a Multilingual Perspective. 2009. vi, 206 pp.

183 NURMI, Arja, Minna NEVALA and Minna PALANDER-COLLIN (eds.): The Language of Daily Life in England (1400–1800). 2009. vii, 312 pp.

182 NORRICK, Neal R. and Delia CHIARO (eds.): Humor in Interaction. xvii, 231 pp. + index. *Expected August 2009*

181 MASCHLER, Yael: Metalanguage in Interaction. Hebrew discourse markers. xiv, 248 pp. + index. *Expected July 2009*

180 JONES, Kimberly and Tsuyoshi ONO (eds.): Style Shifting in Japanese. 2008. vii, 335 pp.

179 SIMÕES LUCAS FREITAS, Elsa: Taboo in Advertising. 2008. xix, 214 pp.

178 SCHNEIDER, Klaus P. and Anne BARRON (eds.): Variational Pragmatics. A focus on regional varieties in pluricentric languages. 2008. vii, 371 pp.

177 RUE, Yong-Ju and Grace ZHANG: Request Strategies. A comparative study in Mandarin Chinese and Korean. 2008. xv, 320 pp.

176 JUCKER, Andreas H. and Irma TAAVITSAINEN (eds.): Speech Acts in the History of English. 2008. viii, 318 pp.

175 GÓMEZ GONZÁLEZ, María de los Ángeles, J. Lachlan MACKENZIE and Elsa M. GONZÁLEZ ÁLVAREZ (eds.): Languages and Cultures in Contrast and Comparison. 2008. xxii, 364 pp.

174 HEYD, Theresa: Email Hoaxes. Form, function, genre ecology. 2008. vii, 239 pp.

173 ZANOTTO, Mara Sophia, Lynne CAMERON and Marilda C. CAVALCANTI (eds.): Confronting Metaphor in Use. An applied linguistic approach. 2008. vii, 315 pp.

172 BENZ, Anton and Peter KÜHNLEIN (eds.): Constraints in Discourse. 2008. vii, 292 pp.

171 FÉLIX-BRASDEFER, J. César: Politeness in Mexico and the United States. A contrastive study of the realization and perception of refusals. 2008. xiv, 195 pp.

170 OAKLEY, Todd and Anders HOUGAARD (eds.): Mental Spaces in Discourse and Interaction. 2008. vi, 262 pp.

169 CONNOR, Ulla, Ed NAGELHOUT and William ROZYCKI (eds.): Contrastive Rhetoric. Reaching to intercultural rhetoric. 2008. viii, 324 pp.

168 PROOST, Kristel: Conceptual Structure in Lexical Items. The lexicalisation of communication concepts in English, German and Dutch. 2007. xii, 304 pp.

167 BOUSFIELD, Derek: Impoliteness in Interaction. 2008. xiii, 281 pp.

166 NAKANE, Ikuko: Silence in Intercultural Communication. Perceptions and performance. 2007. xii, 240 pp.

165 BUBLITZ, Wolfram and Axel HÜBLER (eds.): Metapragmatics in Use. 2007. viii, 301 pp.

164 ENGLEBRETSON, Robert (ed.): Stancetaking in Discourse. Subjectivity, evaluation, interaction. 2007. viii, 323 pp.

163 LYTRA, Vally: Play Frames and Social Identities. Contact encounters in a Greek primary school. 2007. xii, 300 pp.

162 FETZER, Anita (ed.): Context and Appropriateness. Micro meets macro. 2007. vi, 265 pp.

161 CELLE, Agnès and Ruth HUART (eds.): Connectives as Discourse Landmarks. 2007. viii, 212 pp.

160 **FETZER, Anita and Gerda Eva LAUERBACH (eds.):** Political Discourse in the Media. Cross-cultural perspectives. 2007. viii, 379 pp.

159 **MAYNARD, Senko K.:** Linguistic Creativity in Japanese Discourse. Exploring the multiplicity of self, perspective, and voice. 2007. xvi, 356 pp.

158 **WALKER, Terry:** *Thou* and *You* in Early Modern English Dialogues. Trials, Depositions, and Drama Comedy. 2007. xx, 339 pp.

157 **CRAWFORD CAMICIOTTOLI, Belinda:** The Language of Business Studies Lectures. A corpus-assisted analysis. 2007. xvi, 236 pp.

156 **VEGA MORENO, Rosa E.:** Creativity and Convention. The pragmatics of everyday figurative speech. 2007. xii, 249 pp.

155 **HEDBERG, Nancy and Ron ZACHARSKI (eds.):** The Grammar–Pragmatics Interface. Essays in honor of Jeanette K. Gundel. 2007. viii, 345 pp.

154 **HÜBLER, Axel:** The Nonverbal Shift in Early Modern English Conversation. 2007. x, 281 pp.

153 **ARNOVICK, Leslie K.:** Written Reliquaries. The resonance of orality in medieval English texts. 2006. xii, 292 pp.

152 **WARREN, Martin:** Features of Naturalness in Conversation. 2006. x, 272 pp.

151 **SUZUKI, Satoko (ed.):** Emotive Communication in Japanese. 2006. x, 234 pp.

150 **BUSSE, Beatrix:** Vocative Constructions in the Language of Shakespeare. 2006. xviii, 525 pp.

149 **LOCHER, Miriam A.:** Advice Online. Advice-giving in an American Internet health column. 2006. xvi, 277 pp.

148 **FLØTTUM, Kjersti, Trine DAHL and Torodd KINN:** Academic Voices. Across languages and disciplines. 2006. x, 309 pp.

147 **HINRICHS, Lars:** Codeswitching on the Web. English and Jamaican Creole in e-mail communication. 2006. x, 302 pp.

146 **TANSKANEN, Sanna-Kaisa:** Collaborating towards Coherence. Lexical cohesion in English discourse. 2006. ix, 192 pp.

145 **KURHILA, Salla:** Second Language Interaction. 2006. vii, 257 pp.

144 **BÜHRIG, Kristin and Jan D. ten THIJE (eds.):** Beyond Misunderstanding. Linguistic analyses of intercultural communication. 2006. vi, 339 pp.

143 **BAKER, Carolyn, Michael EMMISON and Alan FIRTH (eds.):** Calling for Help. Language and social interaction in telephone helplines. 2005. xviii, 352 pp.

142 **SIDNELL, Jack:** Talk and Practical Epistemology. The social life of knowledge in a Caribbean community. 2005. xvi, 255 pp.

141 **ZHU, Yunxia:** Written Communication across Cultures. A sociocognitive perspective on business genres. 2005. xviii, 216 pp.

140 **BUTLER, Christopher S., María de los Ángeles GÓMEZ GONZÁLEZ and Susana M. DOVAL-SUÁREZ (eds.):** The Dynamics of Language Use. Functional and contrastive perspectives. 2005. xvi, 413 pp.

139 **LAKOFF, Robin T. and Sachiko IDE (eds.):** Broadening the Horizon of Linguistic Politeness. 2005. xii, 342 pp.

138 **MÜLLER, Simone:** Discourse Markers in Native and Non-native English Discourse. 2005. xviii, 290 pp.

137 **MORITA, Emi:** Negotiation of Contingent Talk. The Japanese interactional particles *ne* and *sa*. 2005. xvi, 240 pp.

136 **SASSEN, Claudia:** Linguistic Dimensions of Crisis Talk. Formalising structures in a controlled language. 2005. ix, 230 pp.

135 **ARCHER, Dawn:** Questions and Answers in the English Courtroom (1640–1760). A sociopragmatic analysis. 2005. xiv, 374 pp.

134 **SKAFFARI, Janne, Matti PEIKOLA, Ruth CARROLL, Risto HILTUNEN and Brita WÅRVIK (eds.):** Opening Windows on Texts and Discourses of the Past. 2005. x, 418 pp.

133 **MARNETTE, Sophie:** Speech and Thought Presentation in French. Concepts and strategies. 2005. xiv, 379 pp.

132 **ONODERA, Noriko O.:** Japanese Discourse Markers. Synchronic and diachronic discourse analysis. 2004. xiv, 253 pp.

131 **JANOSCHKA, Anja:** Web Advertising. New forms of communication on the Internet. 2004. xiv, 230 pp.

130 **HALMARI, Helena and Tuija VIRTANEN (eds.):** Persuasion Across Genres. A linguistic approach. 2005. x, 257 pp.

129 **TABOADA, María Teresa:** Building Coherence and Cohesion. Task-oriented dialogue in English and Spanish. 2004. xvii, 264 pp.

128 **CORDELLA, Marisa:** The Dynamic Consultation. A discourse analytical study of doctor–patient communication. 2004. xvi, 254 pp.

127 **BRISARD, Frank, Michael MEEUWIS and Bart VANDENABEELE (eds.):** Seduction, Community, Speech. A Festschrift for Herman Parret. 2004. vi, 202 pp.

126 **WU, Yi'an:** Spatial Demonstratives in English and Chinese. Text and Cognition. 2004. xviii, 236 pp.

125 **LERNER, Gene H. (ed.):** Conversation Analysis. Studies from the first generation. 2004. x, 302 pp.

124 **VINE, Bernadette:** Getting Things Done at Work. The discourse of power in workplace interaction. 2004. x, 278 pp.

123 **MÁRQUEZ REITER, Rosina and María Elena PLACENCIA (eds.):** Current Trends in the Pragmatics of Spanish. 2004. xvi, 383 pp.

122 **GONZÁLEZ, Montserrat:** Pragmatic Markers in Oral Narrative. The case of English and Catalan. 2004. xvi, 410 pp.

121 **FETZER, Anita:** Recontextualizing Context. Grammaticality meets appropriateness. 2004. x, 272 pp.

120 **AIJMER, Karin and Anna-Brita STENSTRÖM (eds.):** Discourse Patterns in Spoken and Written Corpora. 2004. viii, 279 pp.

119 **HILTUNEN, Risto and Janne SKAFFARI (eds.):** Discourse Perspectives on English. Medieval to modern. 2003. viii, 243 pp.

118 **CHENG, Winnie:** Intercultural Conversation. 2003. xii, 279 pp.

117 **WU, Ruey-Jiuan Regina:** Stance in Talk. A conversation analysis of Mandarin final particles. 2004. xvi, 260 pp.

116 **GRANT, Colin B. (ed.):** Rethinking Communicative Interaction. New interdisciplinary horizons. 2003. viii, 330 pp.

115 **KÄRKKÄINEN, Elise:** Epistemic Stance in English Conversation. A description of its interactional functions, with a focus on *I think*. 2003. xii, 213 pp.

114 **KÜHNLEIN, Peter, Hannes RIESER and Henk ZEEVAT (eds.):** Perspectives on Dialogue in the New Millennium. 2003. xii, 400 pp.

113 **PANTHER, Klaus-Uwe and Linda L. THORNBURG (eds.):** Metonymy and Pragmatic Inferencing. 2003. xii, 285 pp.

112 **LENZ, Friedrich (ed.):** Deictic Conceptualisation of Space, Time and Person. 2003. xiv, 279 pp.

111 **ENSINK, Titus and Christoph SAUER (eds.):** Framing and Perspectivising in Discourse. 2003. viii, 227 pp.

110 **ANDROUTSOPOULOS, Jannis K. and Alexandra GEORGAKOPOULOU (eds.):** Discourse Constructions of Youth Identities. 2003. viii, 343 pp.

109 **MAYES, Patricia:** Language, Social Structure, and Culture. A genre analysis of cooking classes in Japan and America. 2003. xiv, 228 pp.

108 **BARRON, Anne:** Acquisition in Interlanguage Pragmatics. Learning how to do things with words in a study abroad context. 2003. xviii, 403 pp.

107 **TAAVITSAINEN, Irma and Andreas H. JUCKER (eds.):** Diachronic Perspectives on Address Term Systems. 2003. viii, 446 pp.

106 **BUSSE, Ulrich:** Linguistic Variation in the Shakespeare Corpus. Morpho-syntactic variability of second person pronouns. 2002. xiv, 344 pp.

105 **BLACKWELL, Sarah:** Implicatures in Discourse. The case of Spanish NP anaphora. 2003. xvi, 303 pp.

104 **BEECHING, Kate:** Gender, Politeness and Pragmatic Particles in French. 2002. x, 251 pp.

103 **FETZER, Anita and Christiane MEIERKORD (eds.):** Rethinking Sequentiality. Linguistics meets conversational interaction. 2002. vi, 300 pp.

102 **LEAFGREN, John:** Degrees of Explicitness. Information structure and the packaging of Bulgarian subjects and objects. 2002. xii, 252 pp.

101 **LUKE, K. K. and Theodossia-Soula PAVLIDOU (eds.):** Telephone Calls. Unity and diversity in conversational structure across languages and cultures. 2002. x, 295 pp.

100 **JASZCZOLT, Katarzyna M. and Ken TURNER (eds.):** Meaning Through Language Contrast. Volume 2. 2003. viii, 496 pp.

99 **JASZCZOLT, Katarzyna M. and Ken TURNER (eds.):** Meaning Through Language Contrast. Volume 1. 2003. xii, 388 pp.

98 DUSZAK, Anna (ed.): Us and Others. Social identities across languages, discourses and cultures. 2002. viii, 522 pp.

97 MAYNARD, Senko K.: Linguistic Emotivity. Centrality of place, the topic-comment dynamic, and an ideology of *pathos* in Japanese discourse. 2002. xiv, 481 pp.

96 HAVERKATE, Henk: The Syntax, Semantics and Pragmatics of Spanish Mood. 2002. vi, 241 pp.

95 FITZMAURICE, Susan M.: The Familiar Letter in Early Modern English. A pragmatic approach. 2002. viii, 263 pp.

94 McILVENNY, Paul (ed.): Talking Gender and Sexuality. 2002. x, 332 pp.

93 BARON, Bettina and Helga KOTTHOFF (eds.): Gender in Interaction. Perspectives on femininity and masculinity in ethnography and discourse. 2002. xxiv, 357 pp.

92 GARDNER, Rod: When Listeners Talk. Response tokens and listener stance. 2001. xxii, 281 pp.

91 GROSS, Joan: Speaking in Other Voices. An ethnography of Walloon puppet theaters. 2001. xxviii, 341 pp.

90 KENESEI, István and Robert M. HARNISH (eds.): Perspectives on Semantics, Pragmatics, and Discourse. A Festschrift for Ferenc Kiefer. 2001. xxii, 352 pp.

89 ITAKURA, Hiroko: Conversational Dominance and Gender. A study of Japanese speakers in first and second language contexts. 2001. xviii, 231 pp.

88 BAYRAKTAROĞLU, Arın and Maria SIFIANOU (eds.): Linguistic Politeness Across Boundaries. The case of Greek and Turkish. 2001. xiv, 439 pp.

87 MUSHIN, Ilana: Evidentiality and Epistemological Stance. Narrative Retelling. 2001. xviii, 244 pp.

86 IFANTIDOU, Elly: Evidentials and Relevance. 2001. xii, 225 pp.

85 COLLINS, Daniel E.: Reanimated Voices. Speech reporting in a historical-pragmatic perspective. 2001. xx, 384 pp.

84 ANDERSEN, Gisle: Pragmatic Markers and Sociolinguistic Variation. A relevance-theoretic approach to the language of adolescents. 2001. ix, 352 pp.

83 MÁRQUEZ REITER, Rosina: Linguistic Politeness in Britain and Uruguay. A contrastive study of requests and apologies. 2000. xviii, 225 pp.

82 KHALIL, Esam N.: Grounding in English and Arabic News Discourse. 2000. x, 274 pp.

81 DI LUZIO, Aldo, Susanne GÜNTHNER and Franca ORLETTI (eds.): Culture in Communication. Analyses of intercultural situations. 2001. xvi, 341 pp.

80 UNGERER, Friedrich (ed.): English Media Texts – Past and Present. Language and textual structure. 2000. xiv, 286 pp.

79 ANDERSEN, Gisle and Thorstein FRETHEIM (eds.): Pragmatic Markers and Propositional Attitude. 2000. viii, 273 pp.

78 SELL, Roger D.: Literature as Communication. The foundations of mediating criticism. 2000. xiv, 348 pp.

77 VANDERVEKEN, Daniel and Susumu KUBO (eds.): Essays in Speech Act Theory. 2002. vi, 328 pp.

76 MATSUI, Tomoko: Bridging and Relevance. 2000. xii, 251 pp.

75 PILKINGTON, Adrian: Poetic Effects. A relevance theory perspective. 2000. xiv, 214 pp.

74 TROSBORG, Anna (ed.): Analysing Professional Genres. 2000. xvi, 256 pp.

73 HESTER, Stephen K. and David FRANCIS (eds.): Local Educational Order. Ethnomethodological studies of knowledge in action. 2000. viii, 326 pp.

72 MARMARIDOU, Sophia S.A.: Pragmatic Meaning and Cognition. 2000. xii, 322 pp.

71 GÓMEZ GONZÁLEZ, María de los Ángeles: The Theme–Topic Interface. Evidence from English. 2001. xxiv, 438 pp.

70 SORJONEN, Marja-Leena: Responding in Conversation. A study of response particles in Finnish. 2001. x, 330 pp.

69 NOH, Eun-Ju: Metarepresentation. A relevance-theory approach. 2000. xii, 242 pp.

68 ARNOVICK, Leslie K.: Diachronic Pragmatics. Seven case studies in English illocutionary development. 2000. xii, 196 pp.

67 TAAVITSAINEN, Irma, Gunnel MELCHERS and Päivi PAHTA (eds.): Writing in Nonstandard English. 2000. viii, 404 pp.

66 JUCKER, Andreas H., Gerd FRITZ and Franz LEBSANFT (eds.): Historical Dialogue Analysis. 1999. viii, 478 pp.

65 COOREN, François: The Organizing Property of Communication. 2000. xvi, 272 pp.

64 SVENNEVIG, Jan: Getting Acquainted in Conversation. A study of initial interactions. 2000. x, 384 pp.

63 BUBLITZ, Wolfram, Uta LENK and Eija VENTOLA (eds.): Coherence in Spoken and Written Discourse. How to create it and how to describe it. Selected papers from the International Workshop on Coherence, Augsburg, 24-27 April 1997. 1999. xiv, 300 pp.